Everybody! It's the last volume!!

Thank you so much for supporting me for so long!! I will not forget these past dreamlike nine years I've spent together with all of you!! I wonder what I'll do next... (*smirk*).

— Takeshi Konomi, 2009

About Takeshi Konomi

Takeshi Konomi exploded onto the manga scene with the incredible **THE PRINCE OF TENNIS**. His refined art style and sleek character designs proved popular with **Weekly Shonen Jump** readers, and **THE PRINCE OF TENNIS** became the number one sports manga in Japan almost overnight. Its cast of fascinating male tennis players attracted legions of female readers even though it was originally intended to be a boys' comic. The manga continues to be a success in Japan and has inspired a hit anime series, as well as several video games and mountains of merchandise.

THE PRINCE OF TENNIS
VOL. 42
SHONEN JUMP Manga Edition

STORY AND ART BY
TAKESHI KONOMI

Translation/Joe Yamazaki
Touch-up Art & Lettering/Vanessa Satone
Design/Sam Elzway
Editor/Daniel Gillespie

Published by VIZ Media, LLC
P.O. Box 77010
San Francisco, CA 94107

10 9 8 7 6 5 4 3 2 1
First printing, July 2011

PARENTAL ADVISORY
THE PRINCE OF TENNIS is
rated A and is suitable for
readers of all ages.
ratings.viz.com

THE WORLD'S
MOST POPULAR MANGA

www.shonenjump.com

www.viz.com

SEIGAKU T

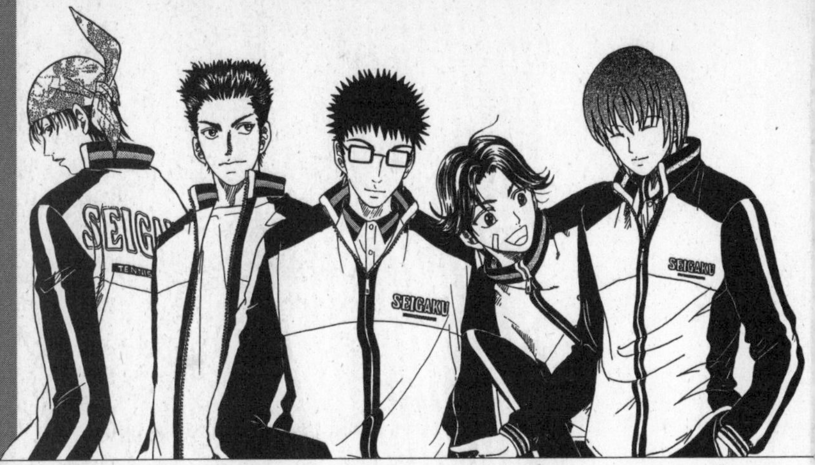
SEIGAKU
TENNIS
SEIGAKU
SEIGAKU

• KAORU KAIDO • TAKESHI MOMOSHIRO • SADAHARU INUI • EIJI KIKUMARU • SHUSUKE FUJI •

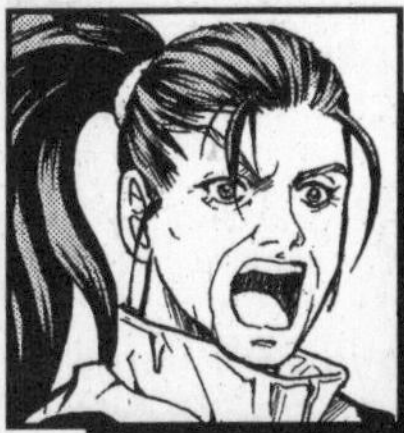
SEISHUN ACADEMY TENNIS COACH
SUMIRE RYUZAKI

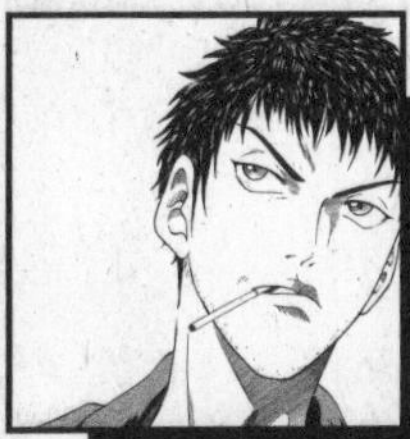
RYOMA ECHIZEN'S FATHER
NANJIRO ECHIZEN

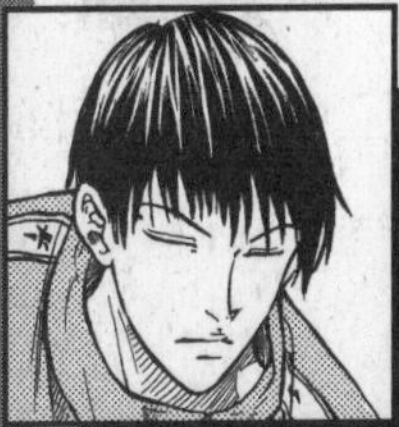
RIKKAI
RENJI YANAGI

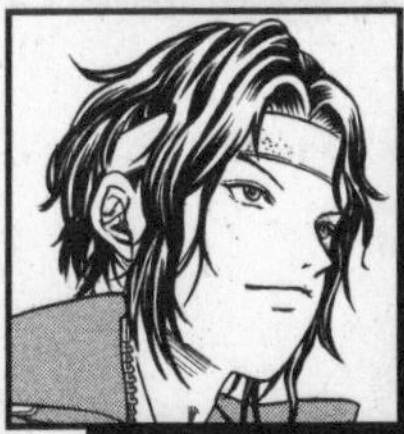
RIKKAI
SEIICHI YUKIMURA

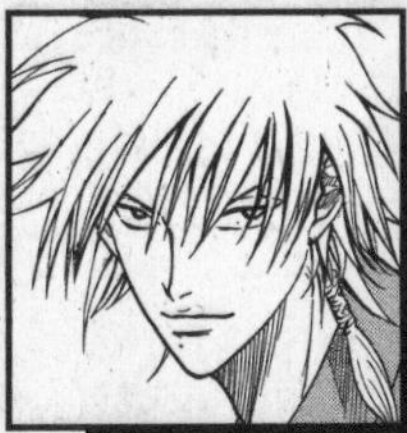
RIKKAI
MASAHARU NIO

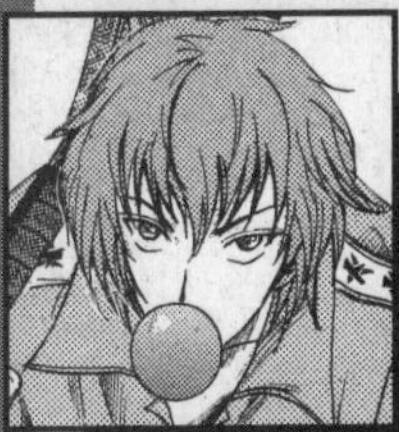
RIKKAI
BUNTA MARUI

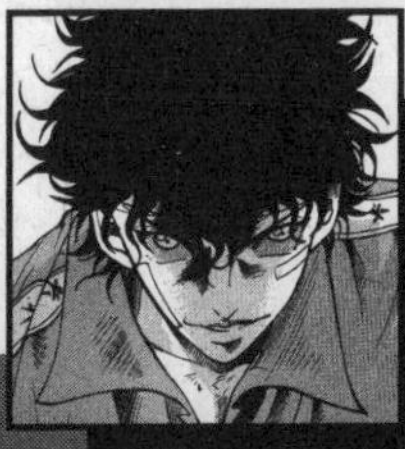
RIKKAI
AKAYA KIRIHARA

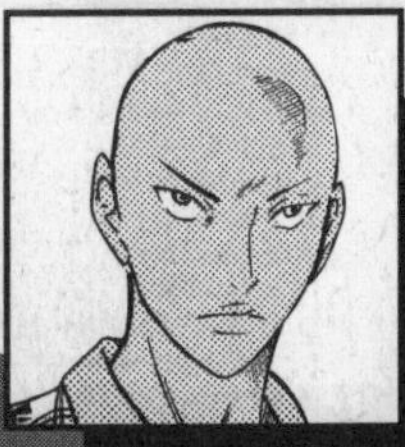
RIKKAI
JACKAL KUWAHARA

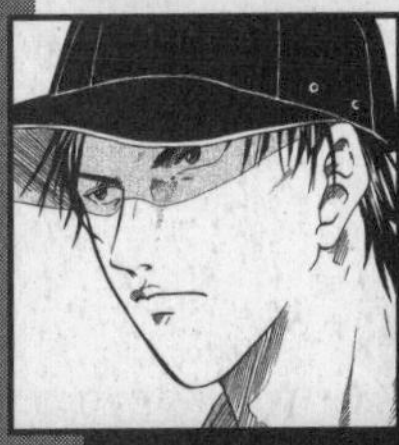
RIKKAI
GENICHIRO SANADA

CONTENTS

Vol. 42
Dear Prince

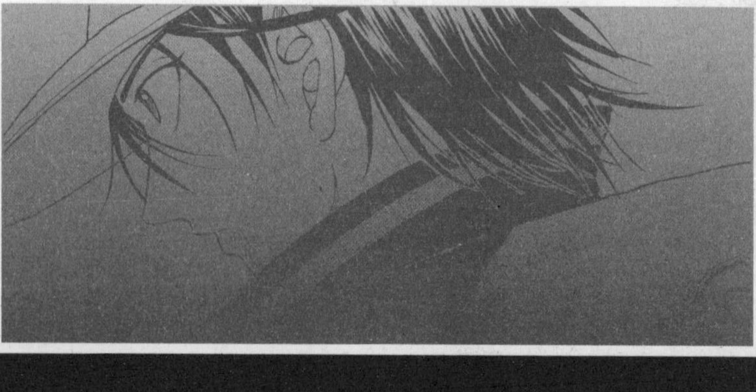

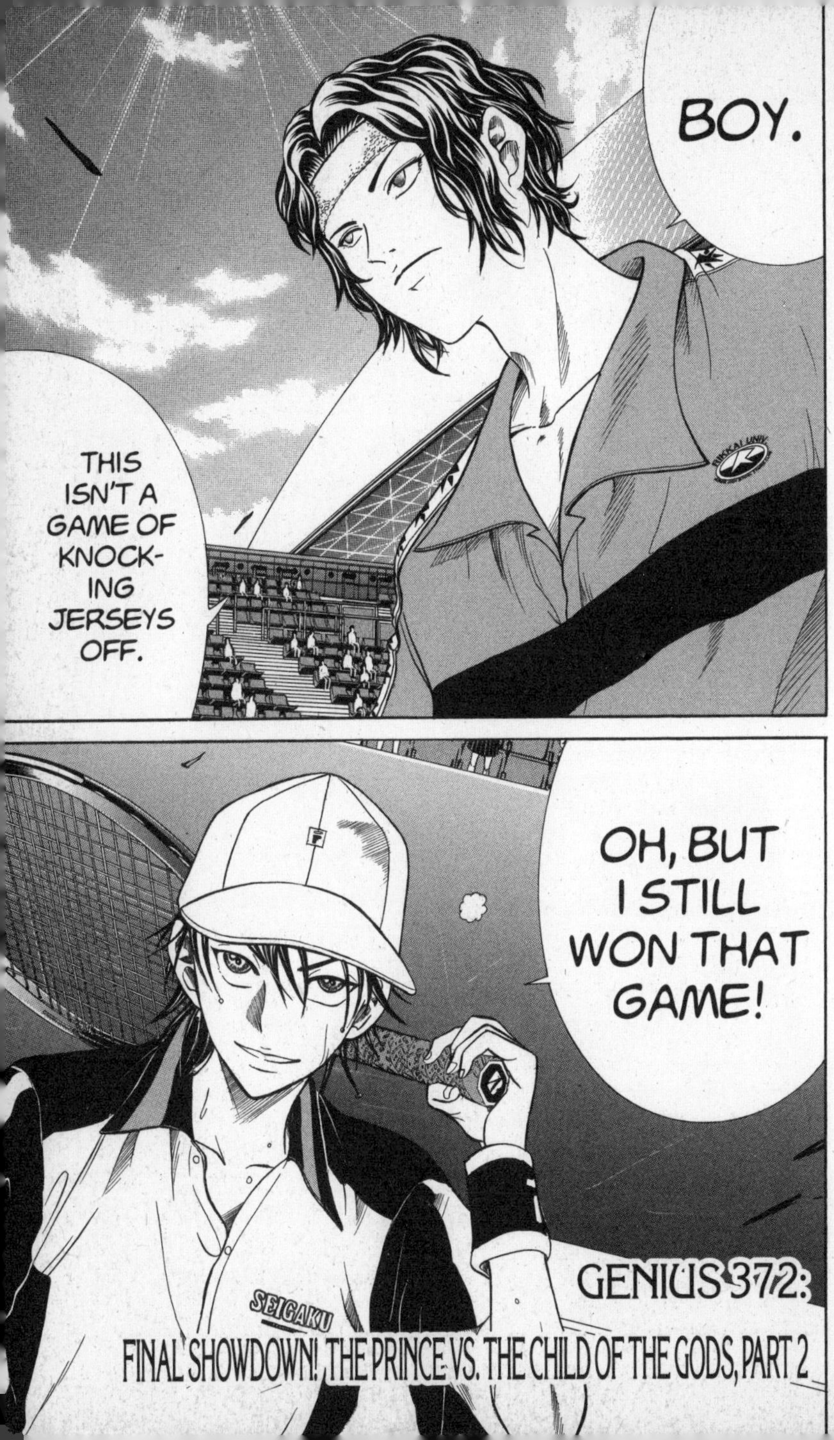
BOY.
THIS ISN'T A GAME OF KNOCK-ING JERSEYS OFF.
OH, BUT I STILL WON THAT GAME!
SEIGAKU
GENIUS 372:
FINAL SHOWDOWN! THE PRINCE VS. THE CHILD OF THE GODS, PART 2

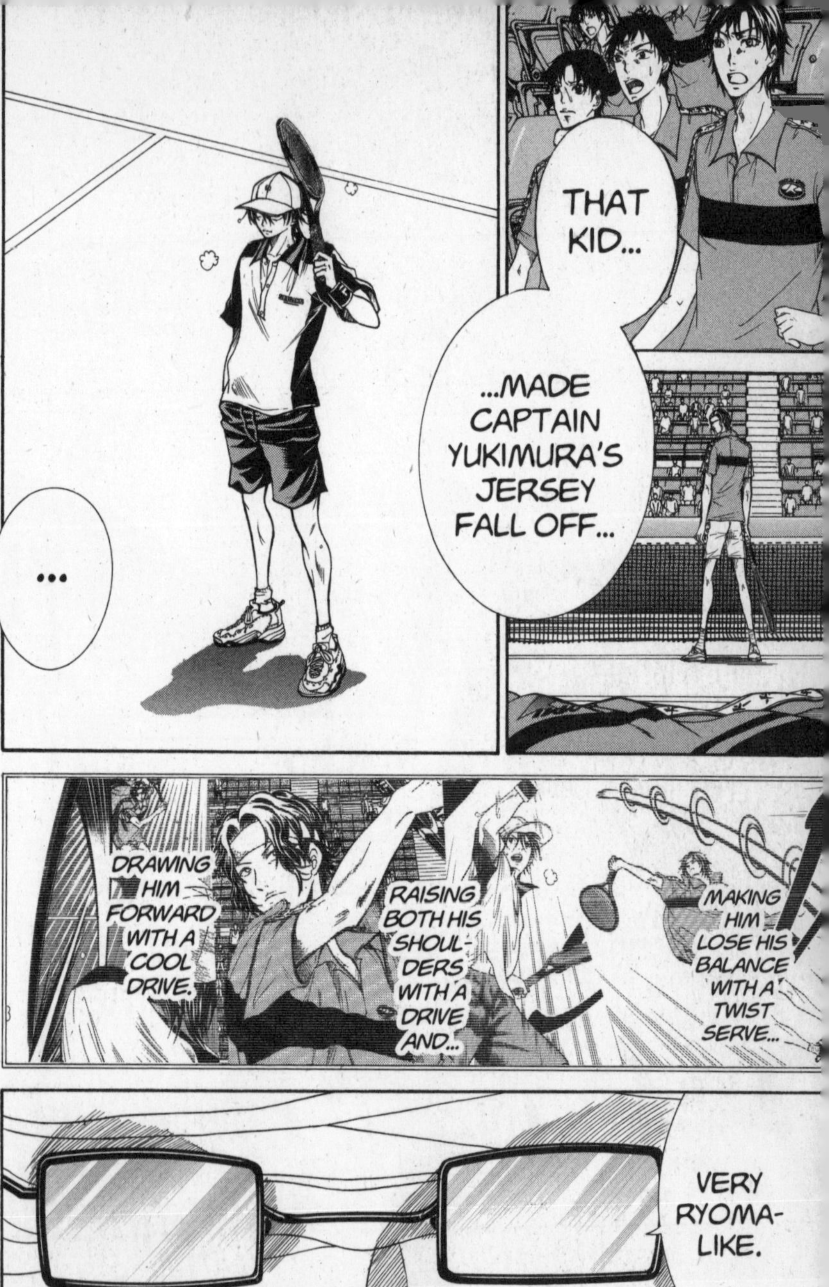
THAT KID...
...MADE CAPTAIN YUKIMURA'S JERSEY FALL OFF...
...
MAKING HIM LOSE HIS BALANCE WITH A TWIST SERVE...
RAISING BOTH HIS SHOULDERS WITH A DRIVE AND...
DRAWING HIM FORWARD WITH A COOL DRIVE.
VERY RYOMA-LIKE.

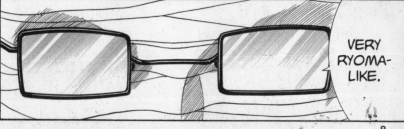

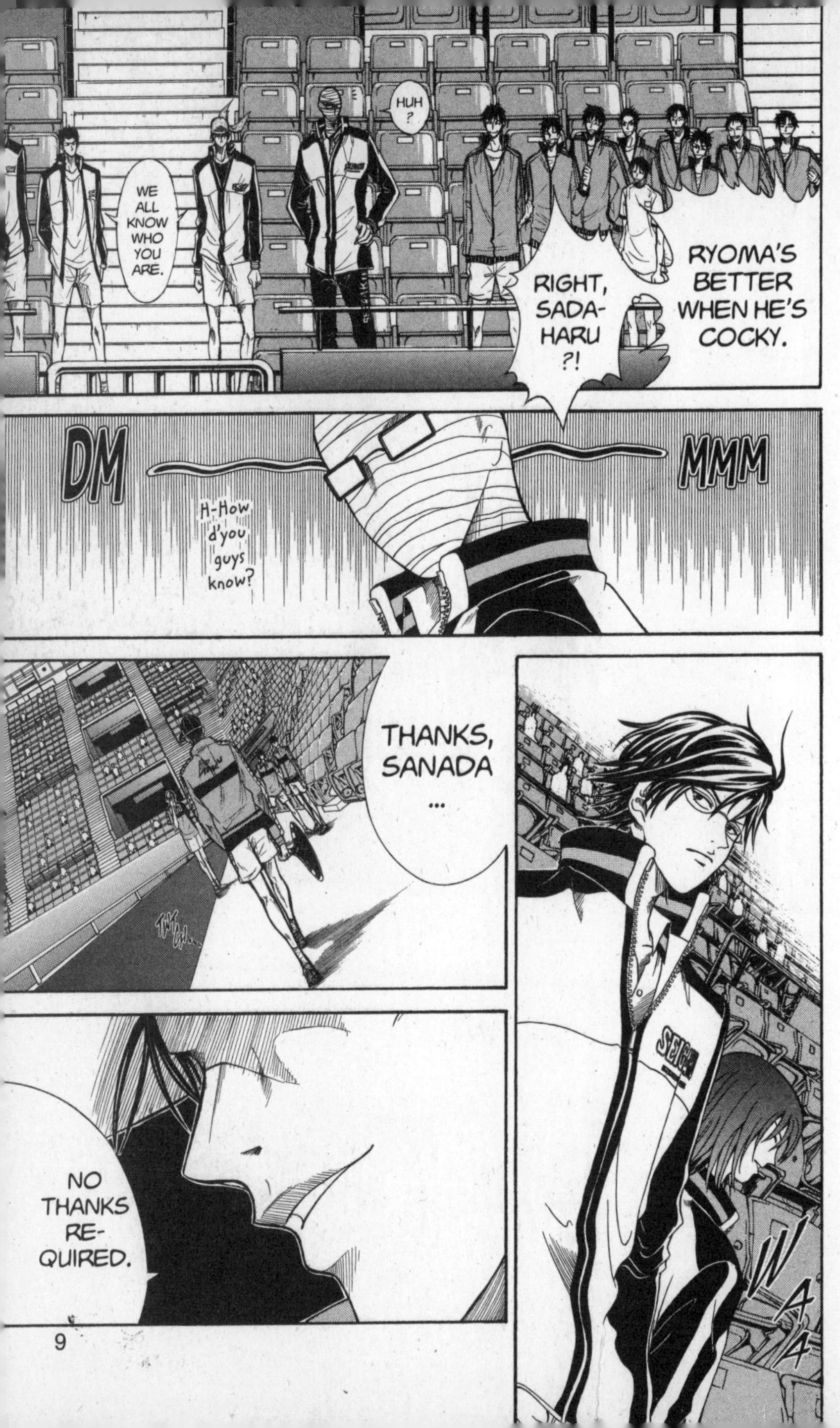
RYOMA'S BETTER WHEN HE'S COCKY.
RIGHT, SADAHARU?!
HUH?
WE ALL KNOW WHO YOU ARE.
DMMMM
H-How d'you guys know?
WAAA
THANKS, SANADA...
NO THANKS REQUIRED.

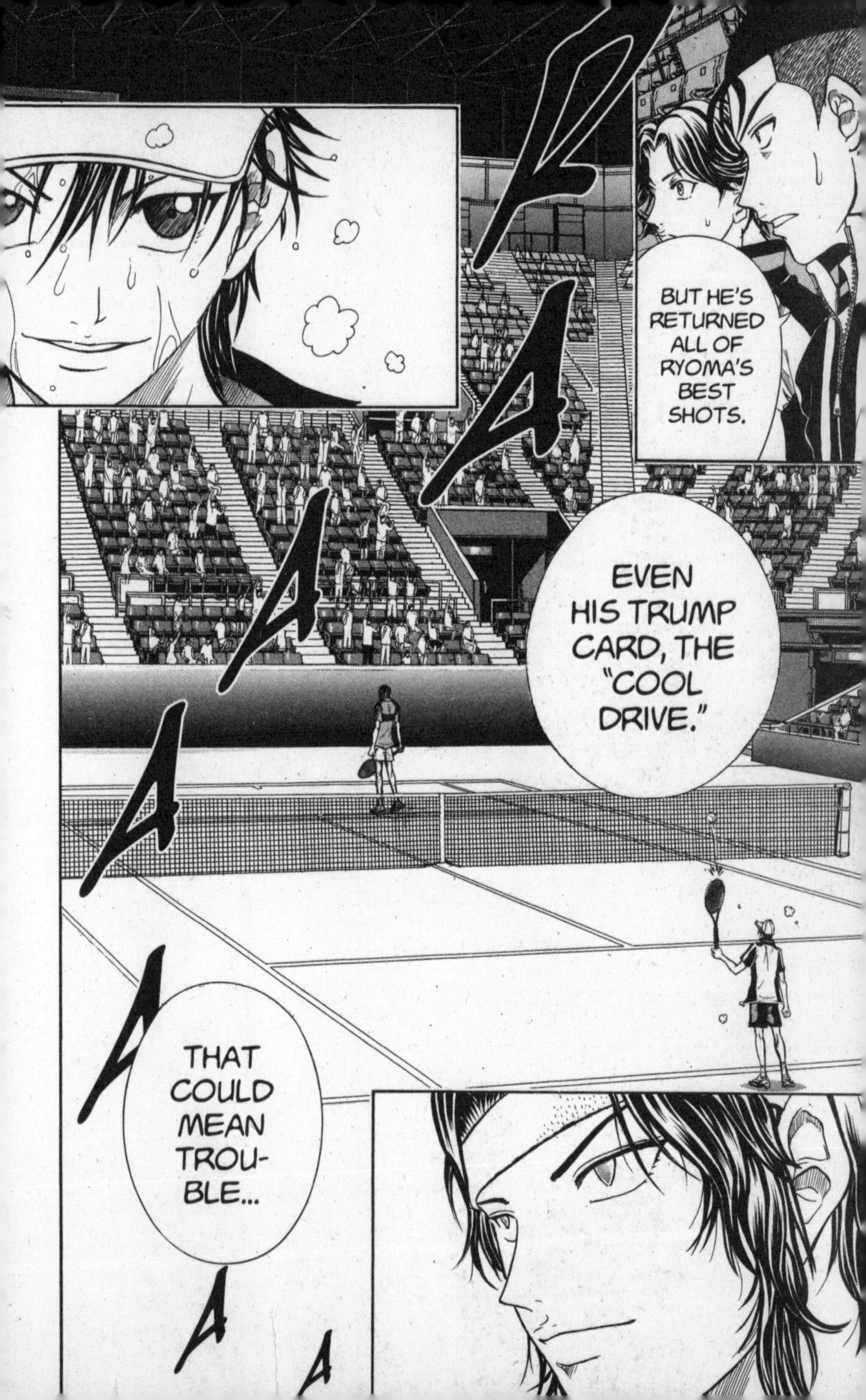
BUT HE'S RETURNED ALL OF RYOMA'S BEST SHOTS.
EVEN HIS TRUMP CARD, THE "COOL DRIVE."
THAT COULD MEAN TROU-BLE...

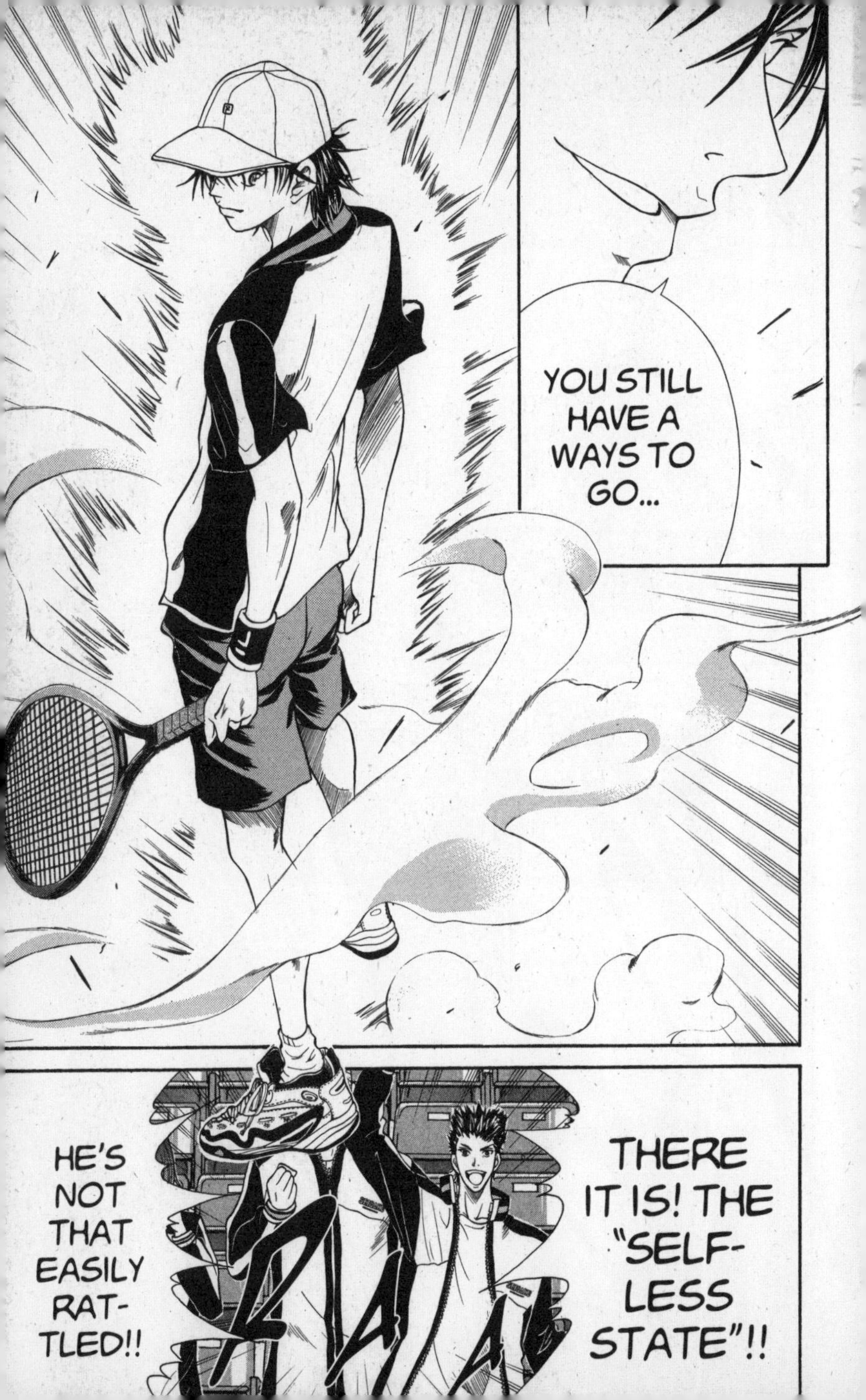
YOU STILL HAVE A WAYS TO GO...
THERE IT IS! THE "SELF-LESS STATE"!!
HE'S NOT THAT EASILY RAT-TLED!!

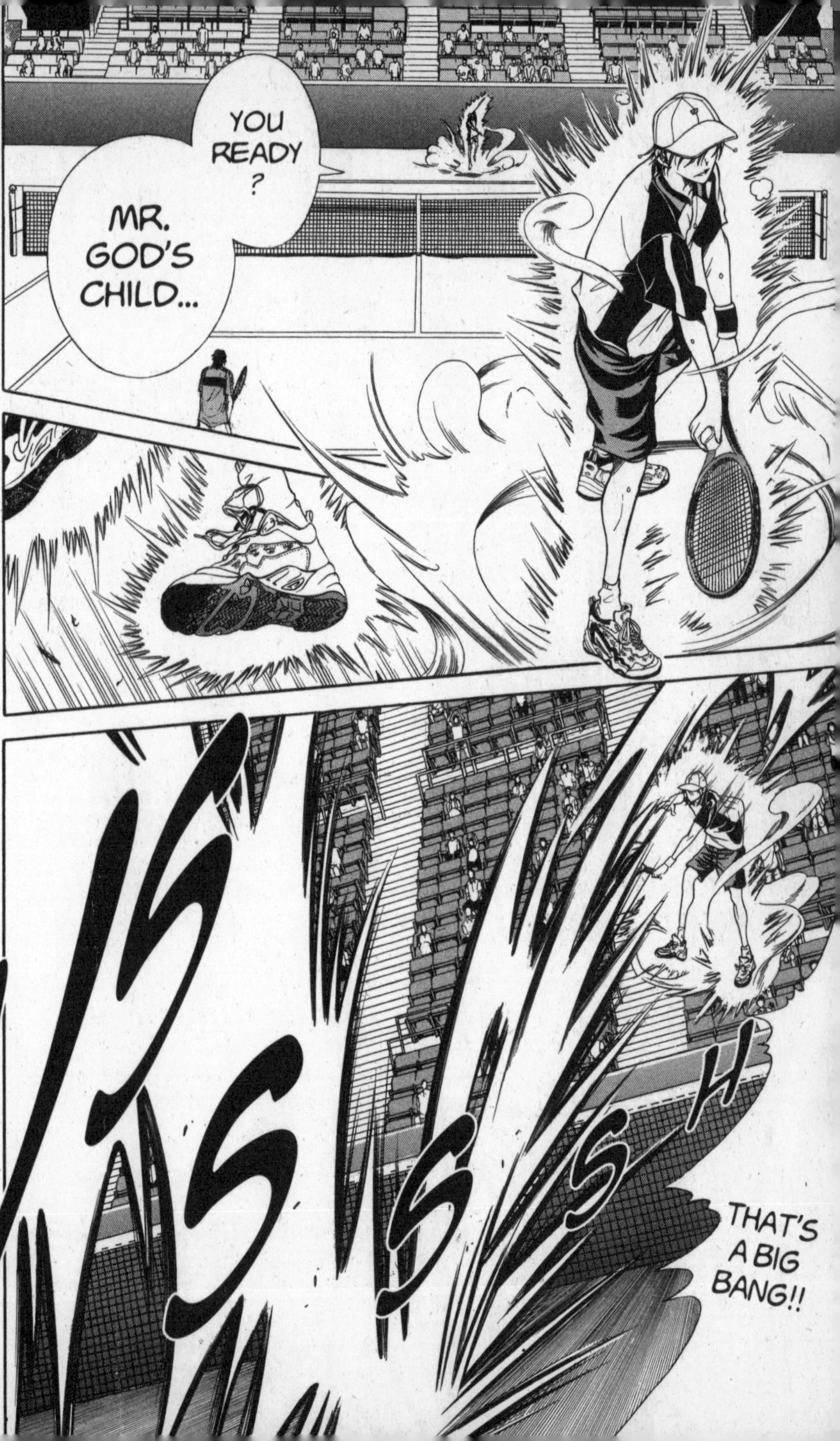

YOU READY?
MR. GOD'S CHILD...
SWISSSH
THAT'S A BIG BANG!!

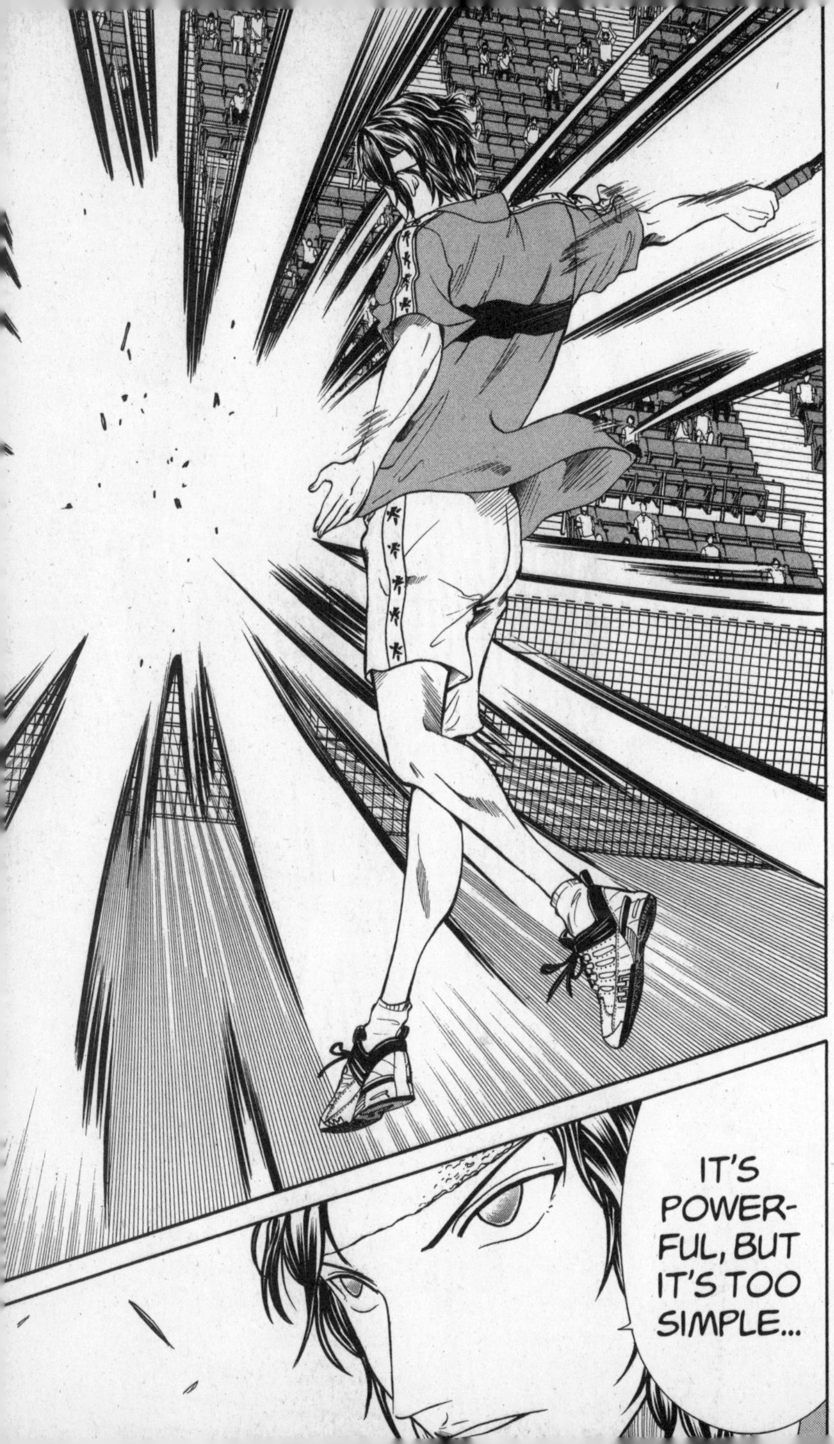
IT'S POWER-FUL, BUT IT'S TOO SIMPLE...

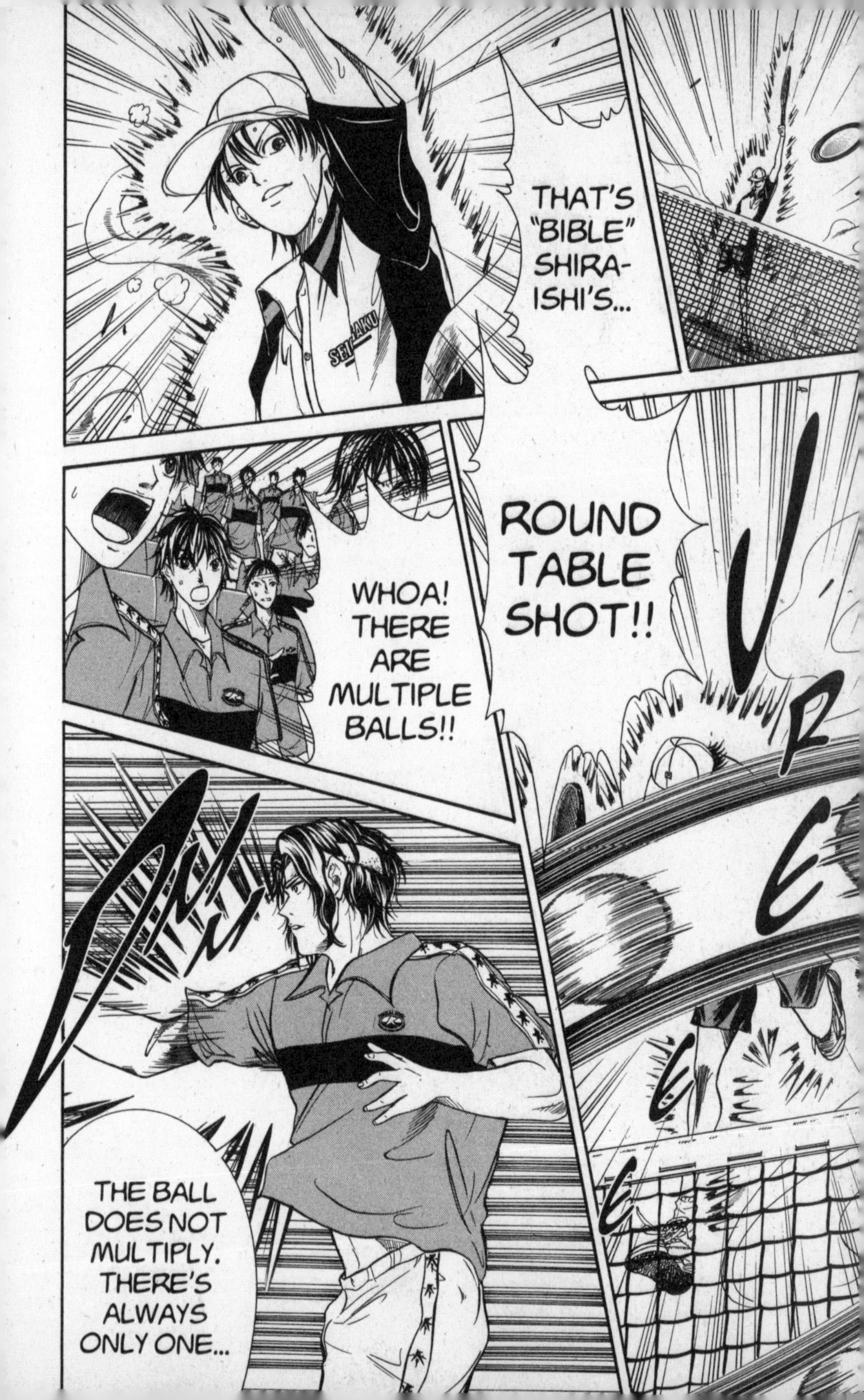
THAT'S "BIBLE" SHIRA-ISHI'S...
ROUND TABLE SHOT!!
WHOA! THERE ARE MULTIPLE BALLS!!
THE BALL DOES NOT MULTIPLY. THERE'S ALWAYS ONLY ONE...

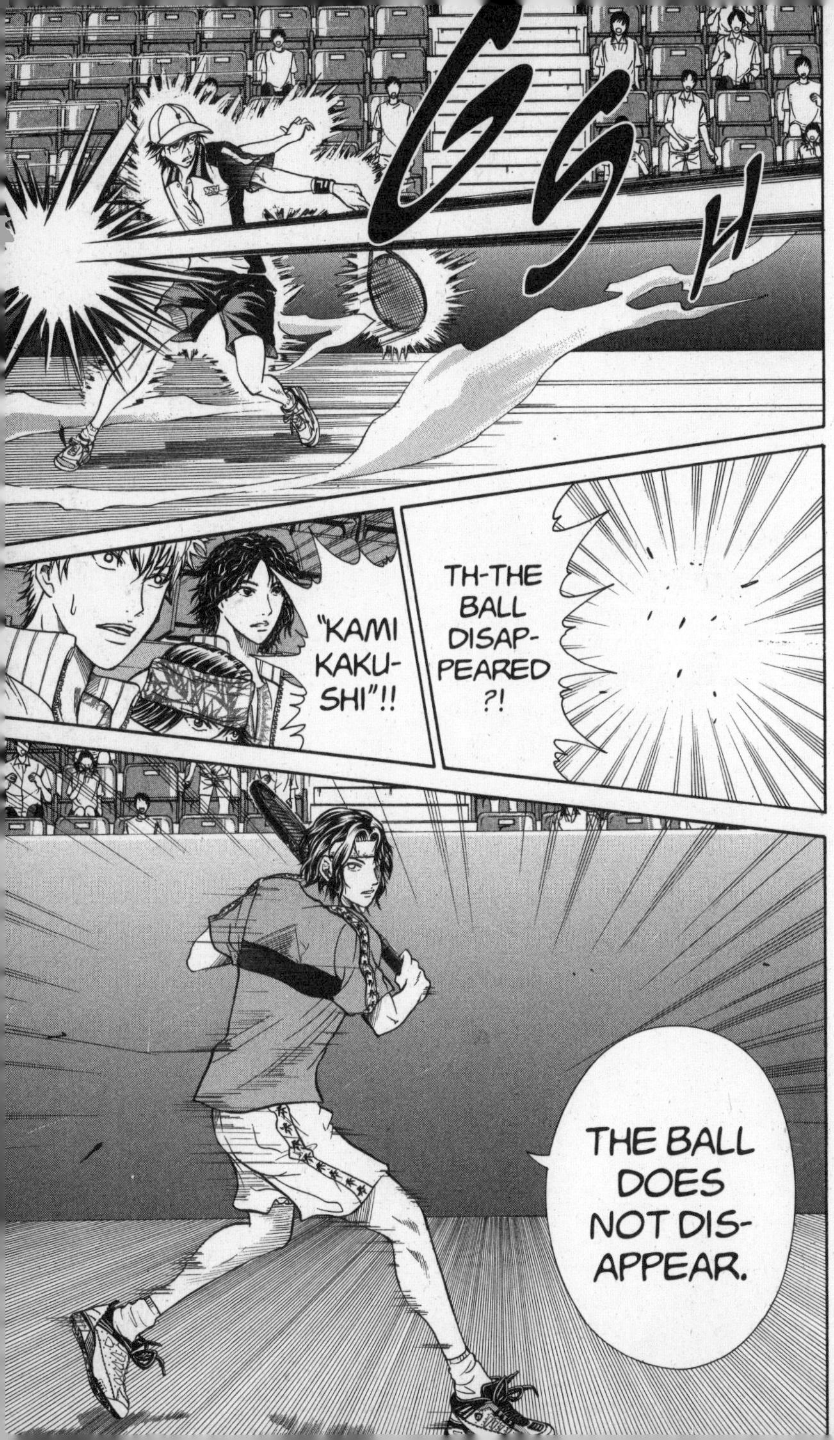
TH-THE BALL DISAP-PEARED ?!
"KAMI KAKU-SHI"!!
THE BALL DOES NOT DIS-APPEAR.

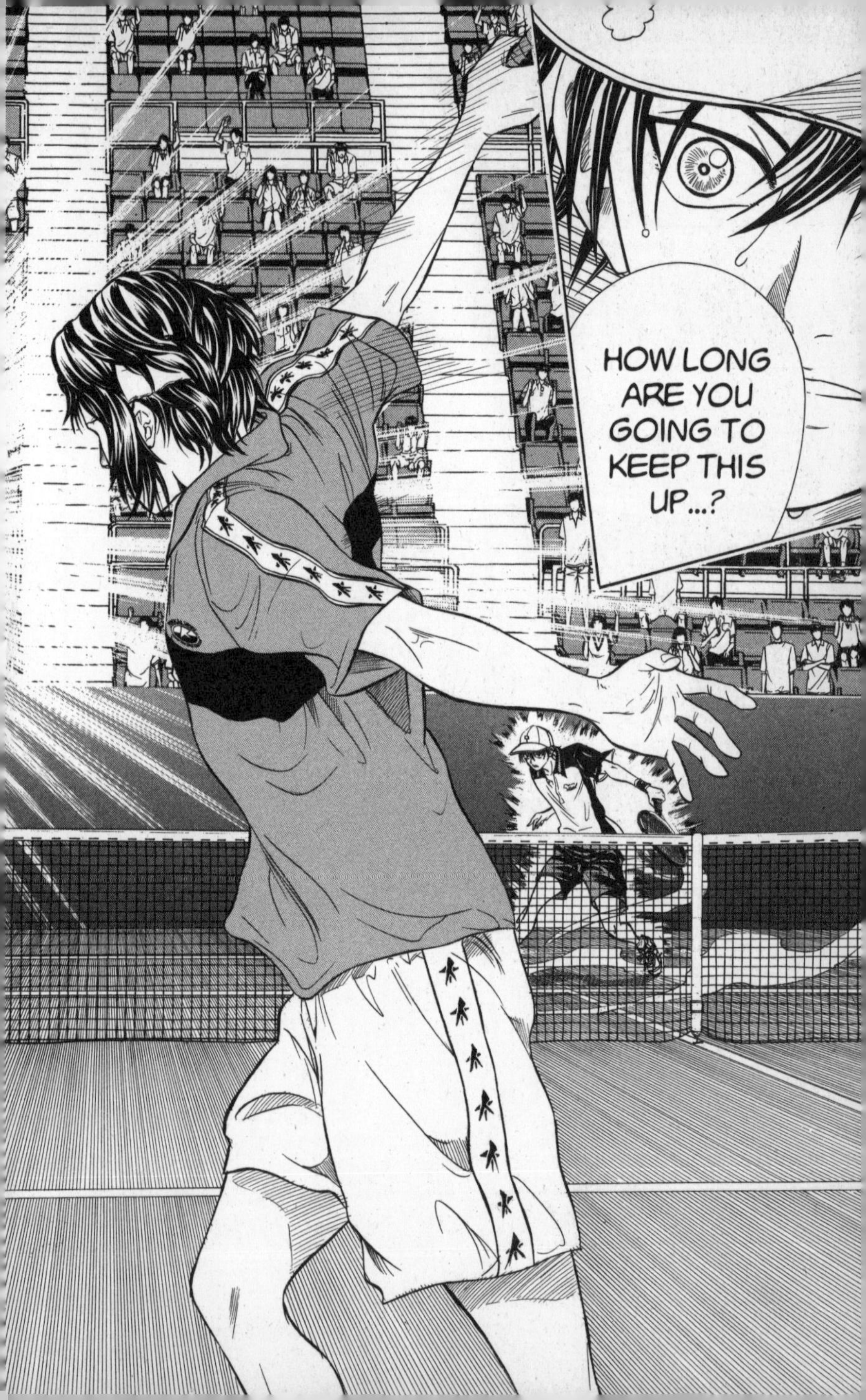
HOW LONG ARE YOU GOING TO KEEP THIS UP...?

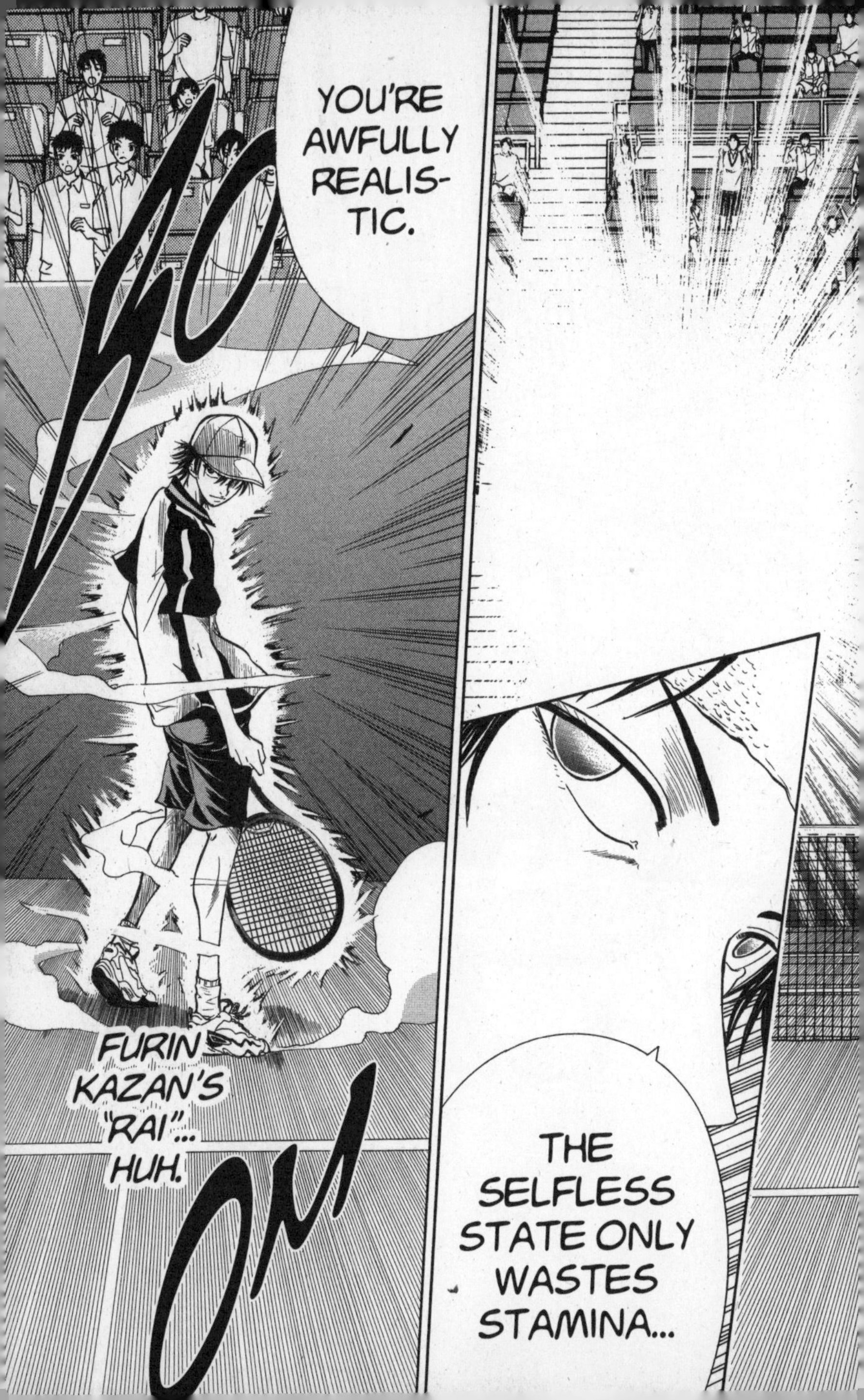
THE SELFLESS STATE ONLY WASTES STAMINA...
YOU'RE AWFULLY REALIS-TIC.
FURIN KAZAN'S "RAI"... HUH.

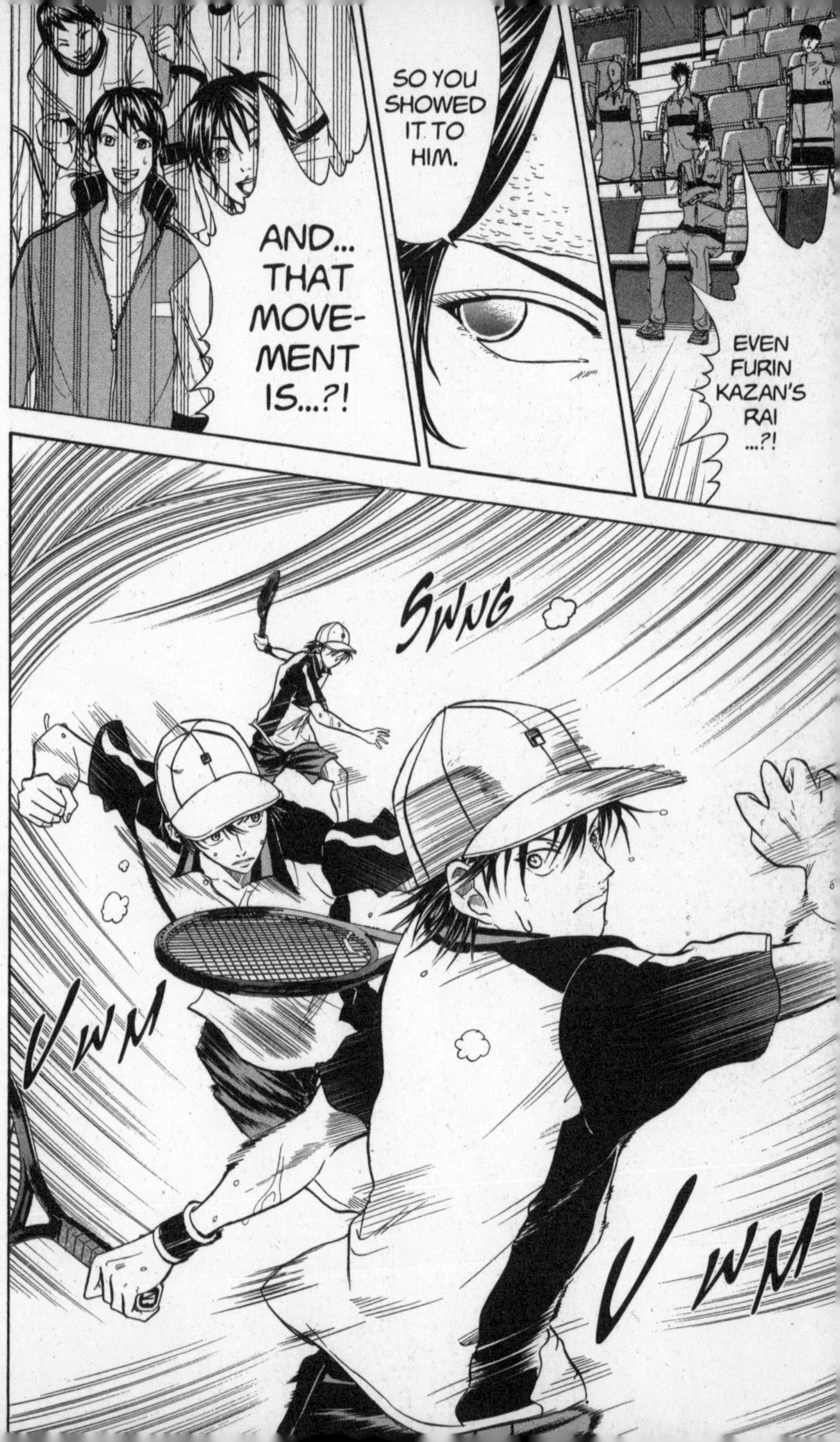
EVEN FURIN KAZAN'S RAI ...?!
SO YOU SHOWED IT TO HIM.
AND... THAT MOVEMENT IS...?!
SWNG
VWM
VWM

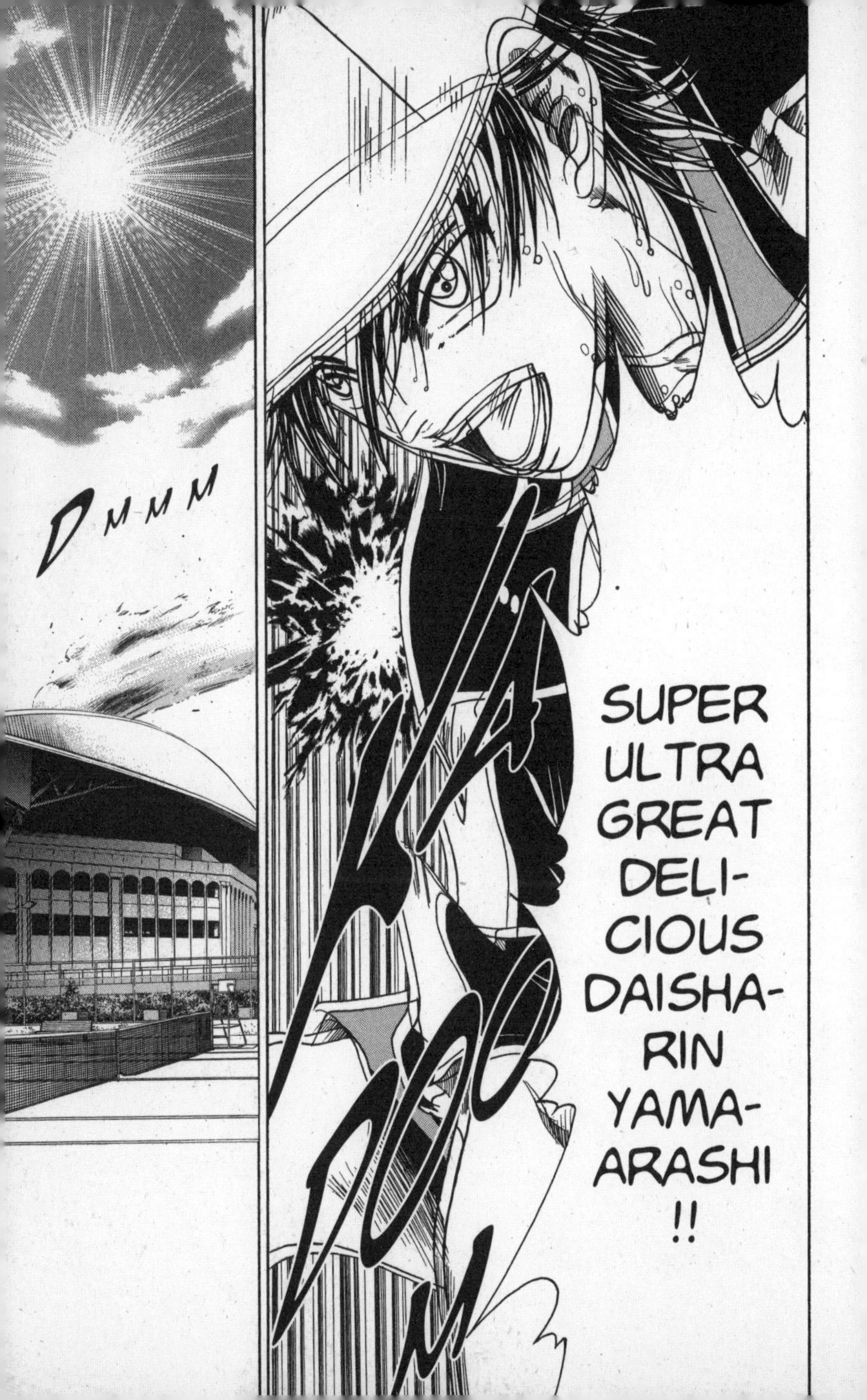
SUPER ULTRA GREAT DELI-CIOUS DAISHA-RIN YAMA-ARASHI !!
DMMM

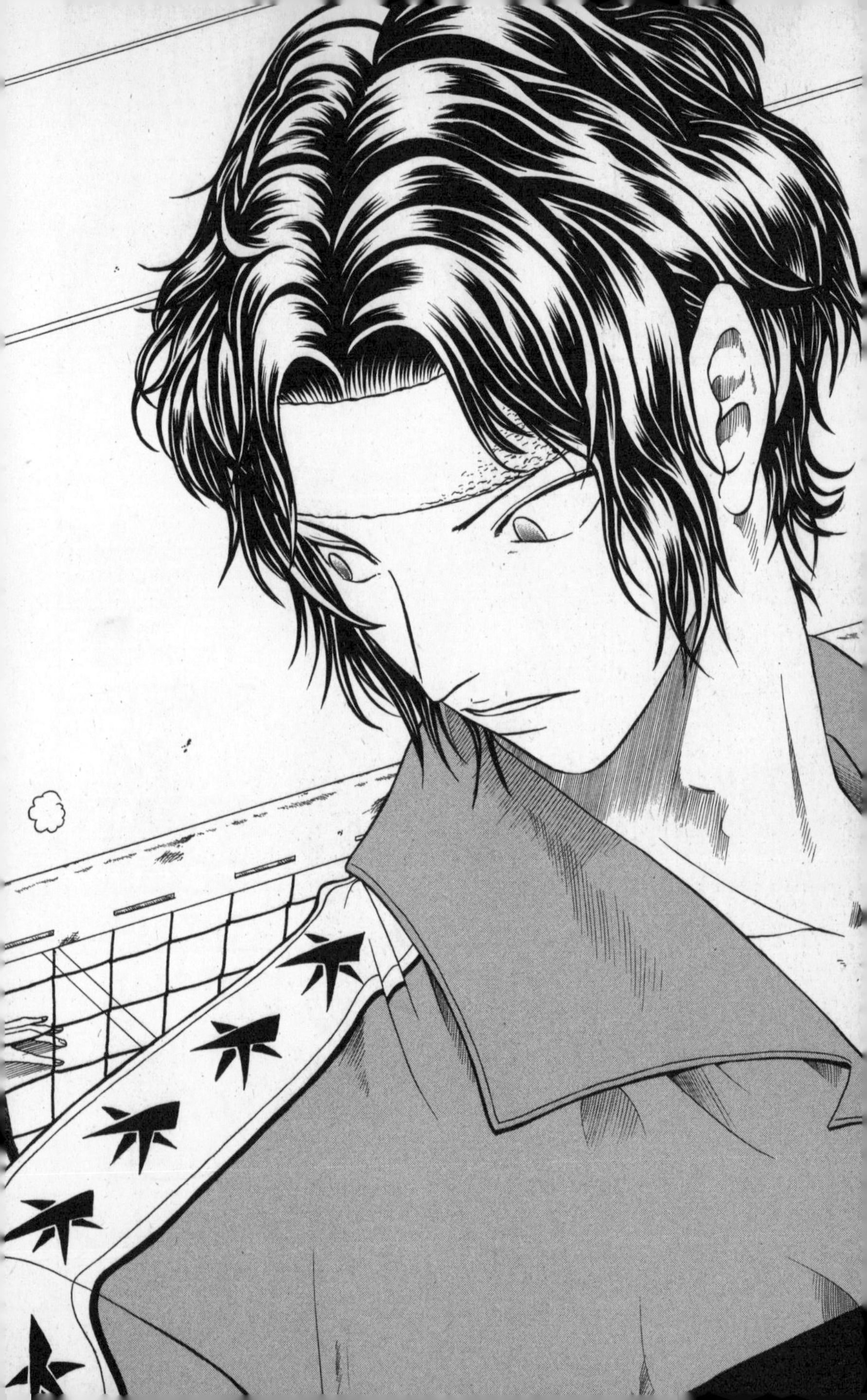

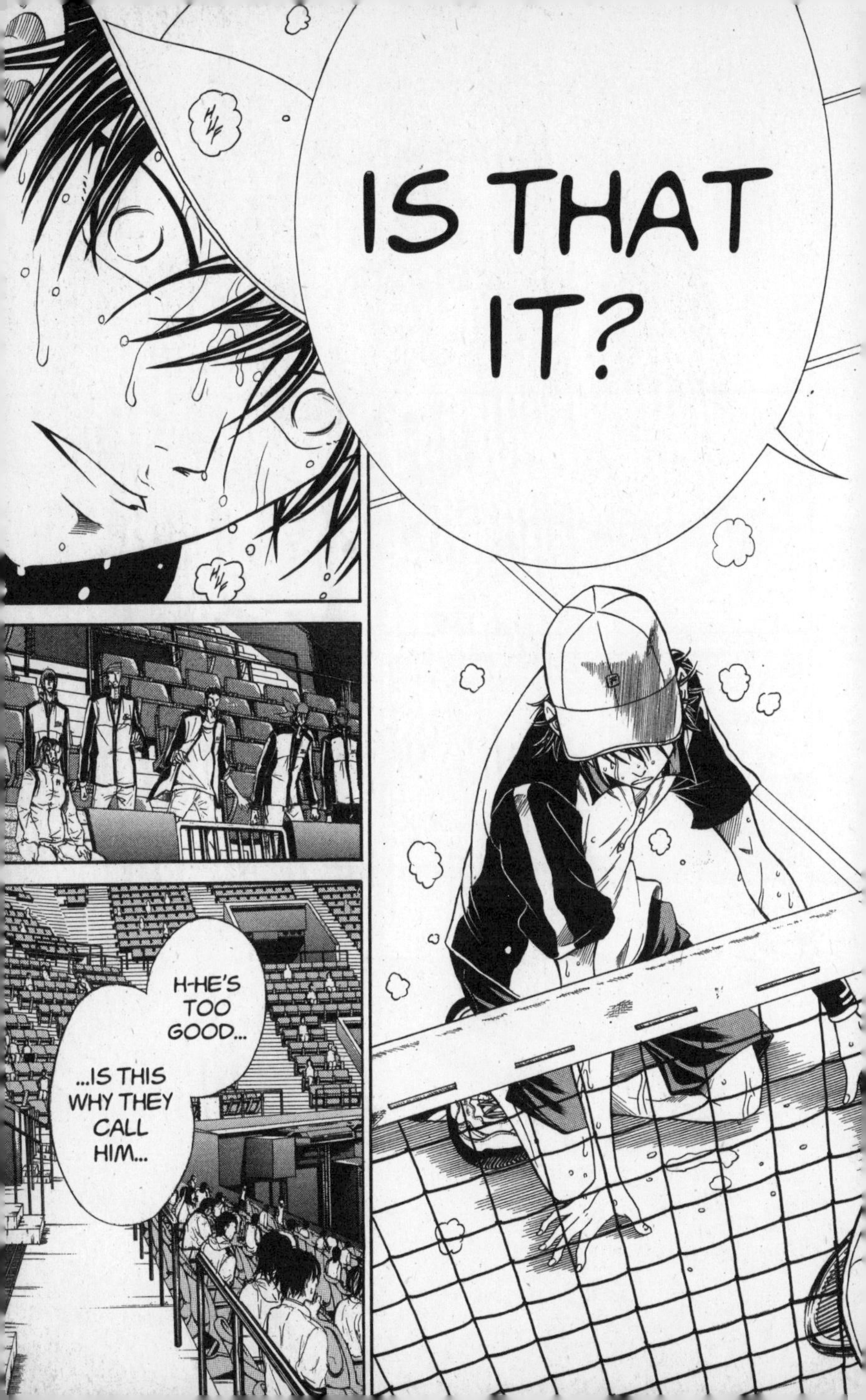
IS THAT IT?
H-HE'S TOO GOOD...
...IS THIS WHY THEY CALL HIM...

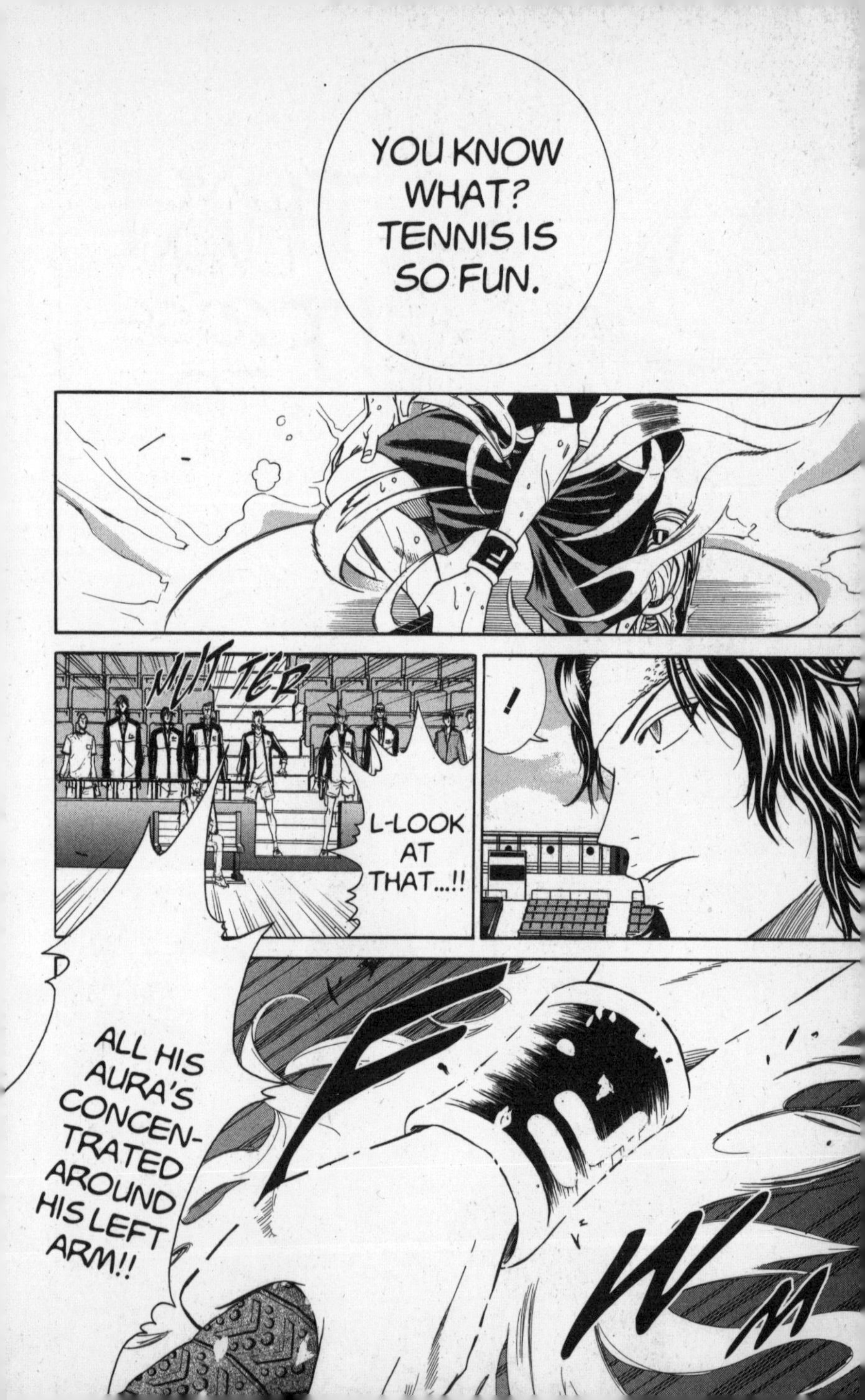
YOU KNOW WHAT? TENNIS IS SO FUN.
!
MUTTER
L-LOOK AT THAT...!!
ALL HIS AURA'S CONCEN-TRATED AROUND HIS LEFT ARM!!

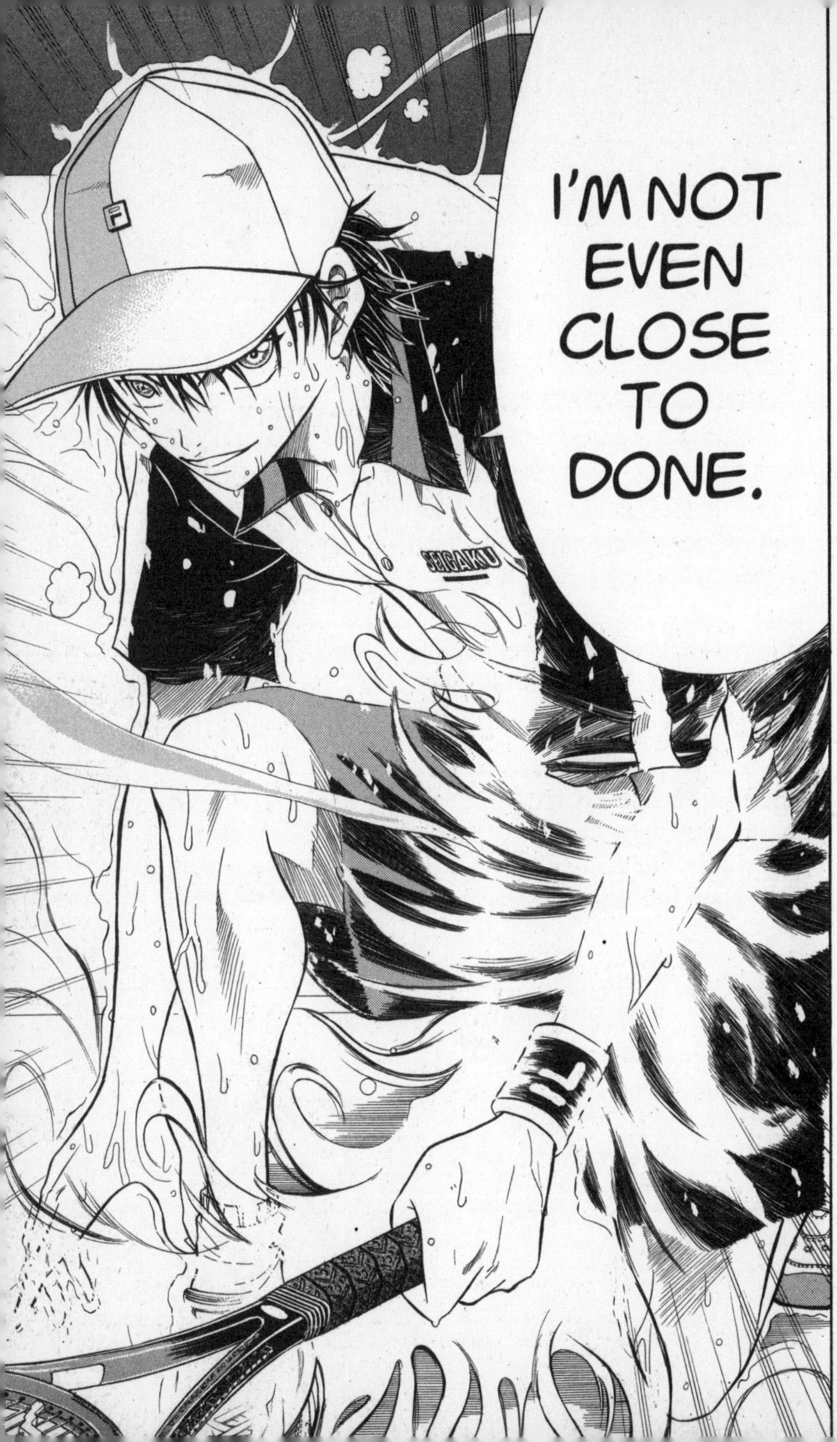
I'M NOT EVEN CLOSE TO DONE.

テニスの王子様
THE PRINCE OF TENNIS

Thank you for reading *The Prince of Tennis* volume 42.

The Prince of Tennis is finally at its final volume!! I was only able to continue this nine-year serial thanks to everybody's support! The last nine years I spent receiving your power was like a dream. I am truly grateful!

Since it began in July of 1997, I wrote each episode as if it was the climax. I spent every week wondering how to surprise and make the readers happy. So I was very happy to receive fan letters telling me I did just that.

I missed a few weeks after hurting my back. To all of you that were waiting in anticipation every week, I'm sorry. I will never forget the kind letters I received from all of you.

I am very fortunate I got to work surrounded by such a warm group of people. I worked with close to fifty different assistants. *The Prince of Tennis* could not have come as far as it did without those people. Thank you.

The voice actors, animation staff, video game staff, cast of the musical, to everybody that was involved, thank you.

And to you all...thank you.

Please continue supporting *The Prince of Tennis*!

テニスの王子様
T.KONOMI
2008.5.12

Send fan letters to: Takeshi Konomi, *The Prince of Tennis*, c/o VIZ Media LLC, P.O. Box 77010, San Francisco, CA 94107

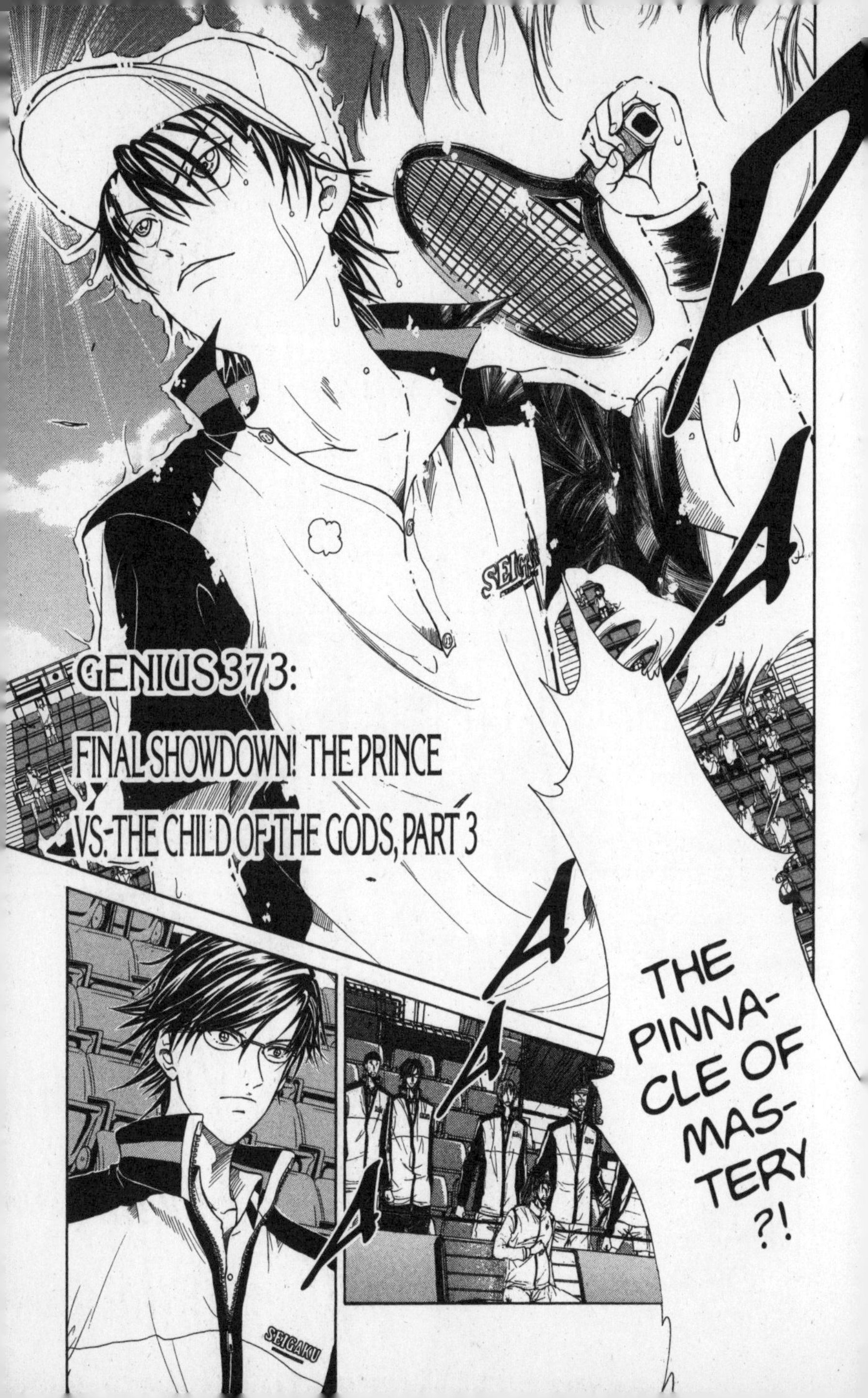
GENIUS 373:
FINAL SHOWDOWN! THE PRINCE VS. THE CHILD OF THE GODS, PART 3
THE PINNACLE OF MASTERY?!
SEIGAKU

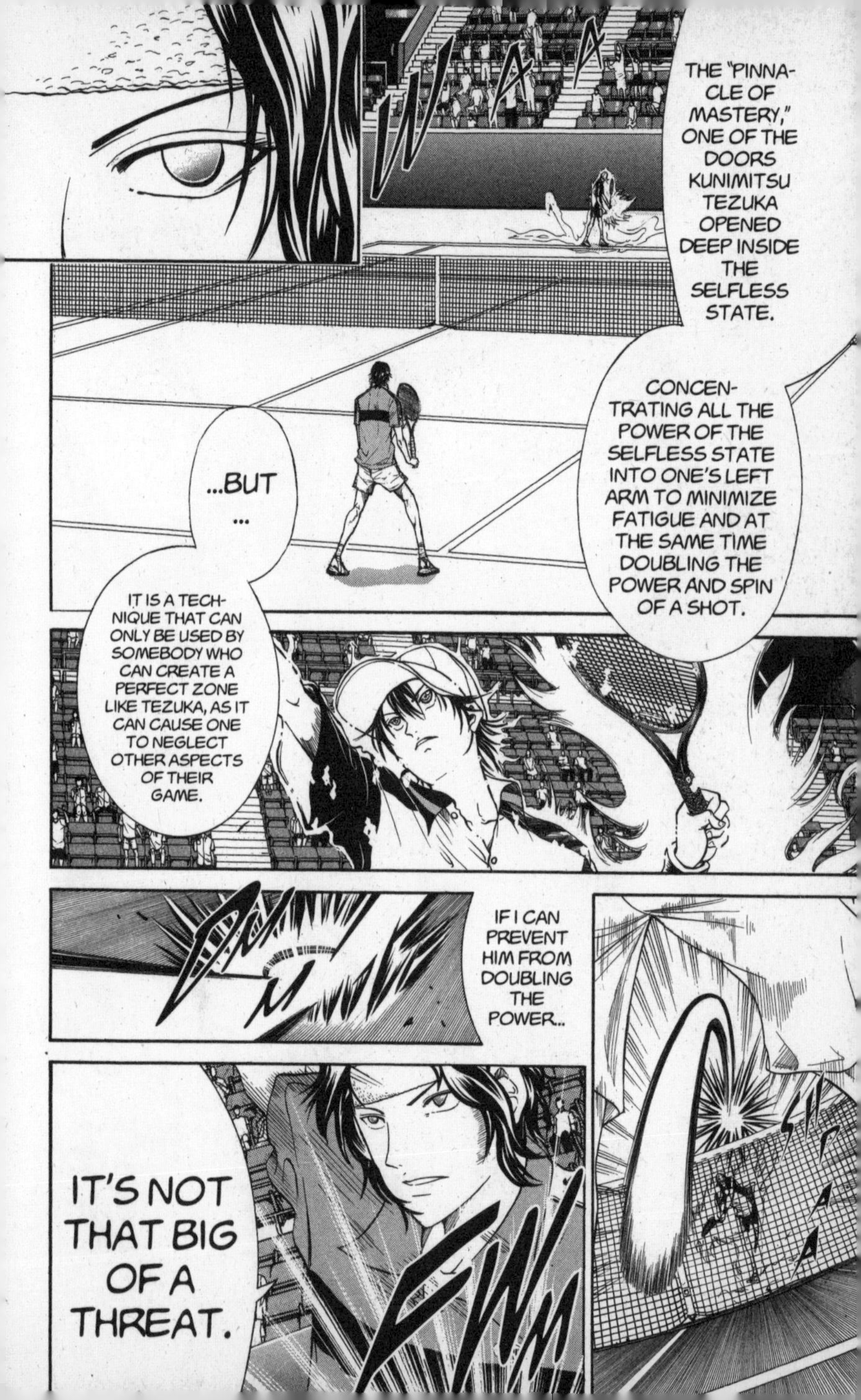
THE "PINNACLE OF MASTERY," ONE OF THE DOORS KUNIMITSU TEZUKA OPENED DEEP INSIDE THE SELFLESS STATE.
CONCENTRATING ALL THE POWER OF THE SELFLESS STATE INTO ONE'S LEFT ARM TO MINIMIZE FATIGUE AND AT THE SAME TIME DOUBLING THE POWER AND SPIN OF A SHOT.
...BUT ...
IT IS A TECHNIQUE THAT CAN ONLY BE USED BY SOMEBODY WHO CAN CREATE A PERFECT ZONE LIKE TEZUKA, AS IT CAN CAUSE ONE TO NEGLECT OTHER ASPECTS OF THEIR GAME.
IF I CAN PREVENT HIM FROM DOUBLING THE POWER...
IT'S NOT THAT BIG OF A THREAT.

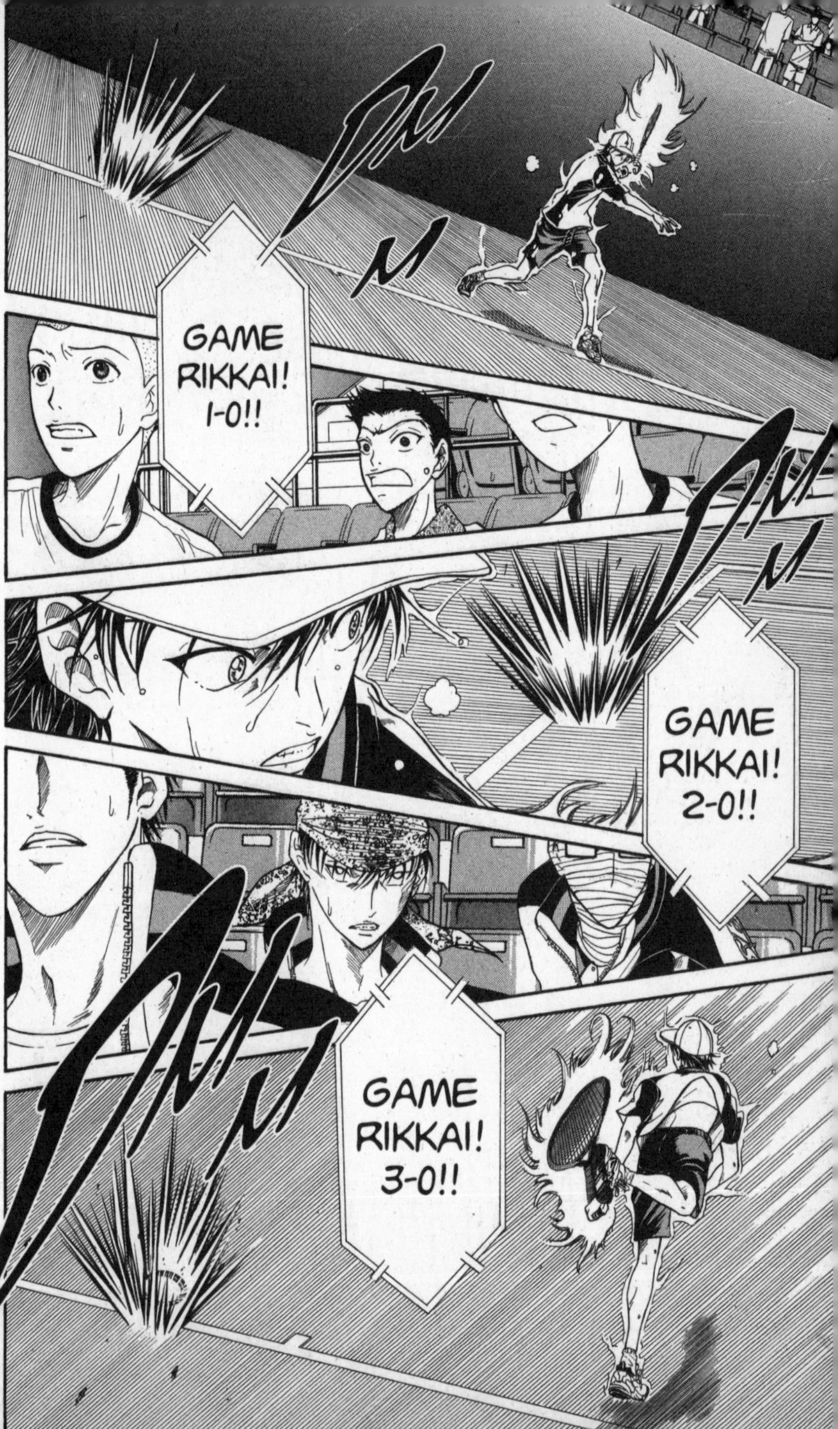
GAME RIKKAI! 1-0!!
GAME RIKKAI! 2-0!!
GAME RIKKAI! 3-0!!

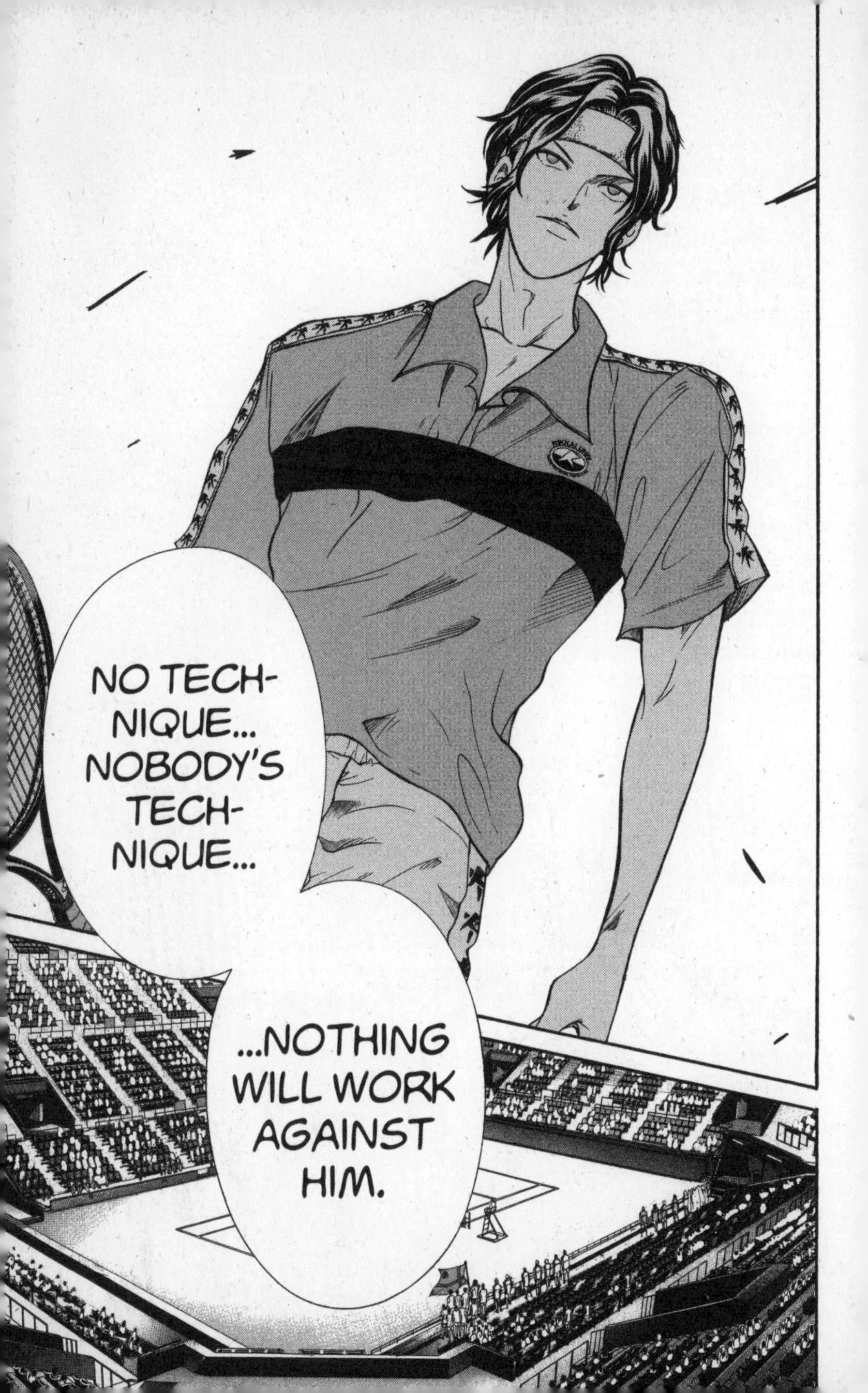
NO TECH-NIQUE... NOBODY'S TECH-NIQUE...
...NOTHING WILL WORK AGAINST HIM.

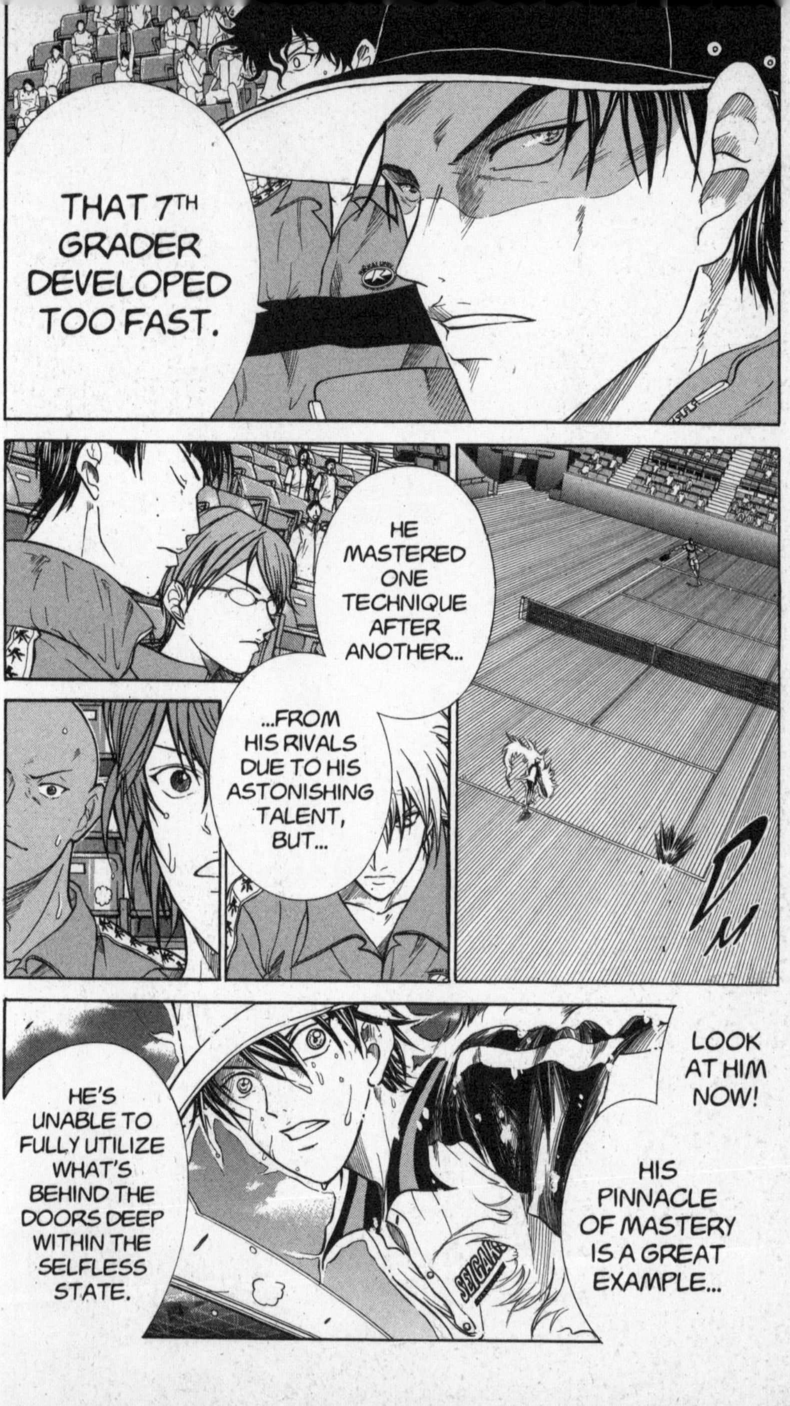
THAT 7TH GRADER DEVELOPED TOO FAST.
HE MASTERED ONE TECHNIQUE AFTER ANOTHER...
...FROM HIS RIVALS DUE TO HIS ASTONISHING TALENT, BUT...
LOOK AT HIM NOW!
HIS PINNACLE OF MASTERY IS A GREAT EXAMPLE...
HE'S UNABLE TO FULLY UTILIZE WHAT'S BEHIND THE DOORS DEEP WITHIN THE SELFLESS STATE.

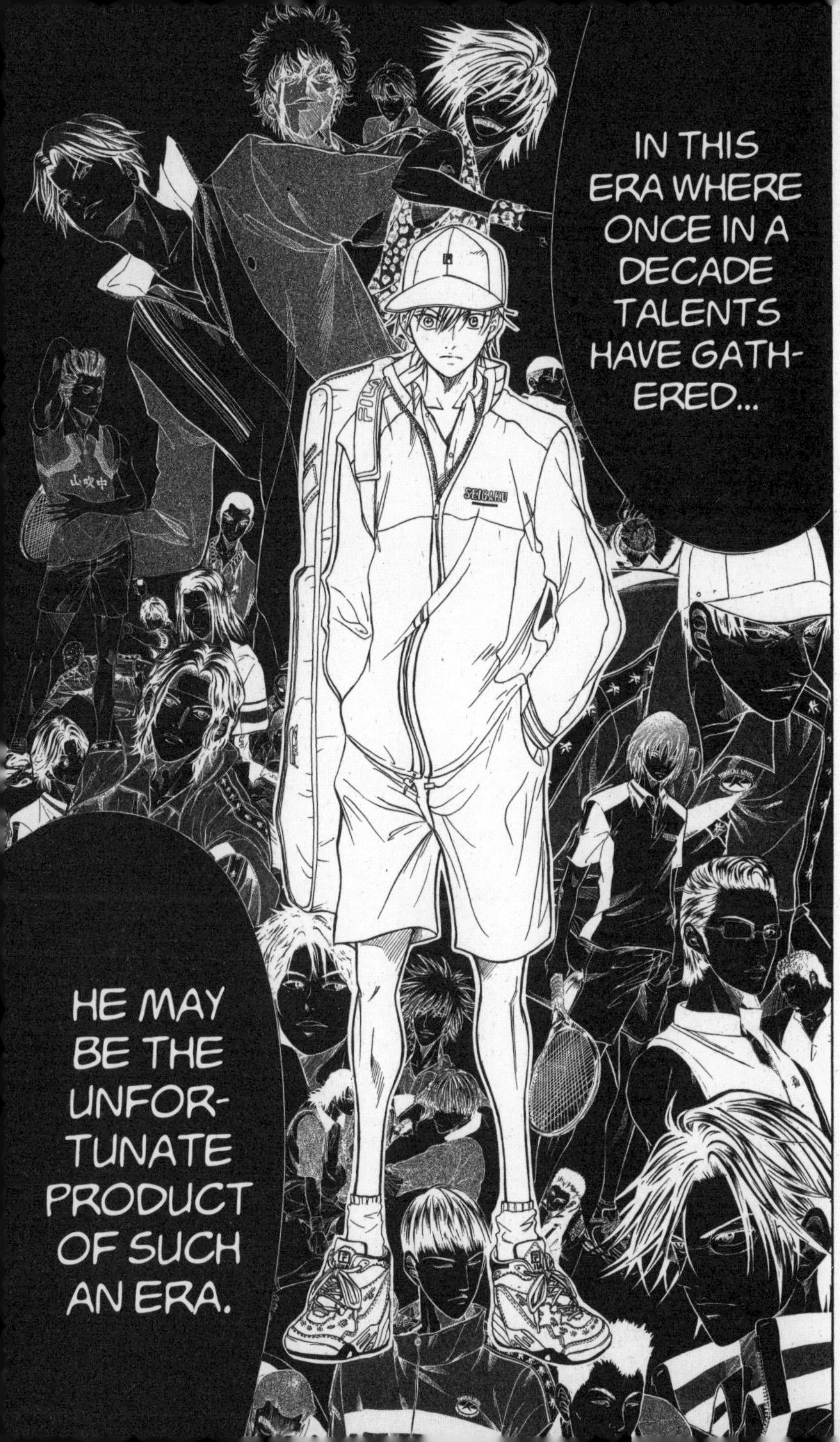
IN THIS ERA WHERE ONCE IN A DECADE TALENTS HAVE GATHERED...
SEIGAKU
HE MAY BE THE UNFORTUNATE PRODUCT OF SUCH AN ERA.

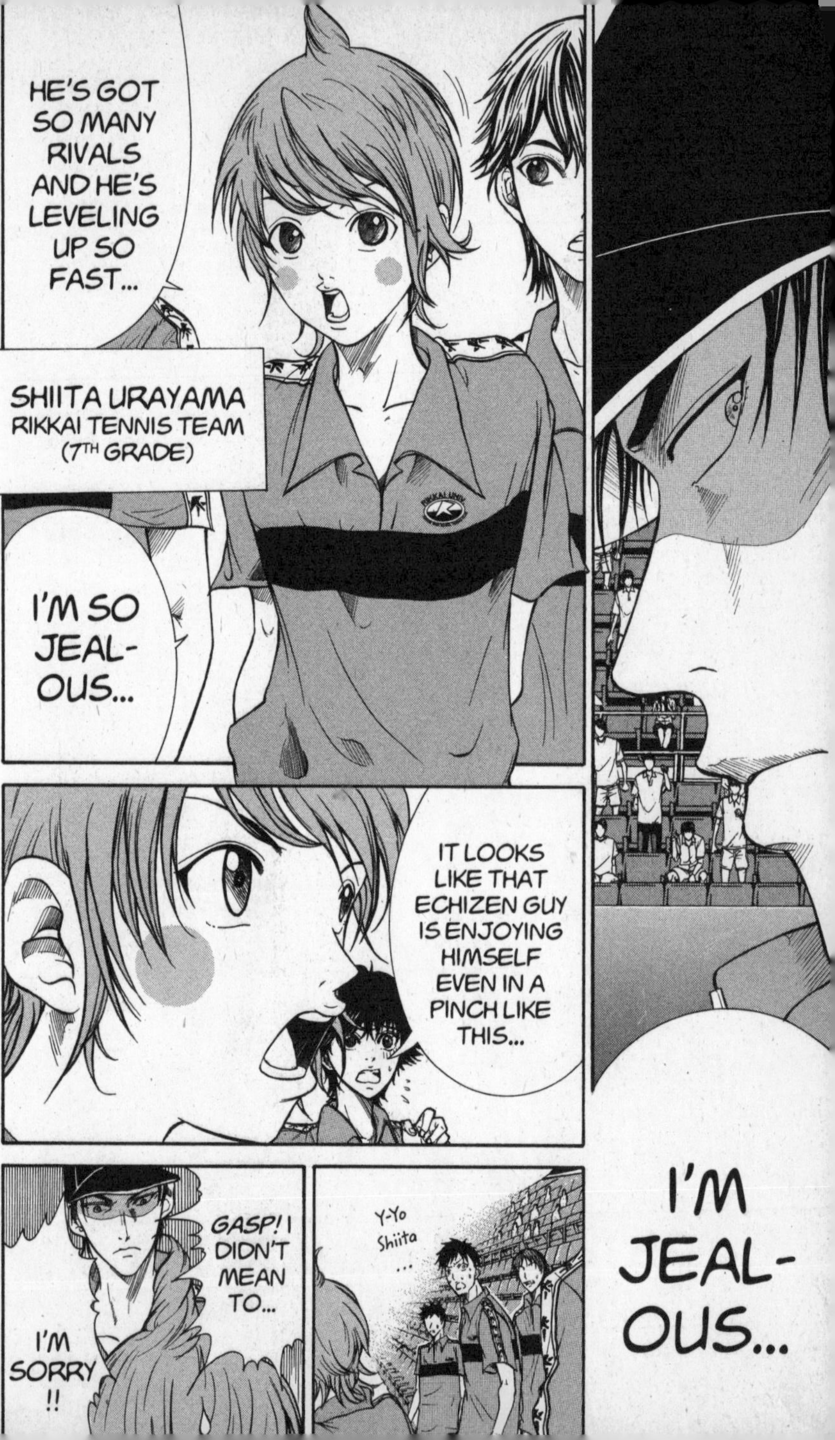

HE'S GOT SO MANY RIVALS AND HE'S LEVELING UP SO FAST...
SHIITA URAYAMA
RIKKAI TENNIS TEAM
(7TH GRADE)
I'M SO JEAL-OUS...
IT LOOKS LIKE THAT ECHIZEN GUY IS ENJOYING HIMSELF EVEN IN A PINCH LIKE THIS...
I'M JEAL-OUS...
Y-Yo Shiita ...
GASP! I DIDN'T MEAN TO...
I'M SORRY !!

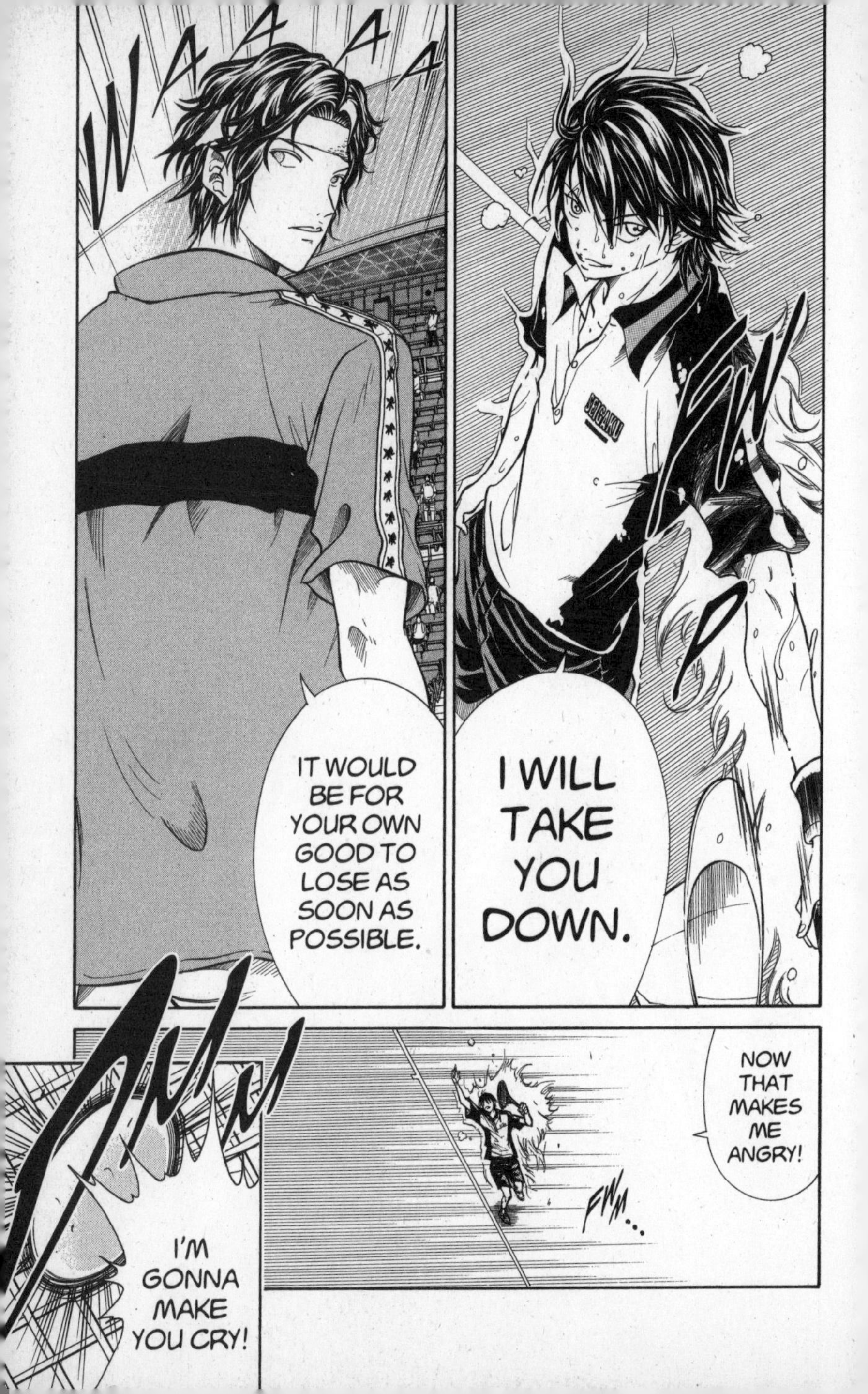
I WILL TAKE YOU DOWN.
WAAAA
IT WOULD BE FOR YOUR OWN GOOD TO LOSE AS SOON AS POSSIBLE.
NOW THAT MAKES ME ANGRY!
FWM...
I'M GONNA MAKE YOU CRY!

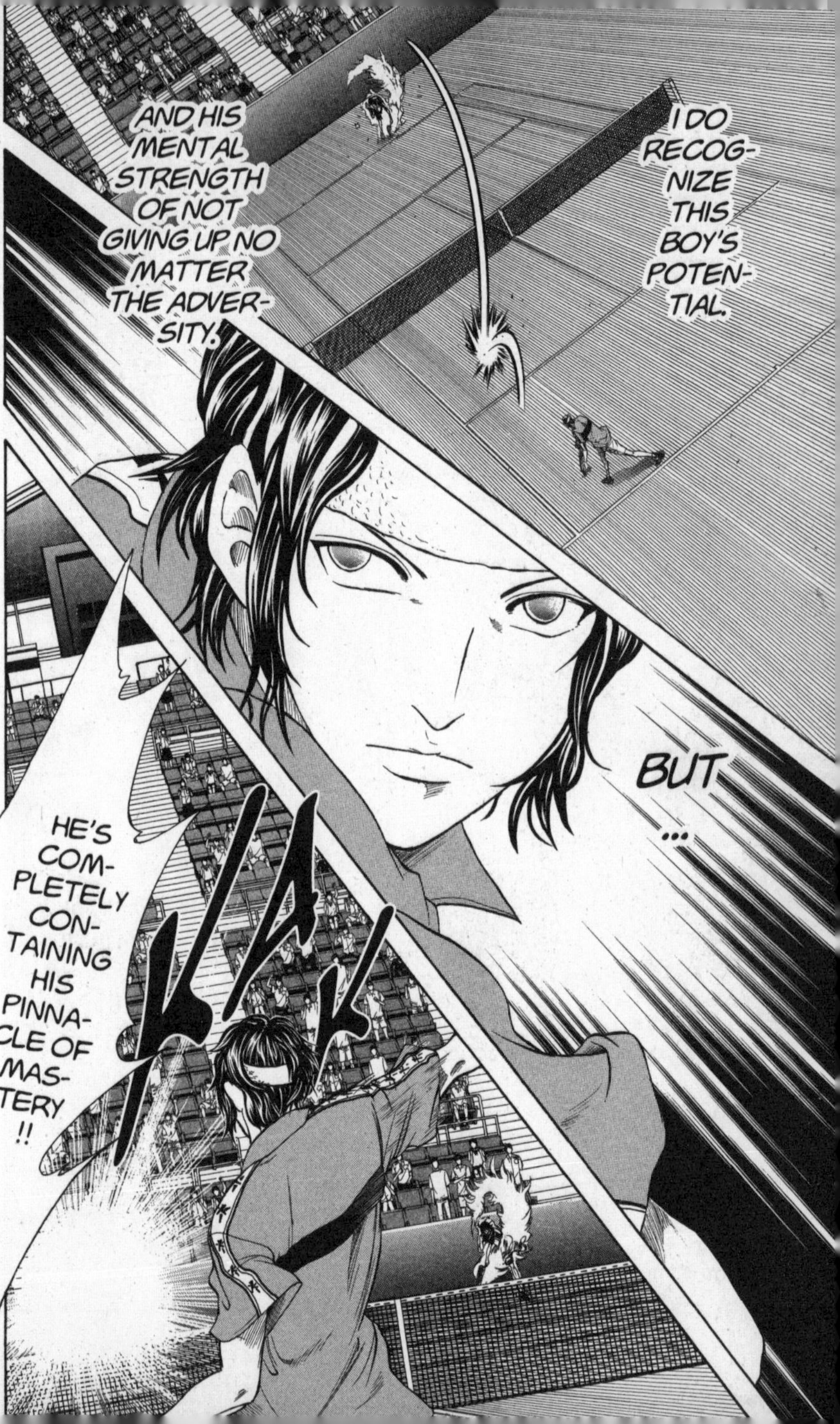
I DO RECOGNIZE THIS BOY'S POTENTIAL.
AND HIS MENTAL STRENGTH OF NOT GIVING UP NO MATTER THE ADVERSITY.
BUT...
HE'S COMPLETELY CONTAINING HIS PINNACLE OF MASTERY!!

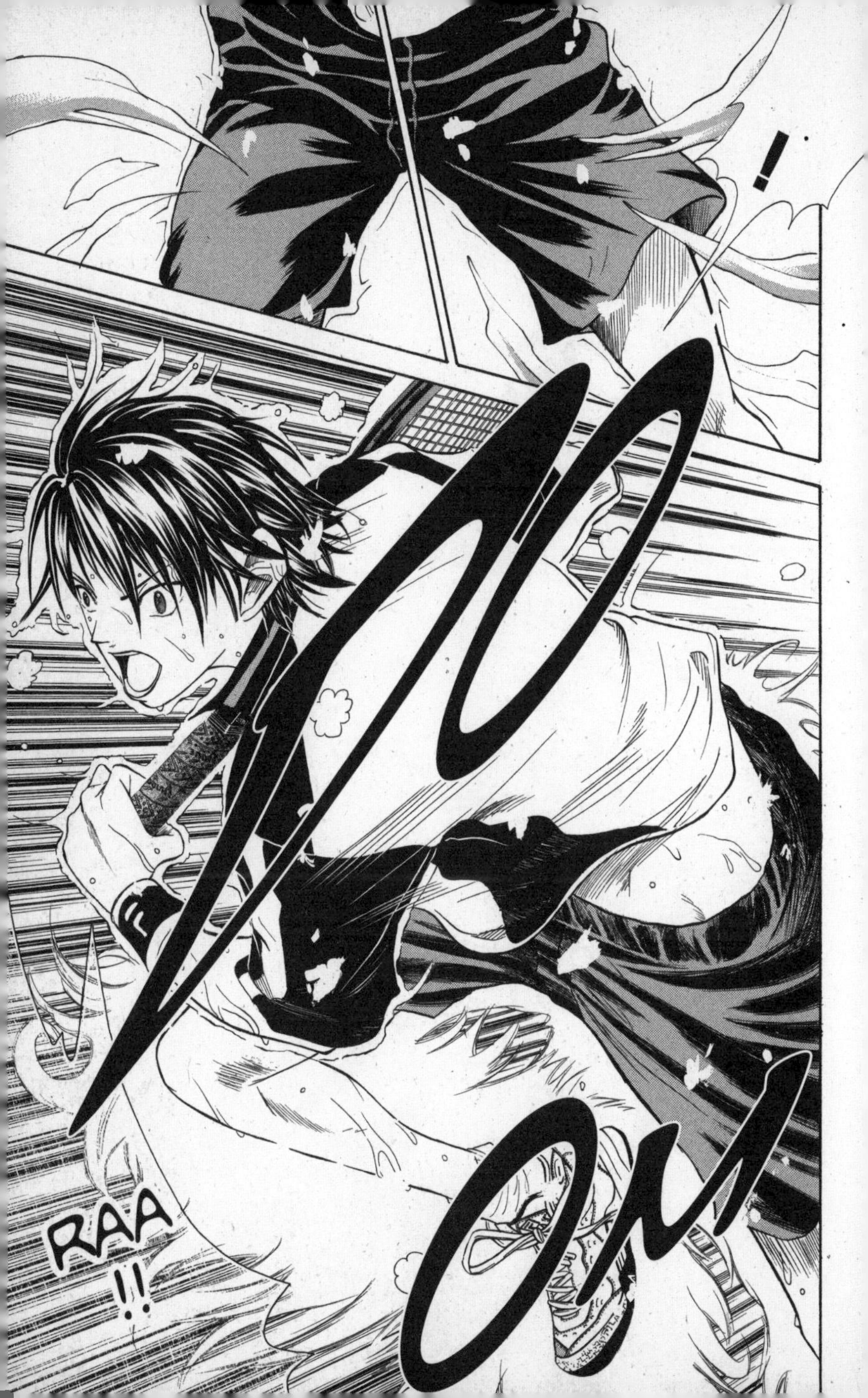
!
RAA !!

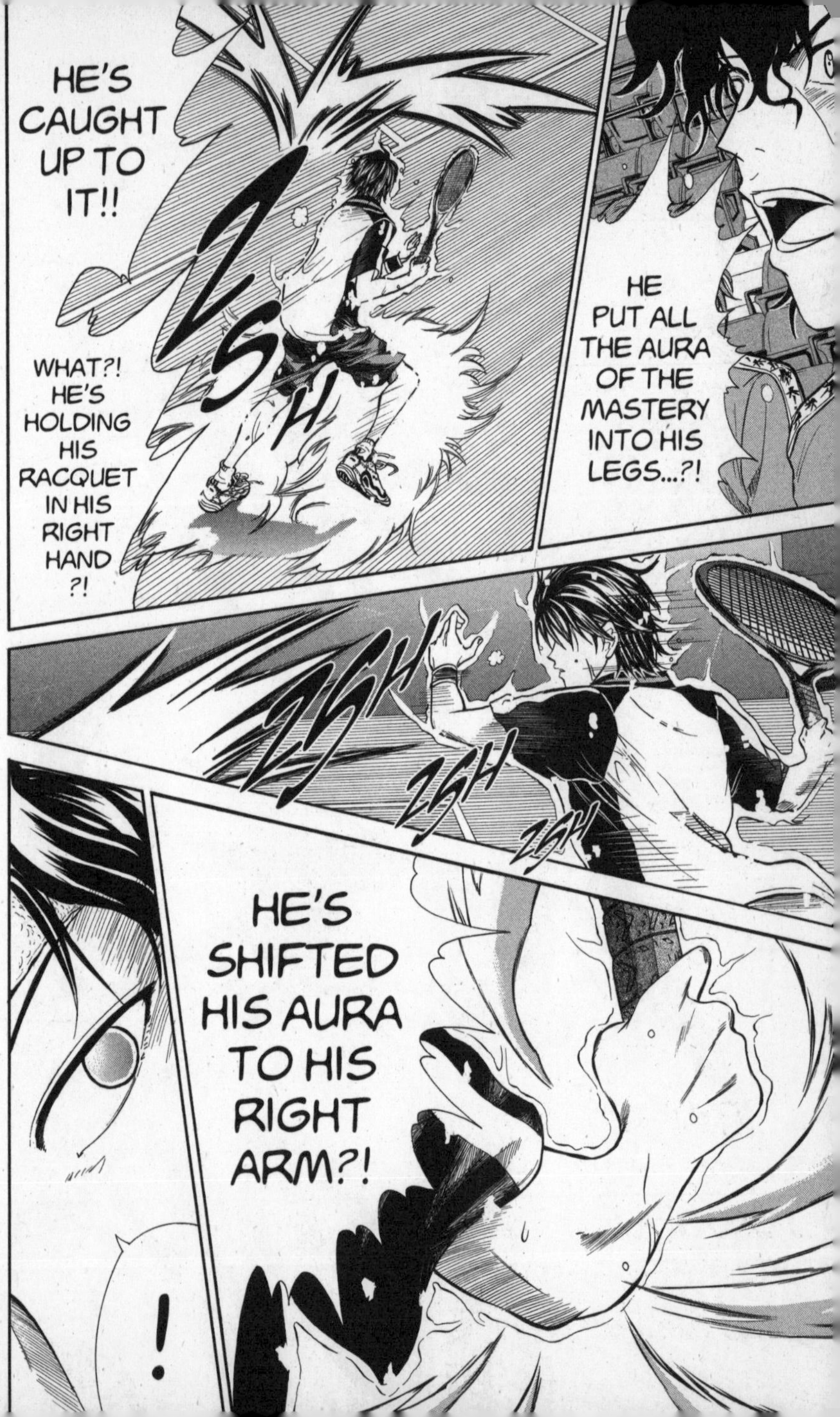
HE PUT ALL THE AURA OF THE MASTERY INTO HIS LEGS...?!
HE'S CAUGHT UP TO IT!!
ZSH
WHAT?! HE'S HOLDING HIS RACQUET IN HIS RIGHT HAND ?!
ZSH
ZSH
ZSH
HE'S SHIFTED HIS AURA TO HIS RIGHT ARM?!
!

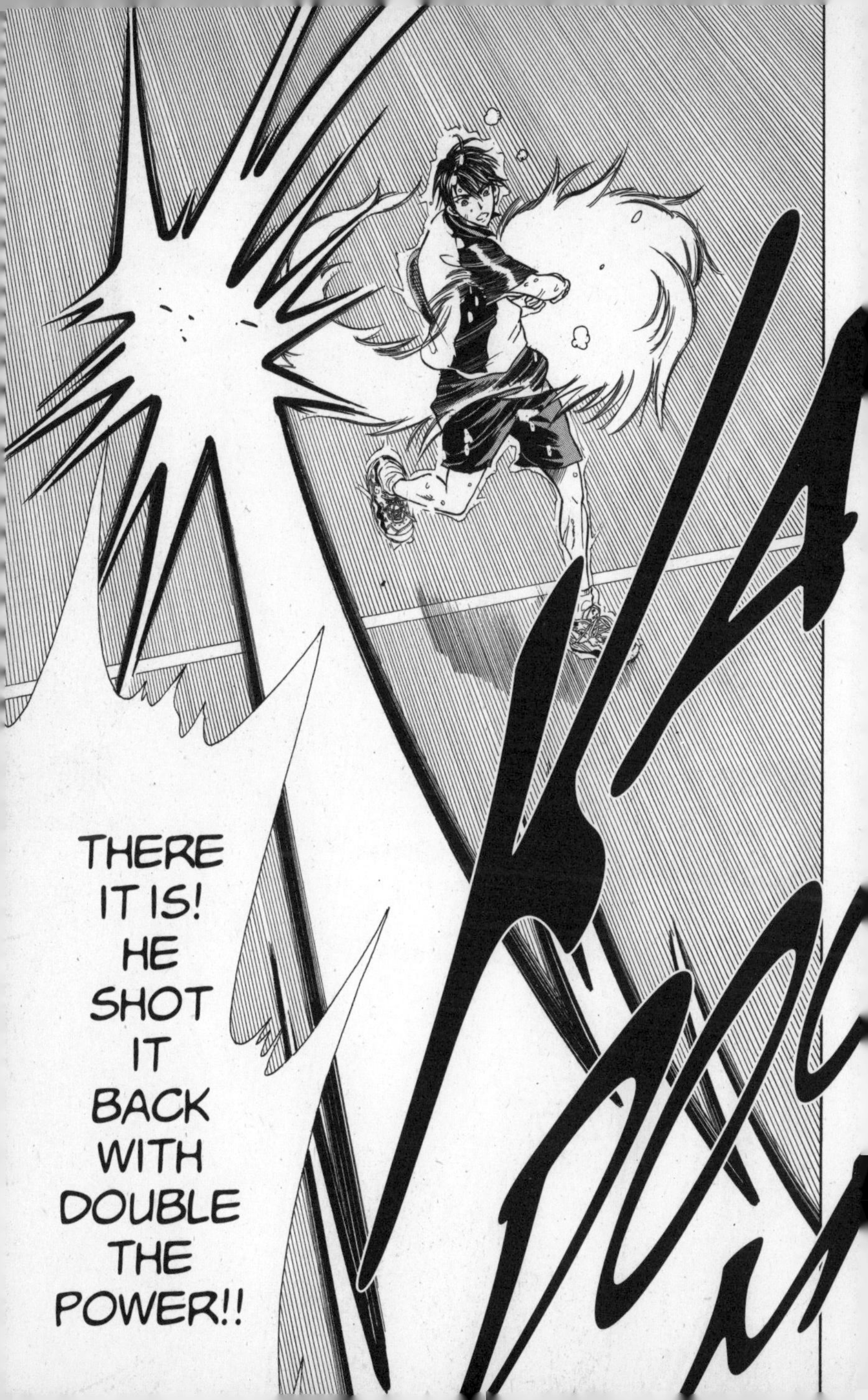
THERE IT IS! HE SHOT IT BACK WITH DOUBLE THE POWER!!

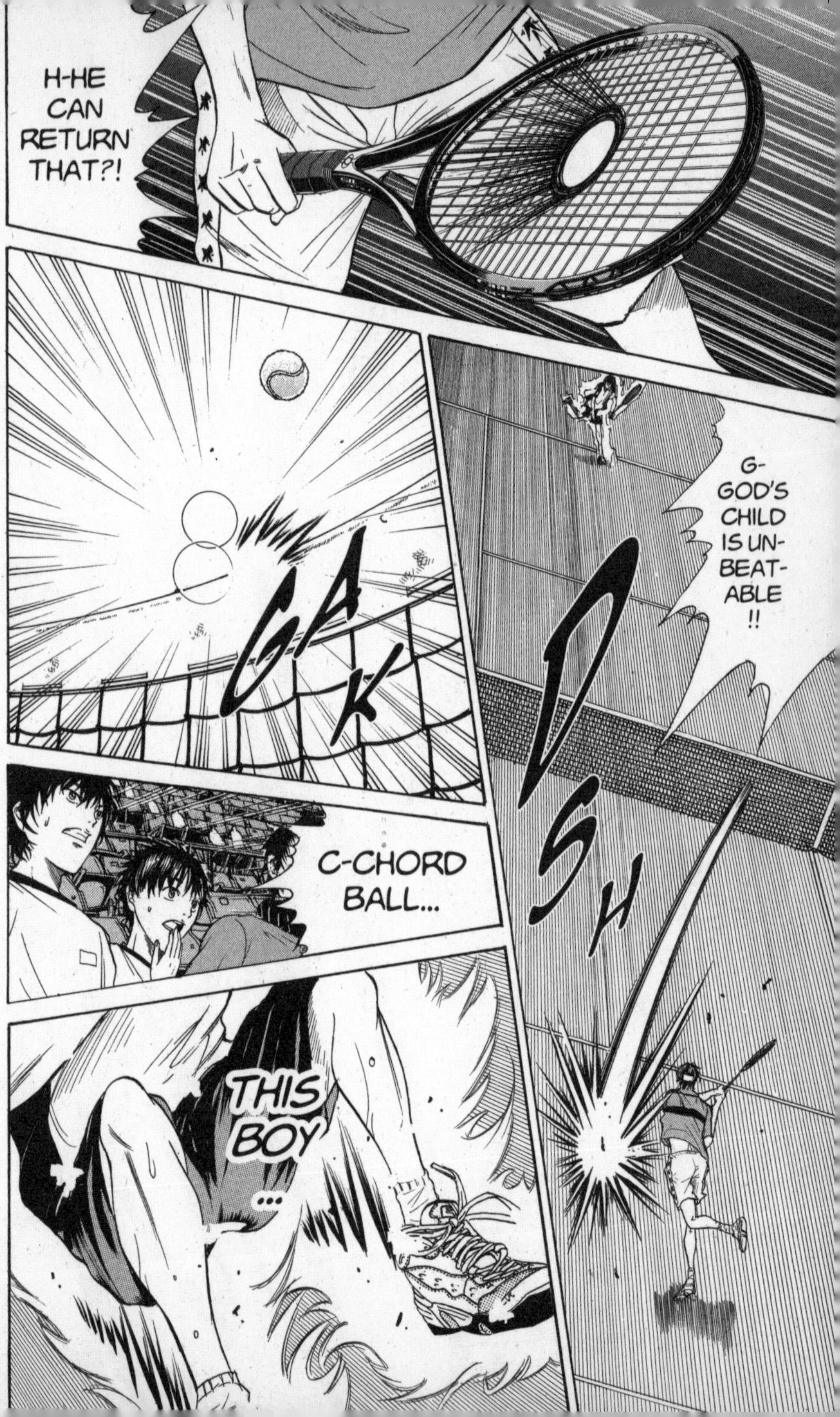
H-HE CAN RETURN THAT?!
G-GOD'S CHILD IS UN-BEAT-ABLE !!
DOSH
GAK
C-CHORD BALL...
THIS BOY ...

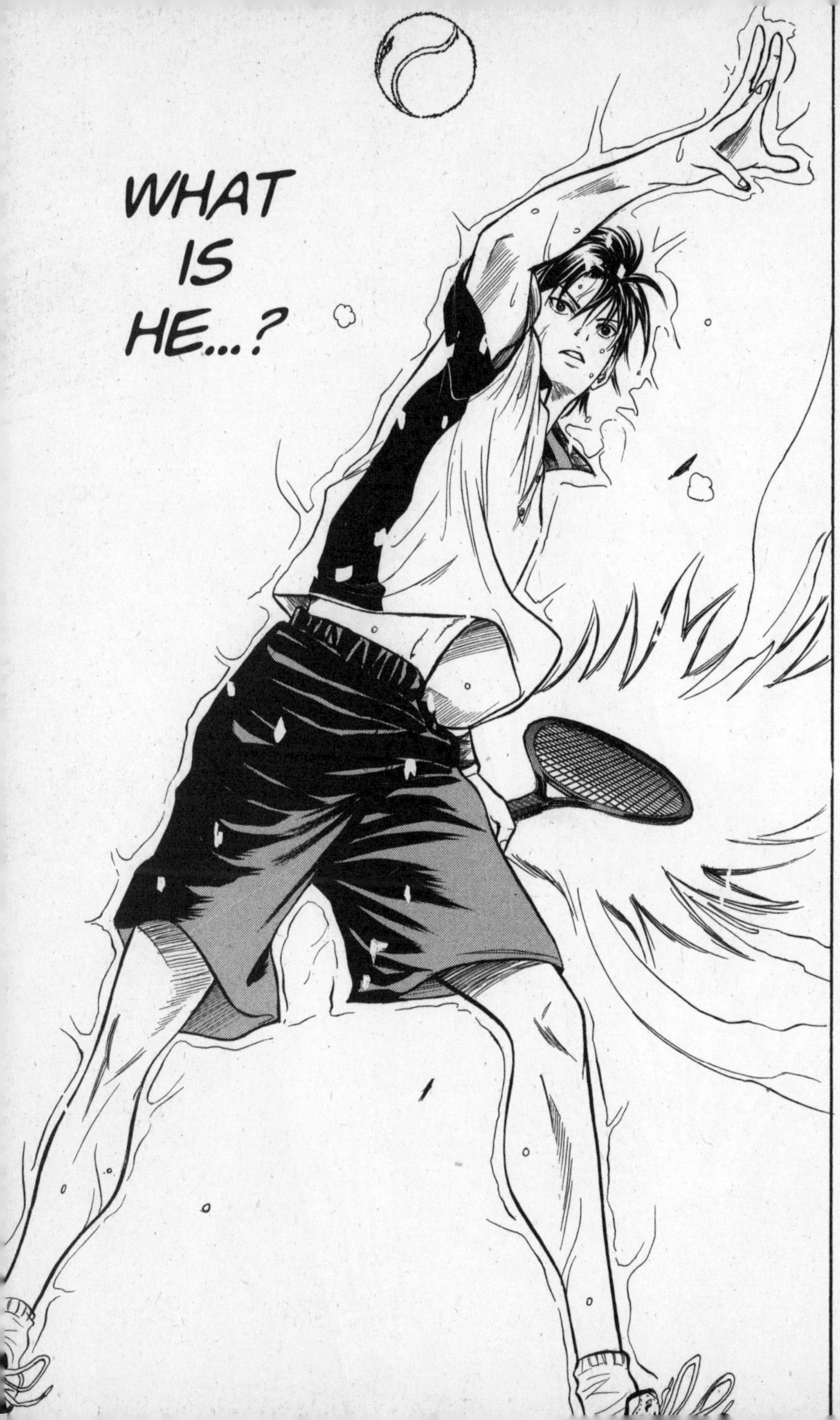
WHAT IS HE...?

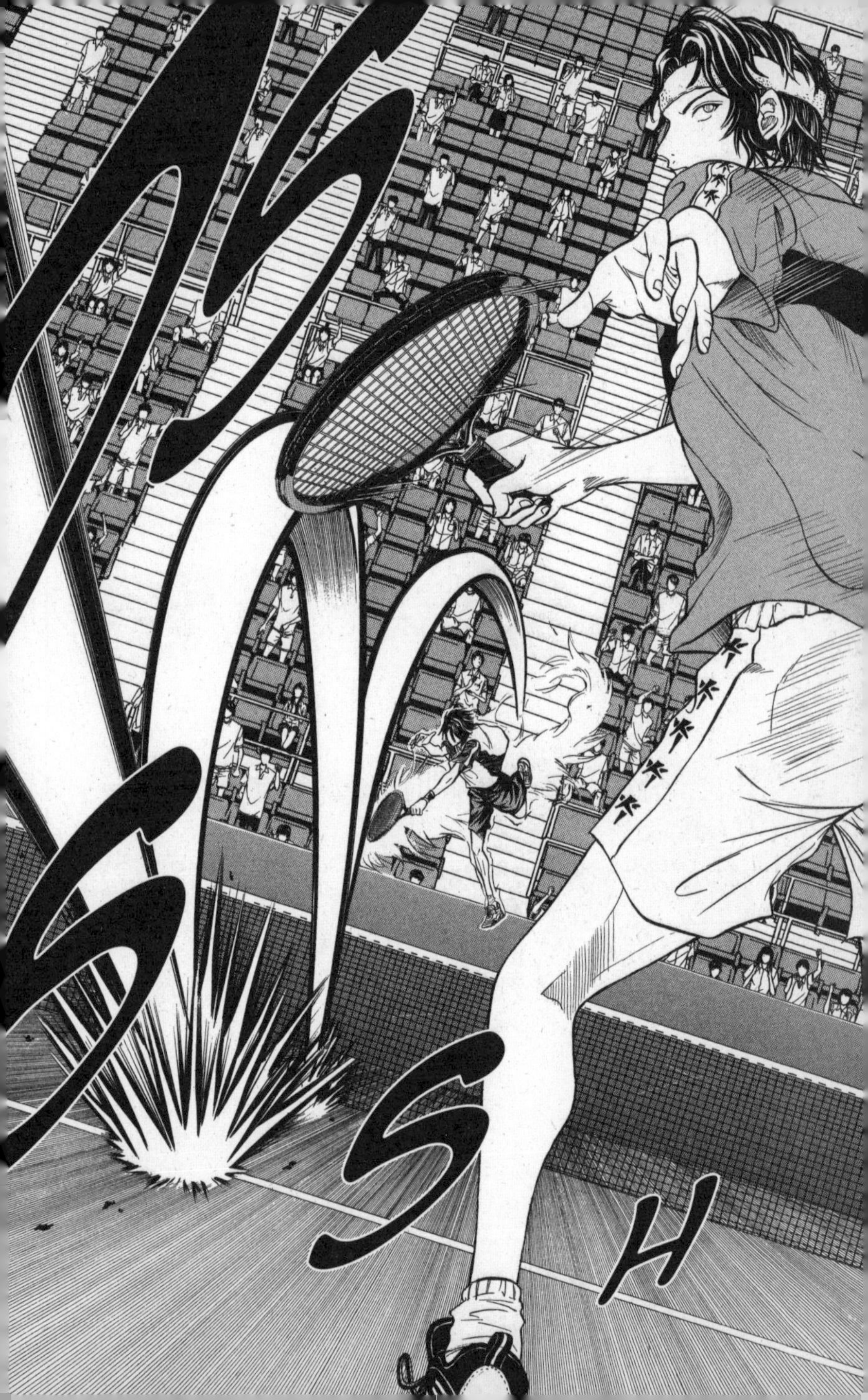

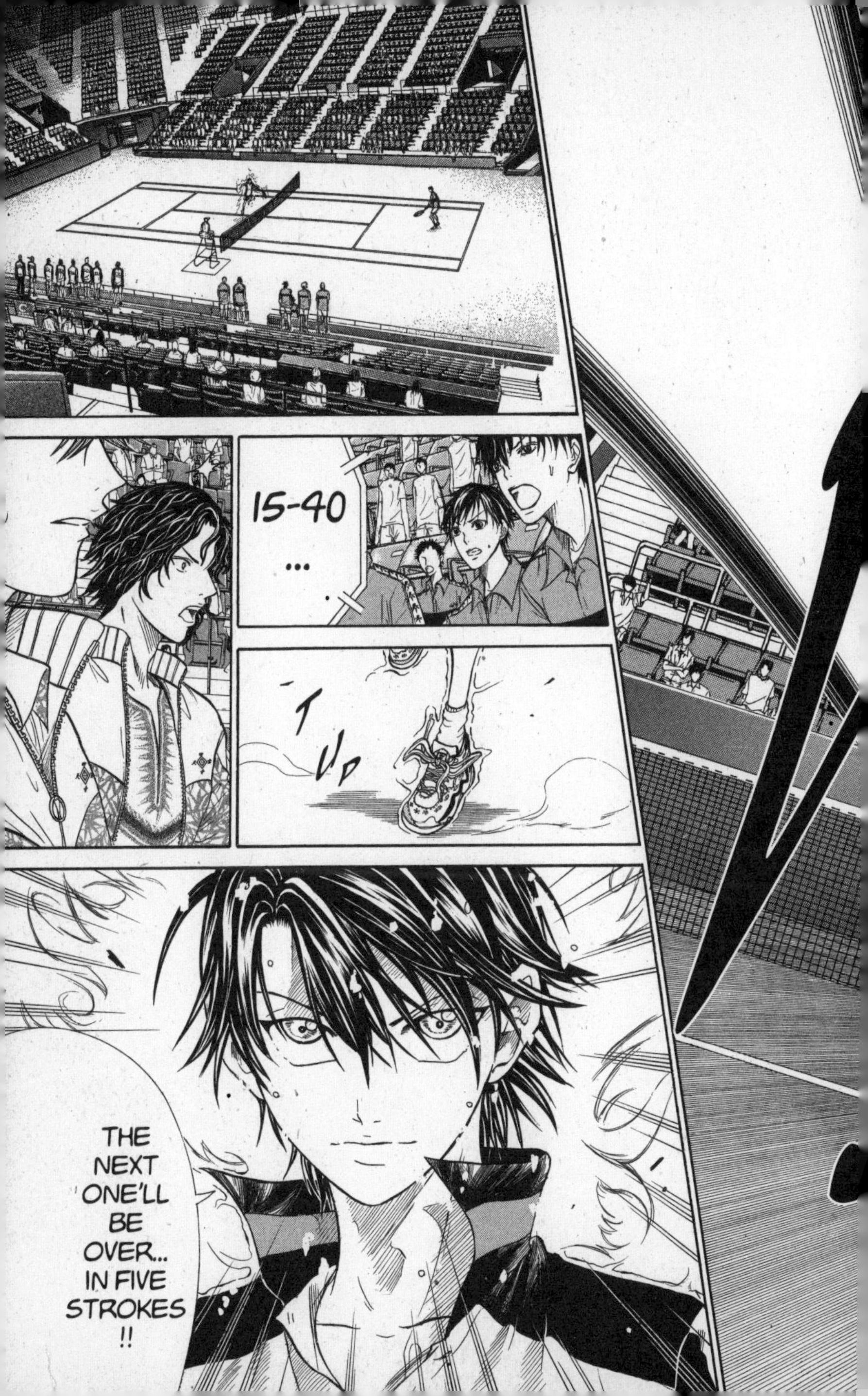
15-40
...
TUD
THE NEXT ONE'LL BE OVER... IN FIVE STROKES!!

2008 Valentine's Day Results!! ①

THANK YOU FOR ALL THE CHOCOLATES!
(2,189 TOTAL)

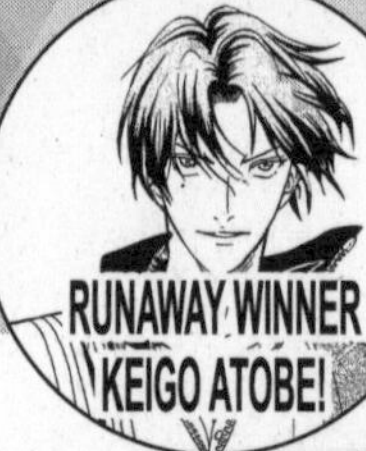
RUNAWAY WINNER
KEIGO ATOBE!

1ST KEIGO ATOBE 323

2ND GENICHIRO SANADA 223

3RD SEIICHI YUKIMURA 219

4TH TAKESHI KONOMI 183

5TH SHUSUKE FUJI 139

6TH KUNIMITSU TEZUKA 112

7TH EIJI KIKUMARU 103

8TH RYOMA ECHIZEN 94

9TH YUUSHI OSHITARI 91

10TH MASAHARU NIO 76

READ THIS WAY

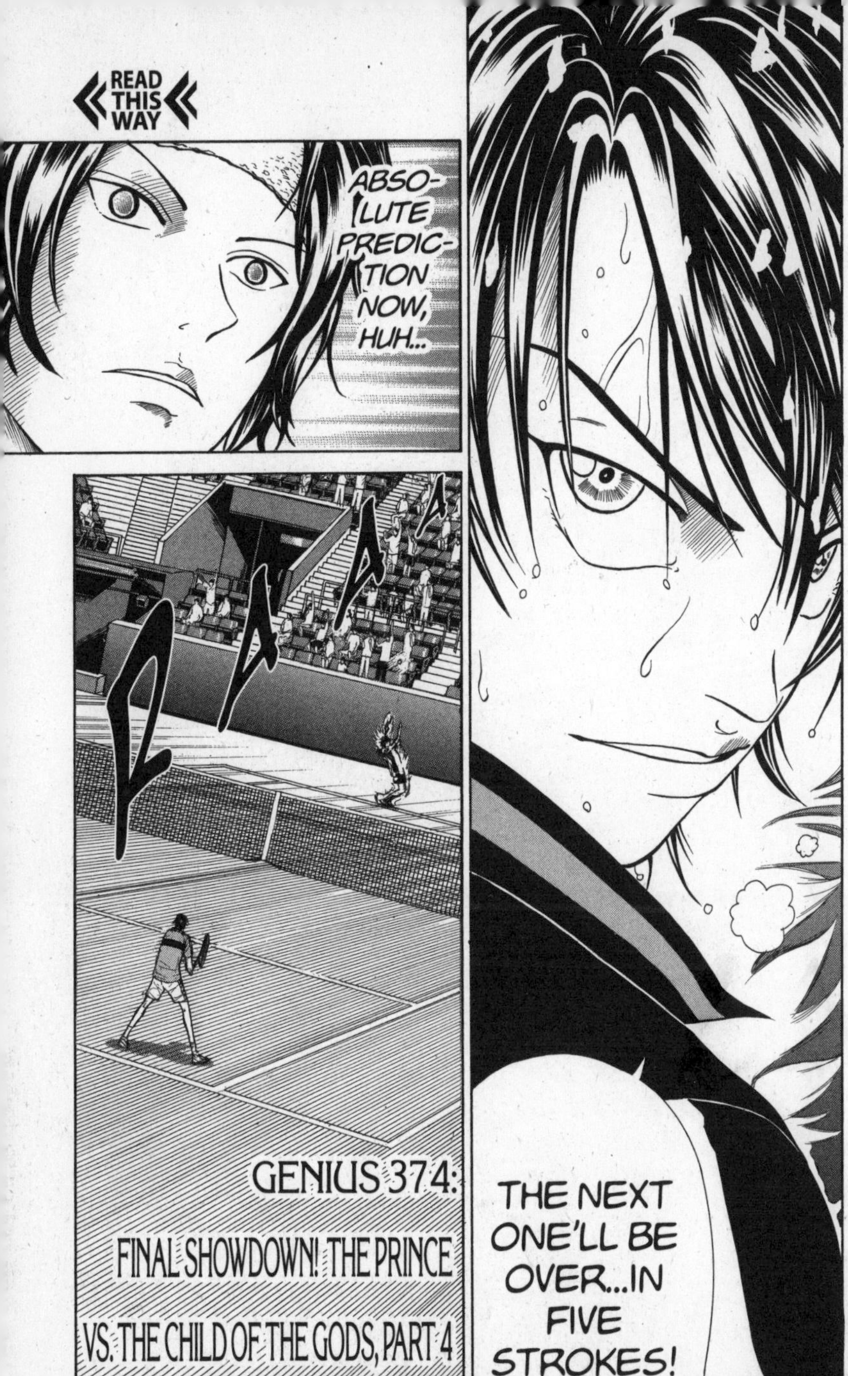
THE NEXT ONE'LL BE OVER...IN FIVE STROKES!
ABSOLUTE PREDICTION NOW, HUH...
GENIUS 374:
FINAL SHOWDOWN! THE PRINCE VS. THE CHILD OF THE GODS, PART 4

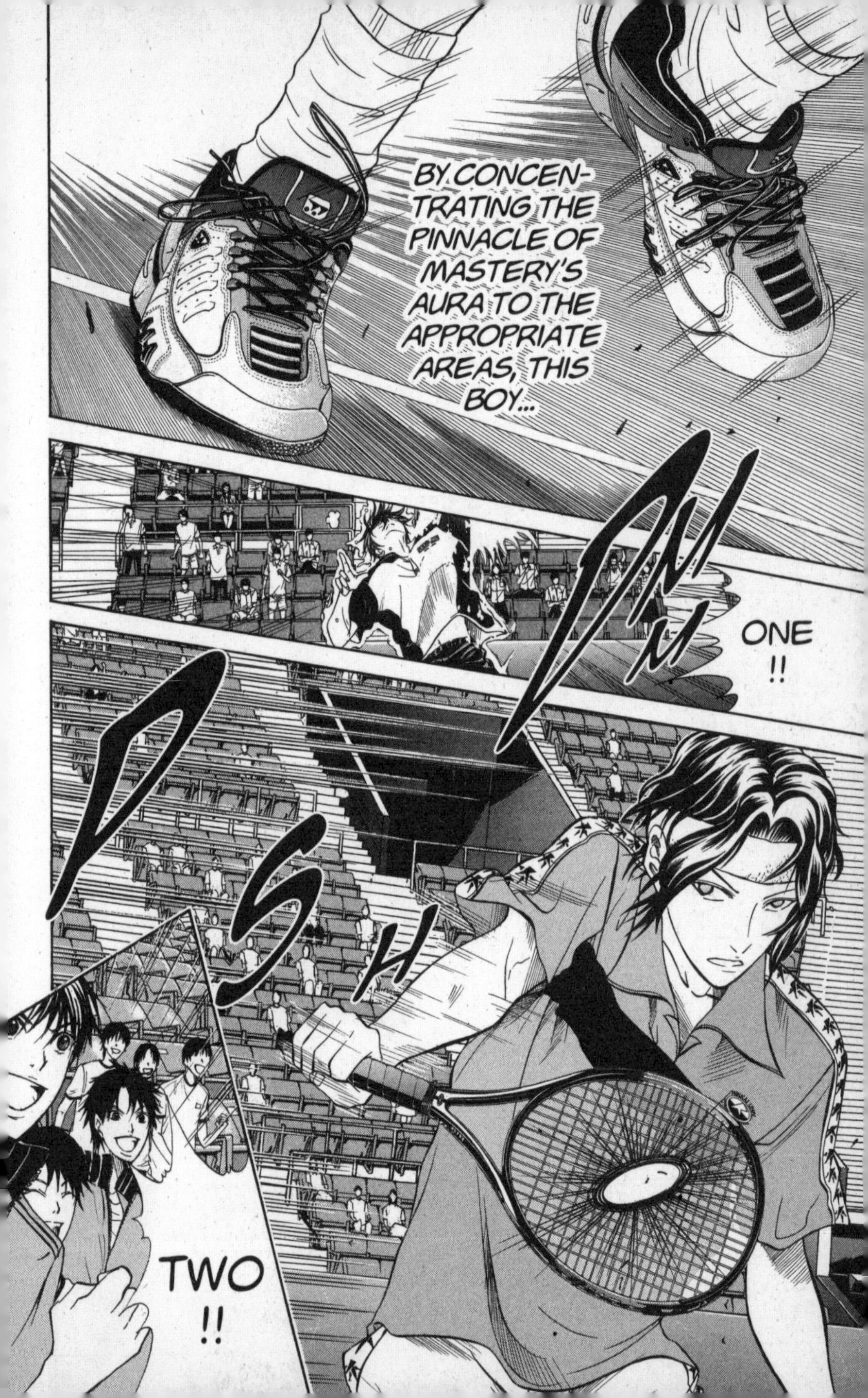
BY CONCEN-TRATING THE PINNACLE OF MASTERY'S AURA TO THE APPROPRIATE AREAS, THIS BOY...
ONE !!
TWO !!

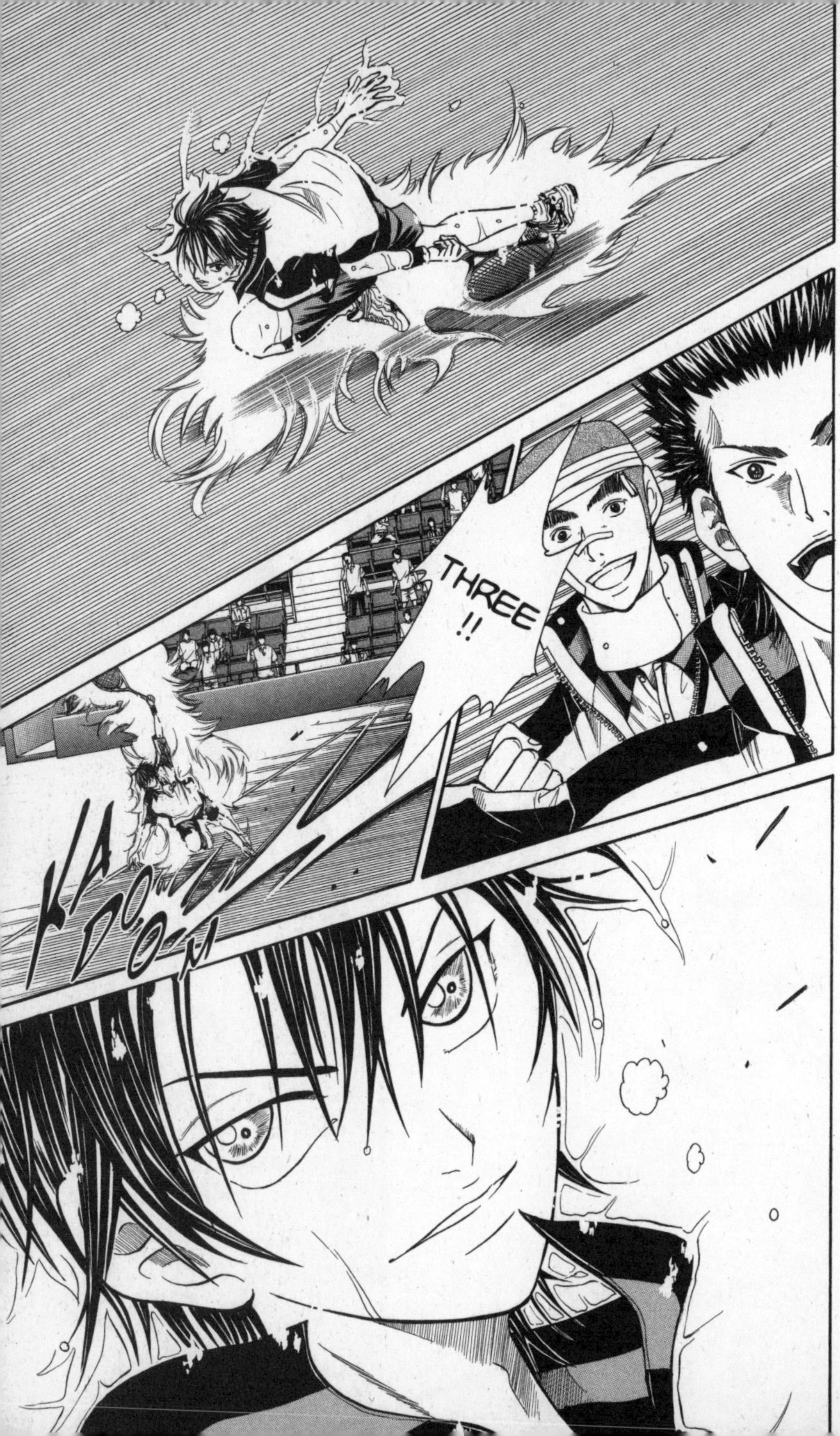
THREE !!
KA DOOM

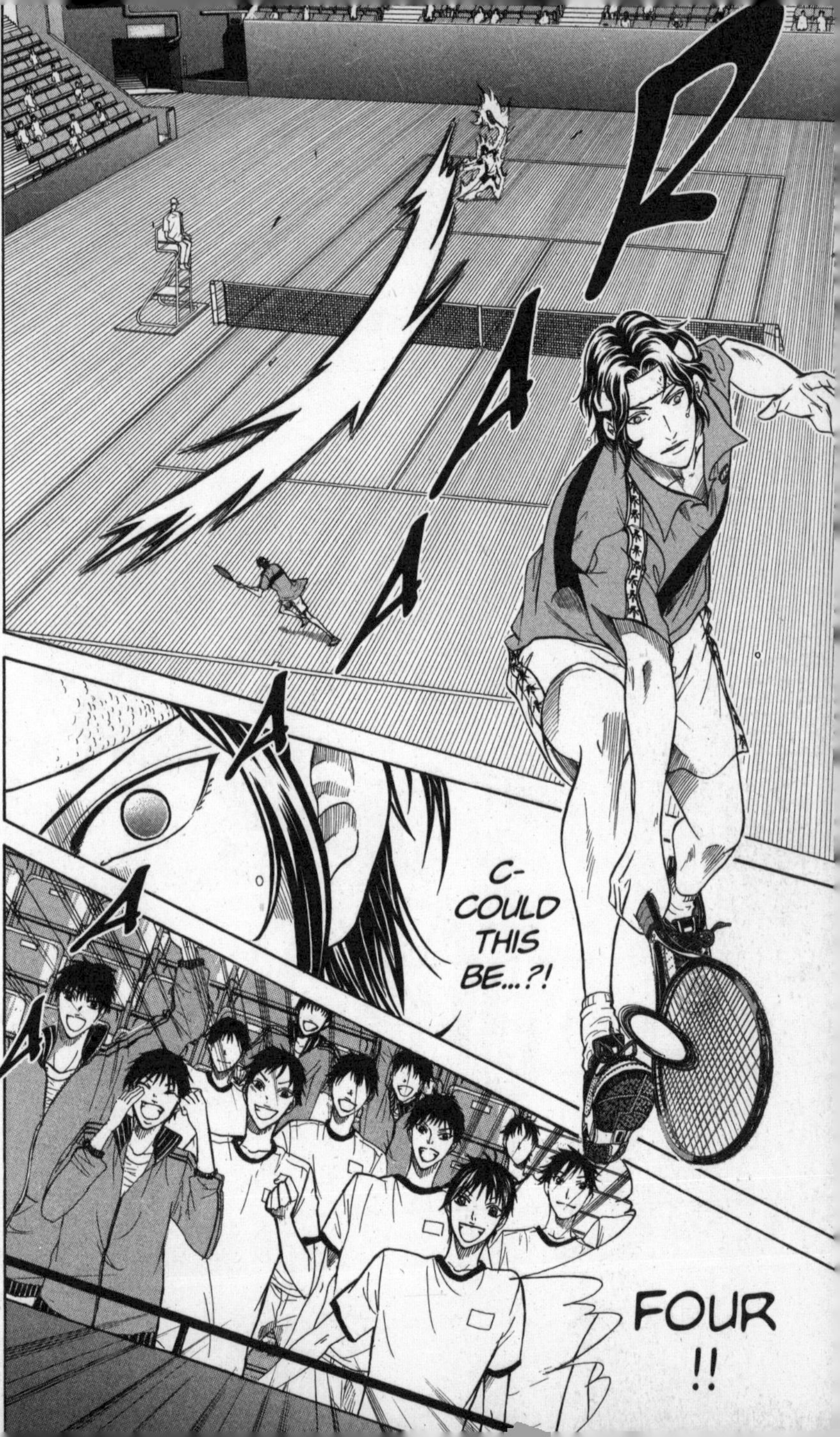
C-COULD THIS BE...?!
FOUR !!

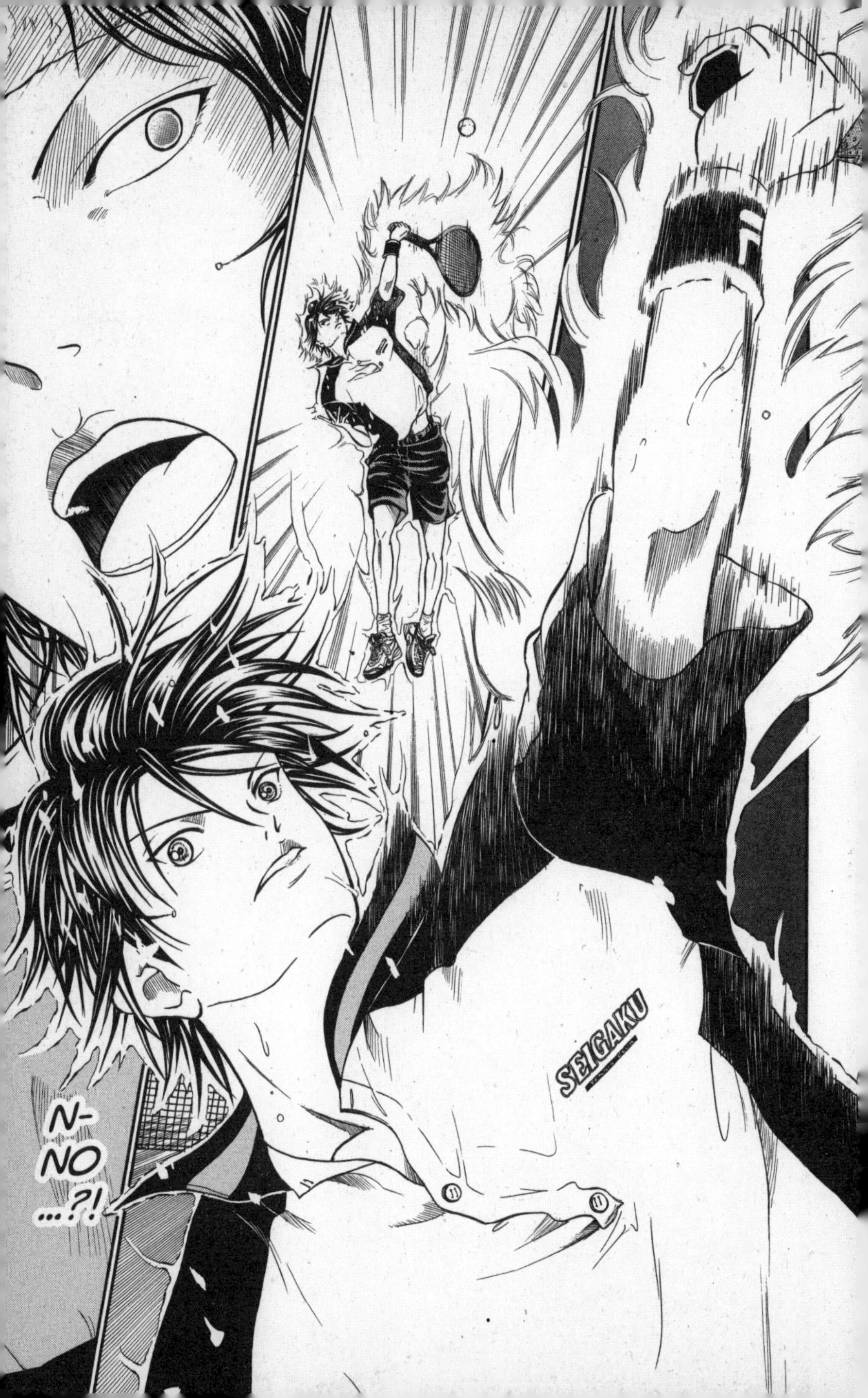
N-NO ...?!
SEIGAKU

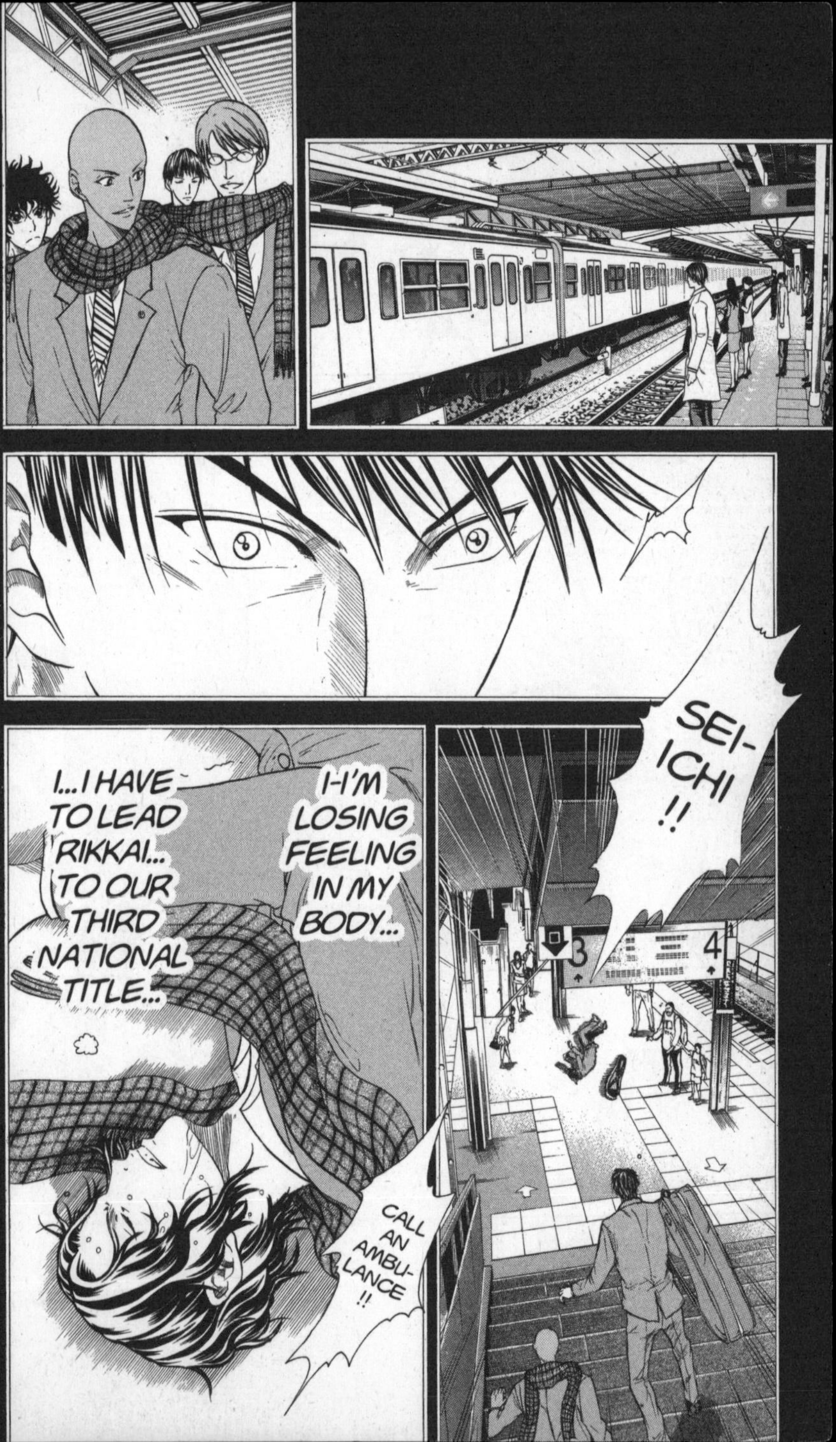
SEI-ICHI!!
I-I'M LOSING FEELING IN MY BODY...
I...I HAVE TO LEAD RIKKAI... TO OUR THIRD NATIONAL TITLE...
CALL AN AMBULANCE!!

READ THIS WAY

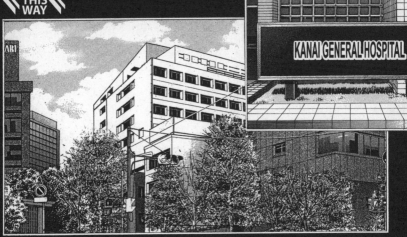

KANAI GENERAL HOSPITAL
...
JUST CONCENTRATE ON GETTING YOURSELF BETTER.
DON'T WORRY, SEIICHI! WE CAN STILL WIN OUR THIRD TITLE WITHOUT YOU!!
THAT'S DEPRESSING IN ITS OWN WAY.
TH-THAT'S NOT HOW I MEANT IT...
HEHE. I'M JUST KIDDING.
HA HA HA HA

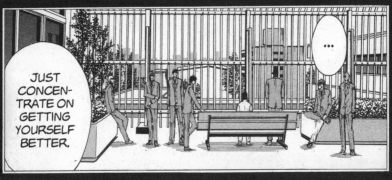

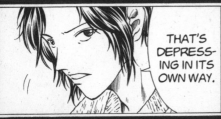

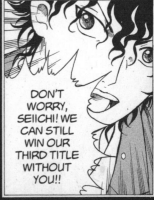

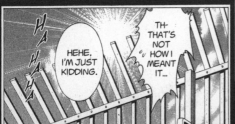

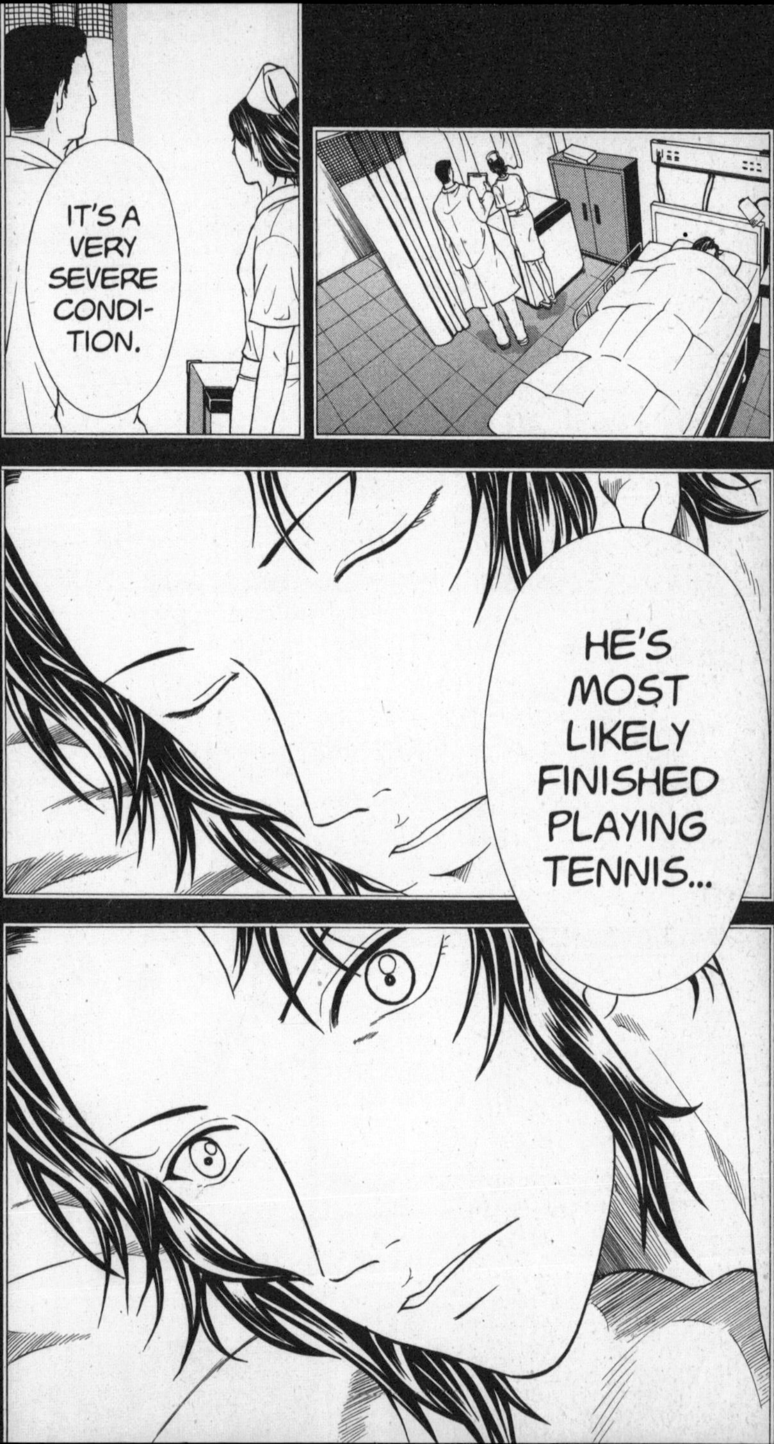
IT'S A VERY SEVERE CONDITION.
HE'S MOST LIKELY FINISHED PLAYING TENNIS...

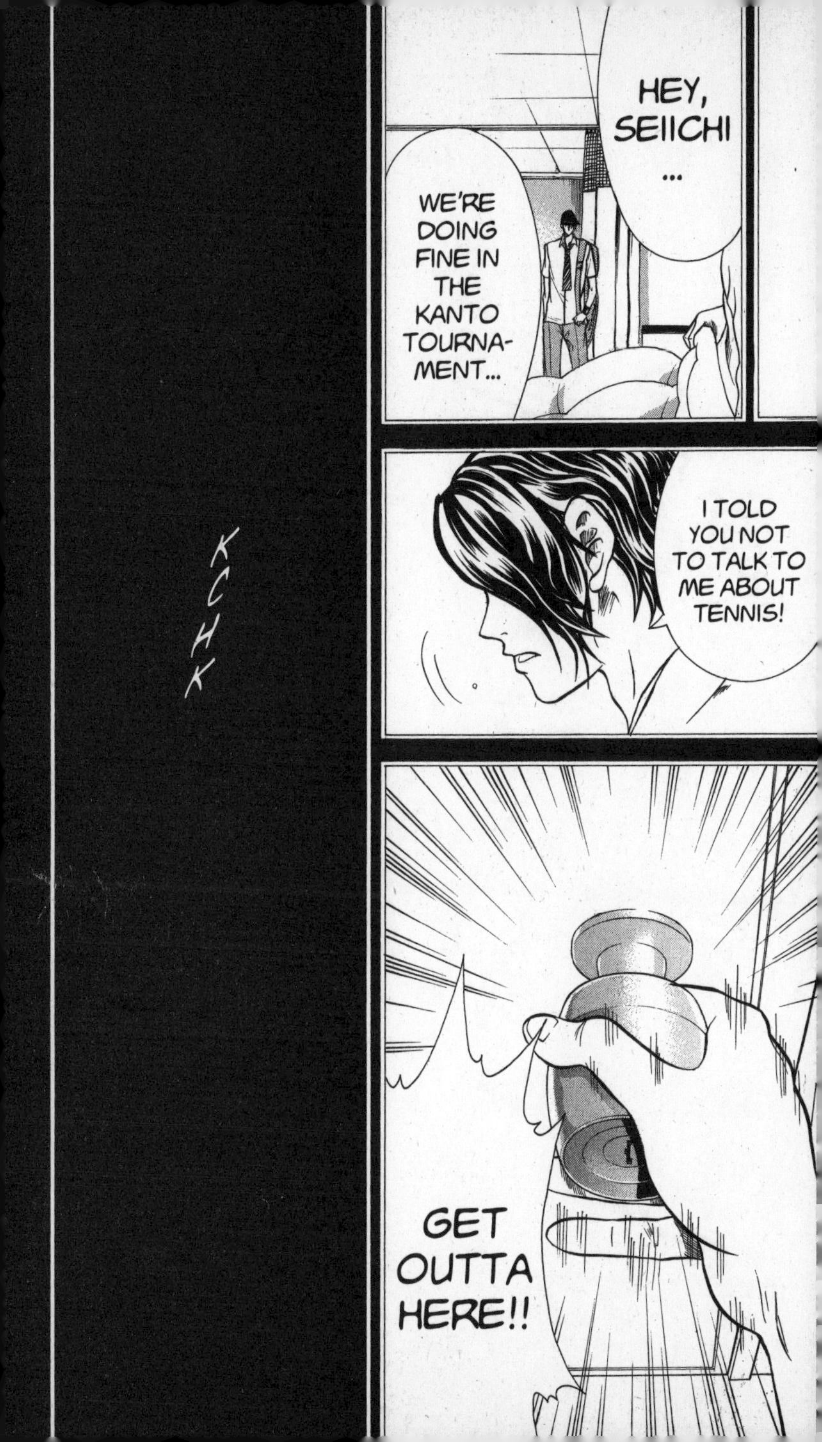
HEY, SEIICHI ...
WE'RE DOING FINE IN THE KANTO TOURNAMENT...
I TOLD YOU NOT TO TALK TO ME ABOUT TENNIS!
GET OUTTA HERE!!
KCHK

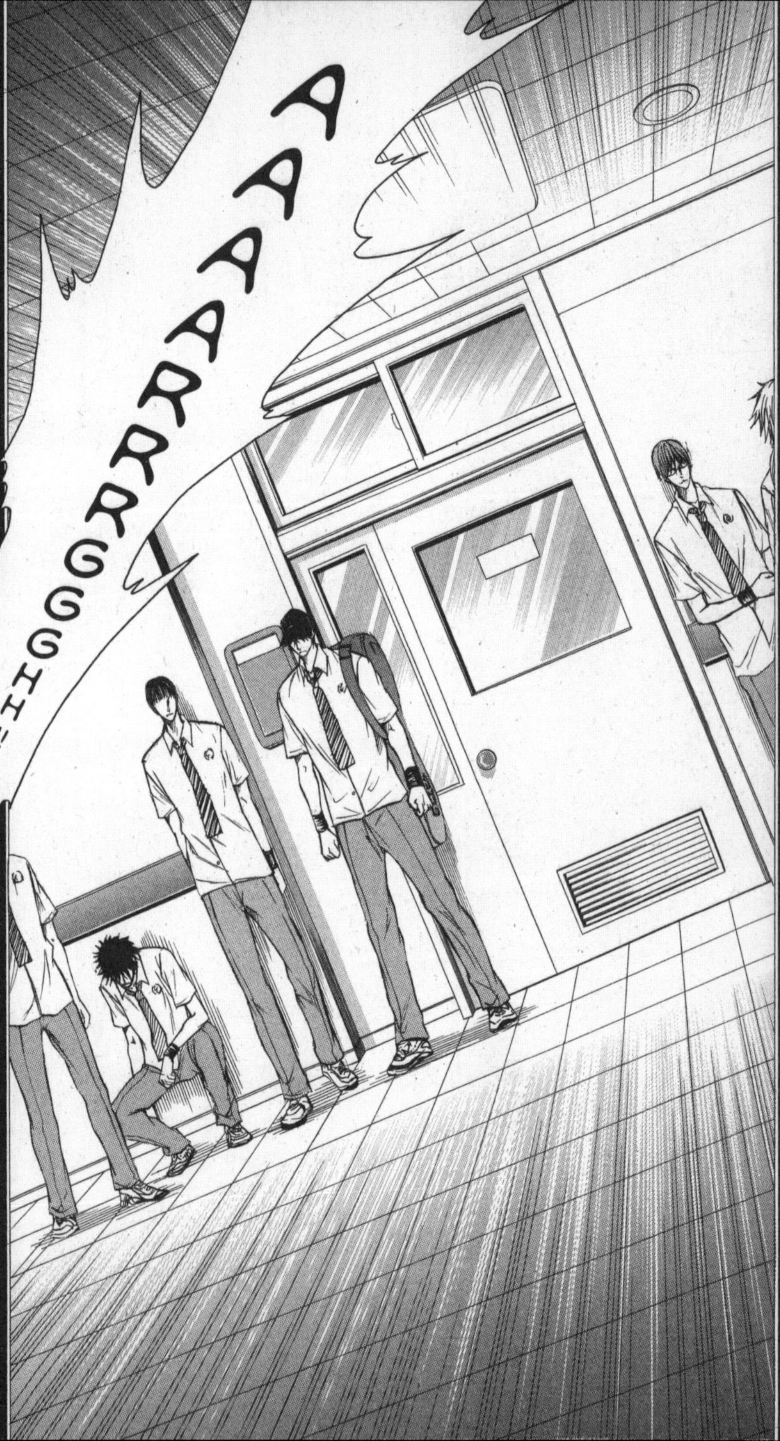
AAAARRRGGGHH!!

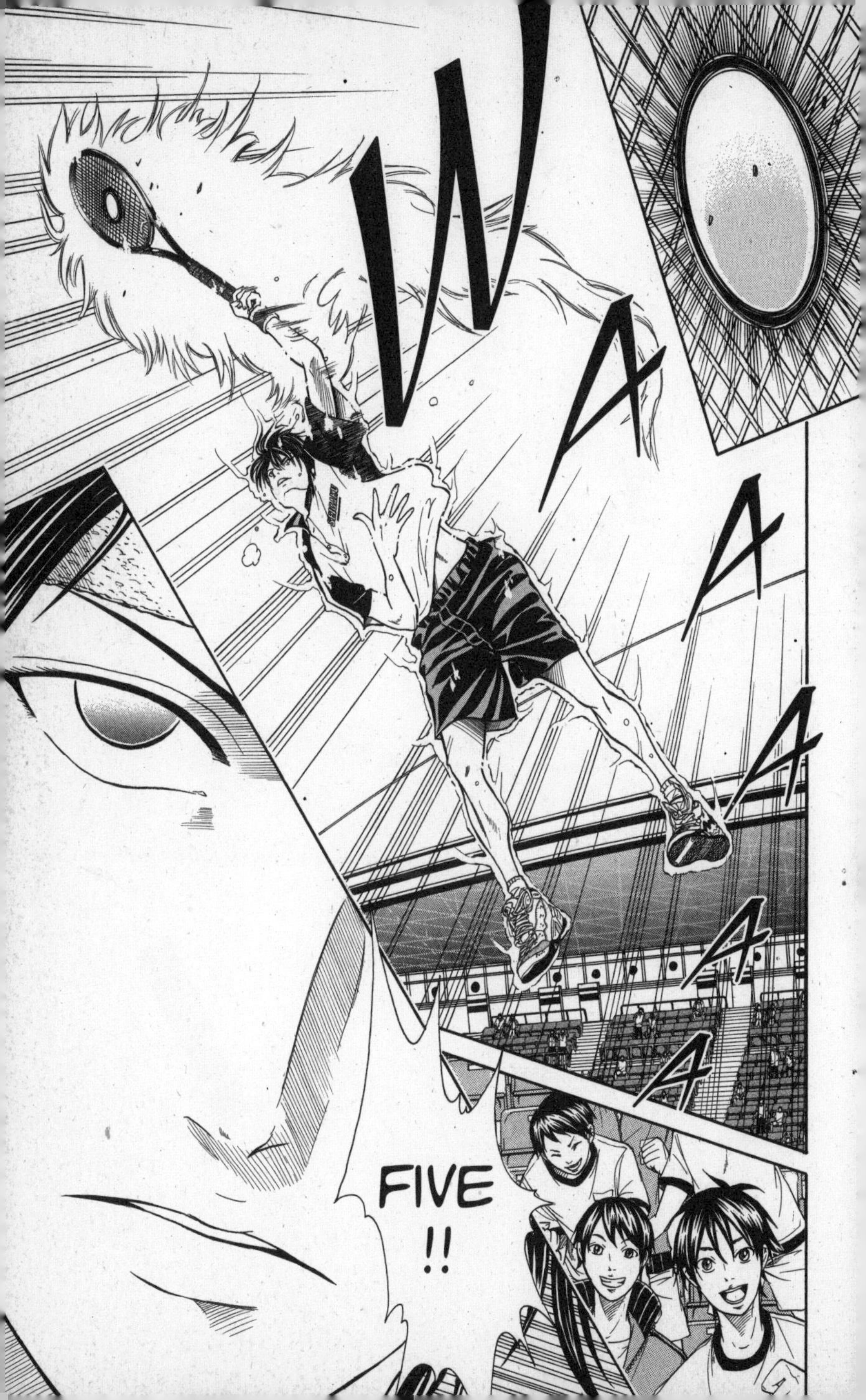
WAAAAAA
FIVE !!

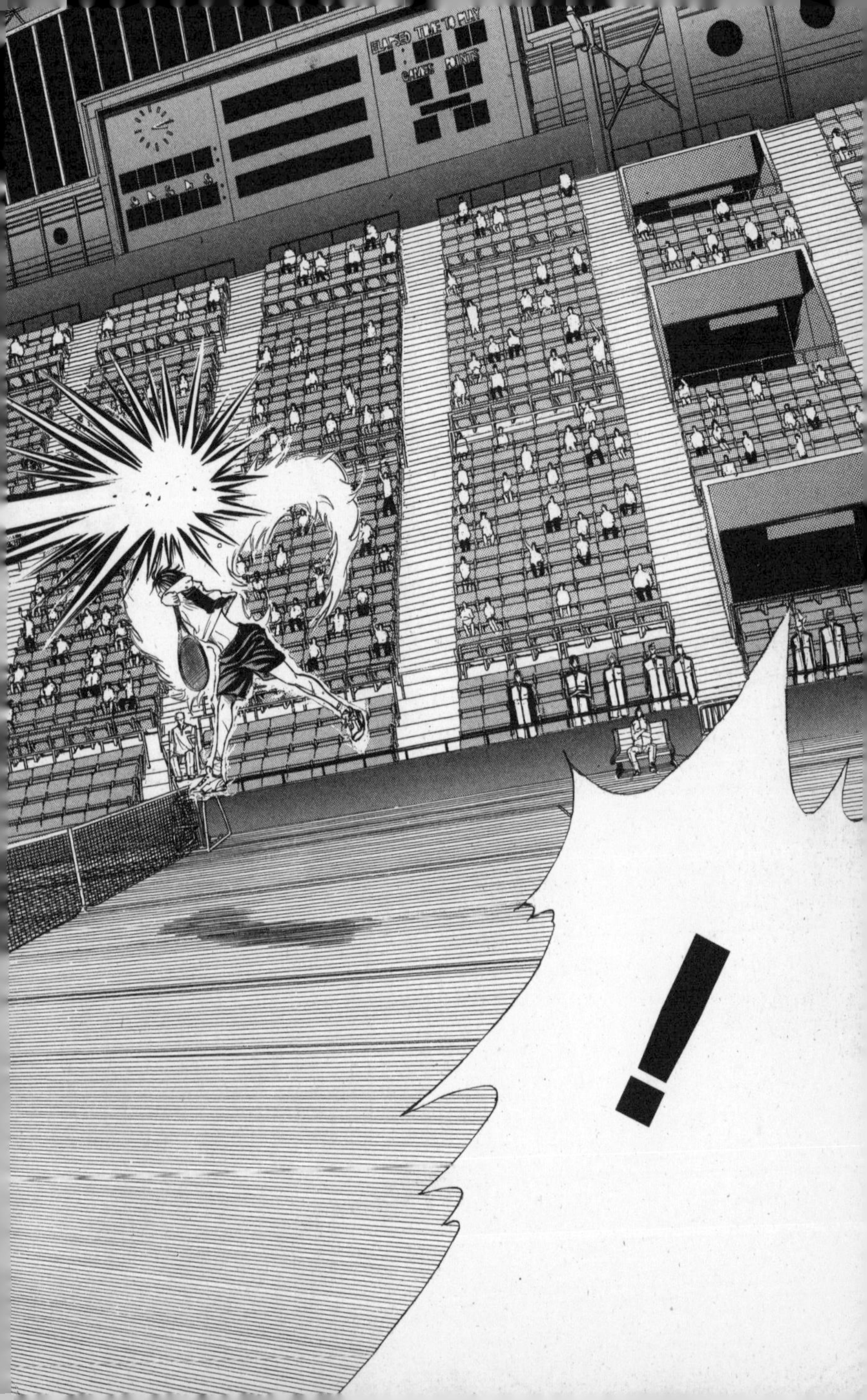
ELAPSED TIME TO PLAY
GAMES
POINTS
!

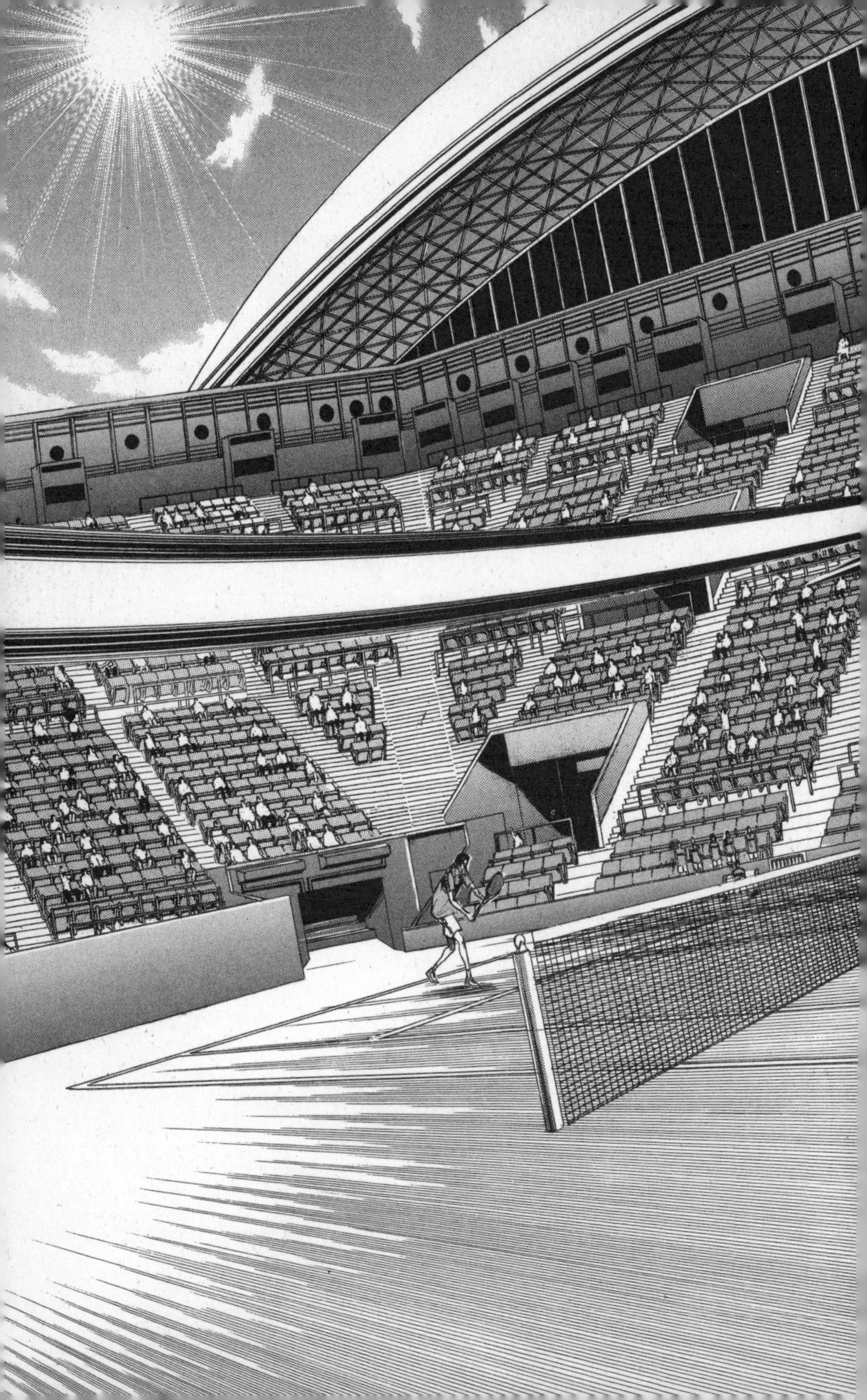

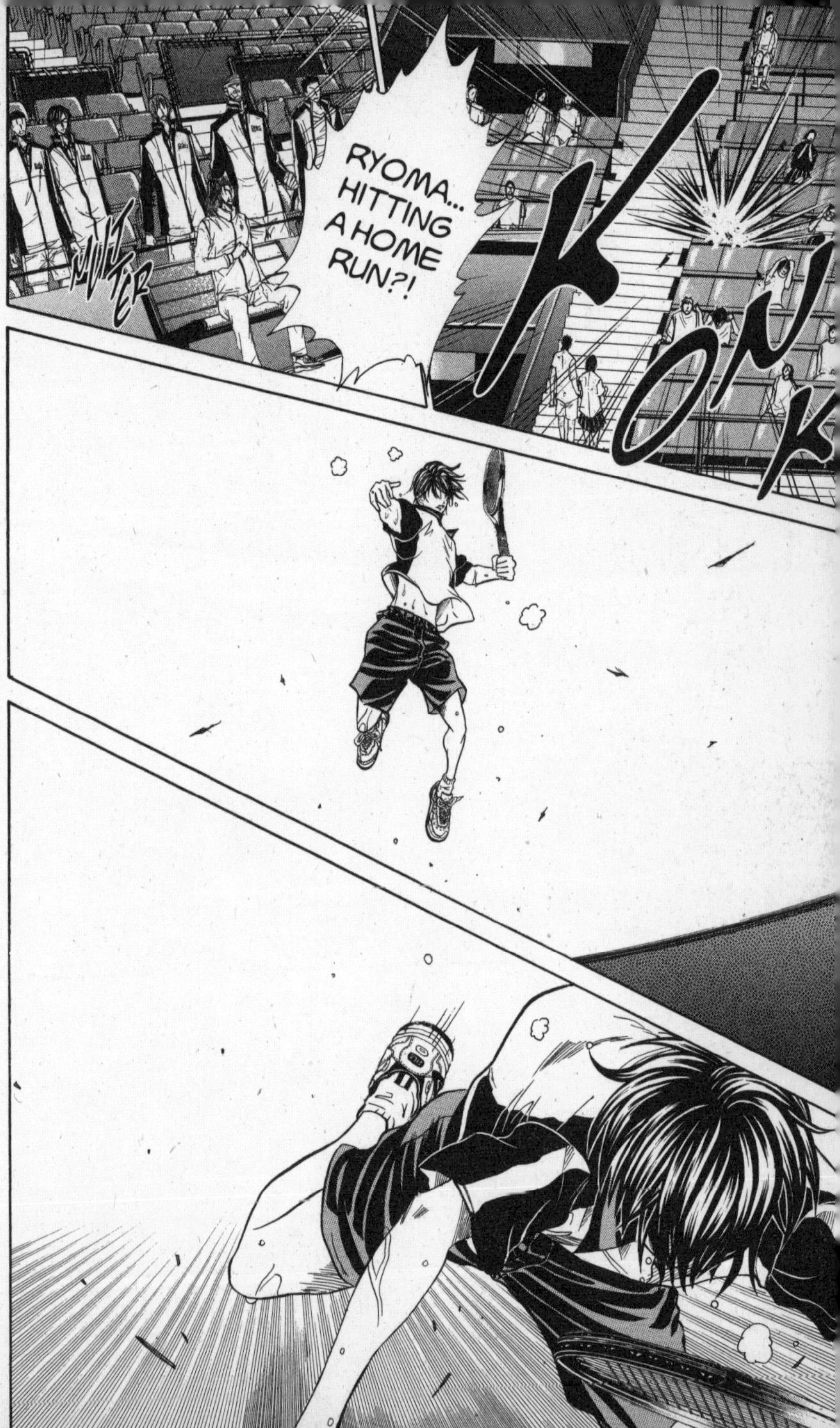
KONK
RYOMA... HITTING A HOME RUN?!
MUTTER

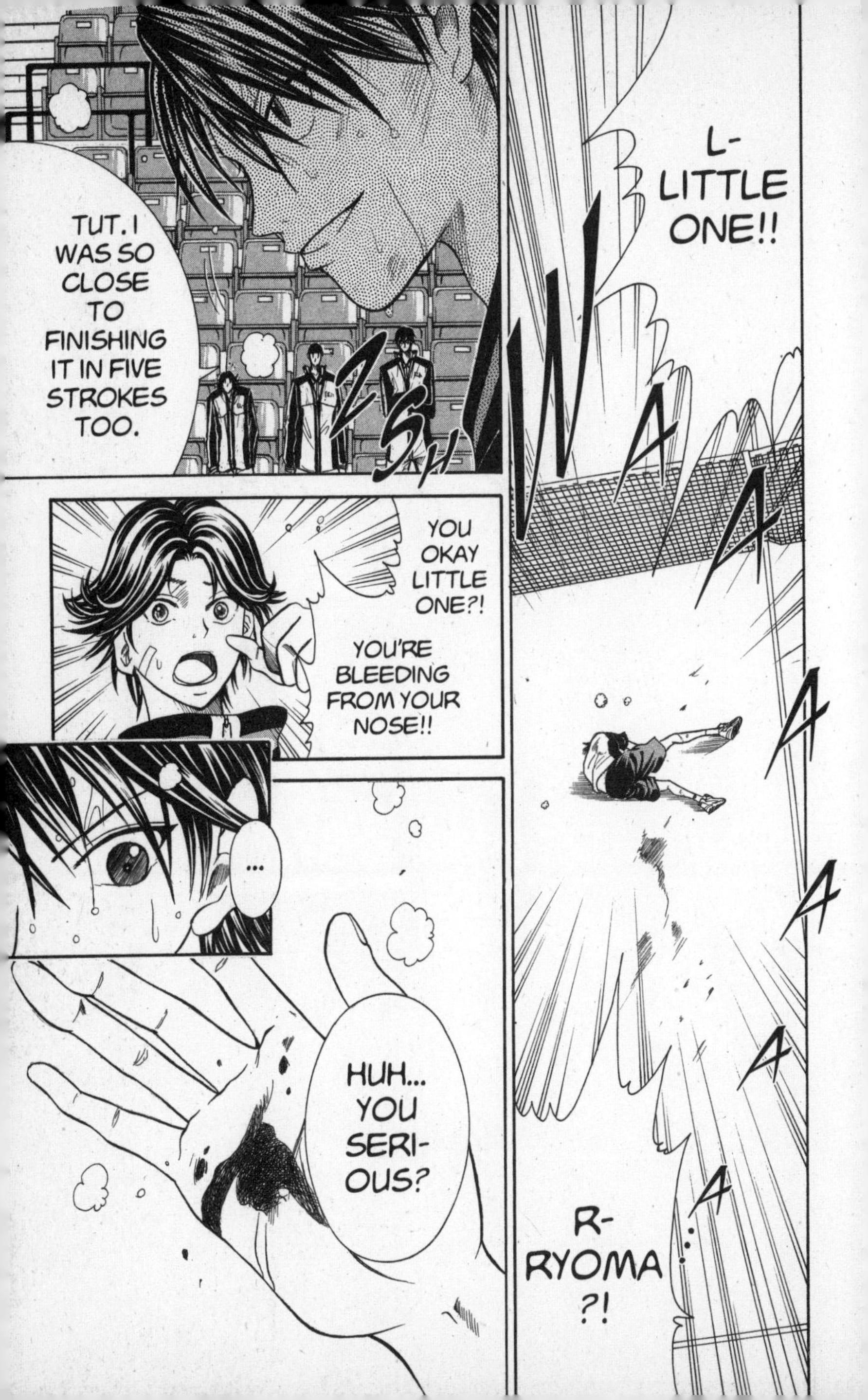
L-LITTLE ONE!!
WAAAAAAA
R-RYOMA?!
TUT. I WAS SO CLOSE TO FINISHING IT IN FIVE STROKES TOO.
ZSH
YOU OKAY LITTLE ONE?!
YOU'RE BLEEDING FROM YOUR NOSE!!
...
HUH... YOU SERIOUS?

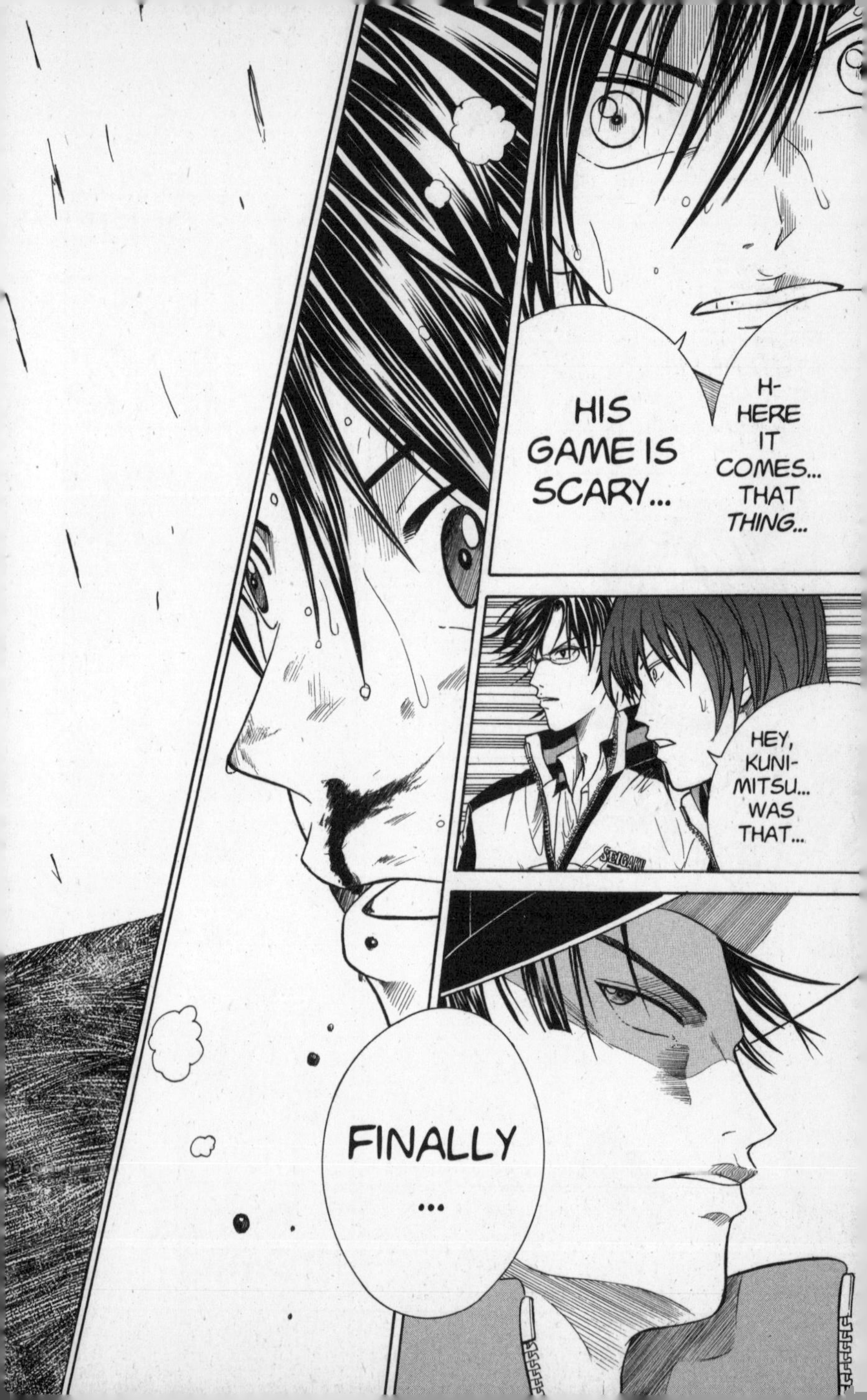
H-HERE IT COMES... THAT THING...
HIS GAME IS SCARY...
HEY, KUNIMITSU... WAS THAT...
FINALLY ...

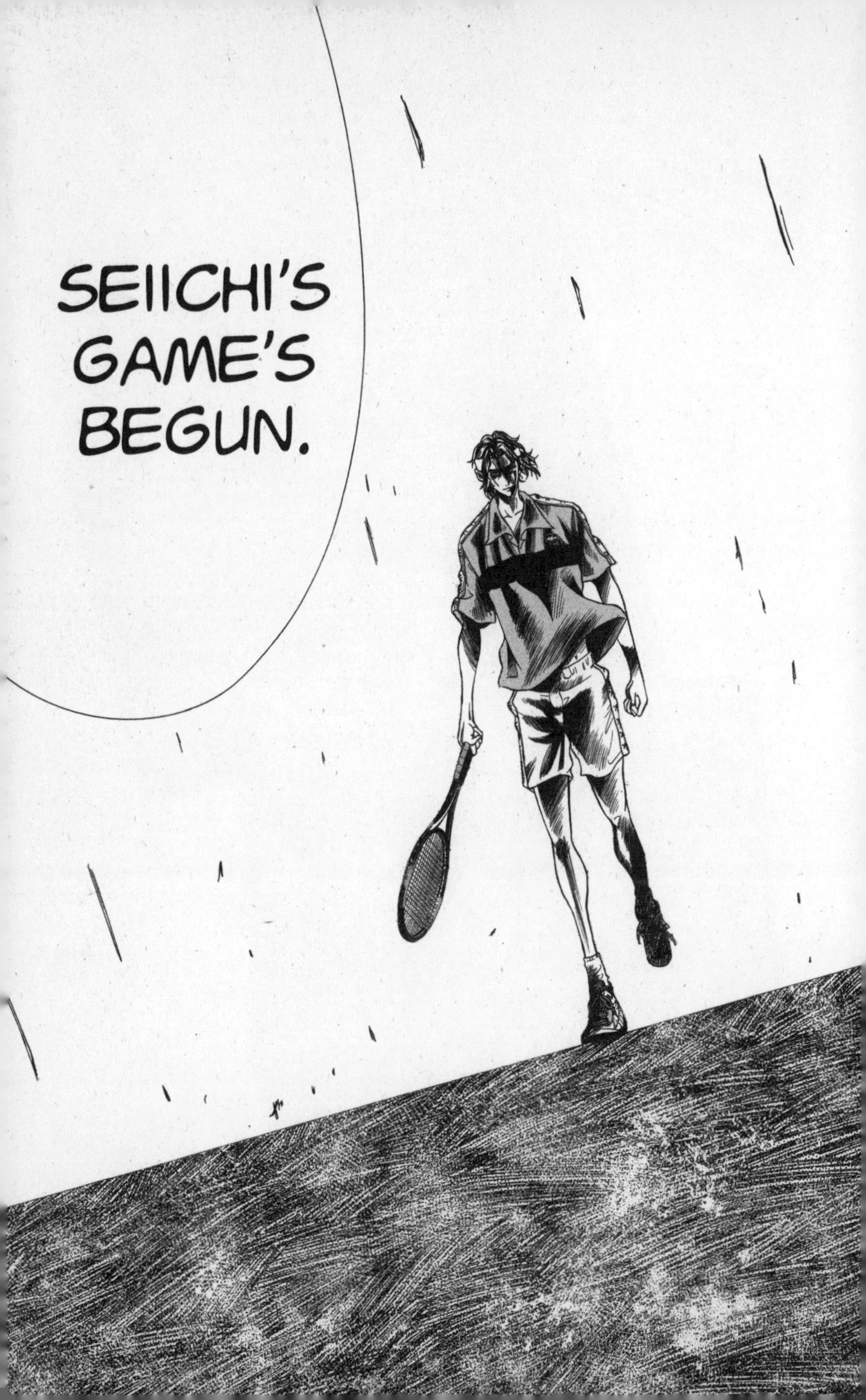
SEIICHI'S GAME'S BEGUN.

2008 Valentine's Day Results!! ②

Rank	Name	Chocolates
11th	Ryo Shishido	59
12th	Akaya Kirihara	48
13th	Hiroshi Yagyu	46
14th	Chotaro Ohtori	41
15th	Gakuto Mukahi	40
16th	Bunta Marui	39
17th	Jiro Akutagawa	38
18th	Sadaharu Inui	28
19th	Wakashi Hiyoshi	22
20th	Kaoru Kaido	19
21st	Rin Hirakoba	18
22nd	Jackal Kuwahara	17
23rd	Kiyosumi Sengoku	16
24th	Shuichiro Oishi	12
25th	Takeshi Momoshiro	11
25th	Yujiro Kai	11
27th	Renji Yanagi	10
27th	Takashi Kawamura	10
27th	Eishiro Kite	10
30th	Kuranosuke Shiraishi	9

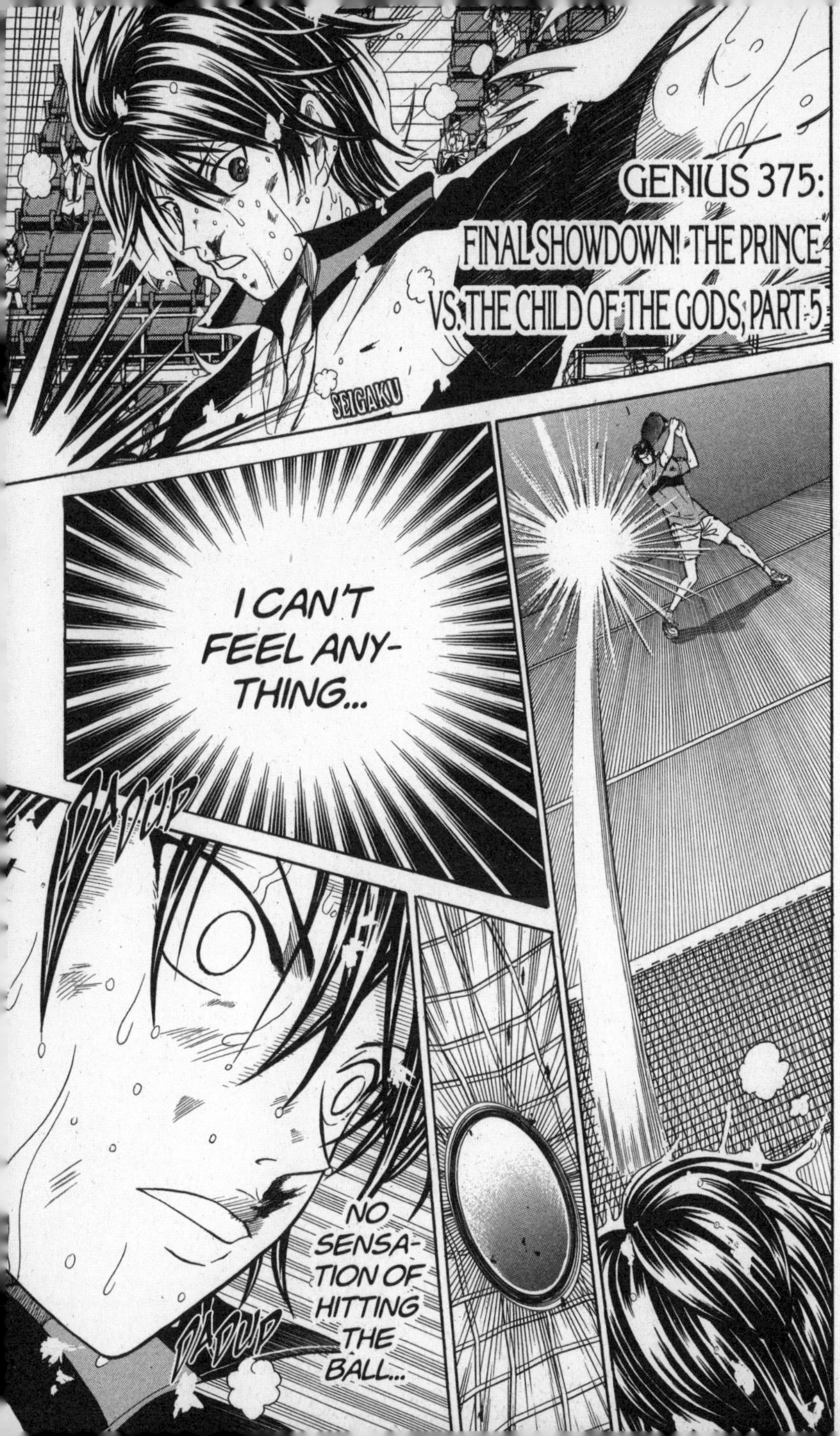
GENIUS 375:
FINAL SHOWDOWN! THE PRINCE VS. THE CHILD OF THE GODS, PART 5
SEIGAKU
I CAN'T FEEL ANYTHING...
NO SENSATION OF HITTING THE BALL...

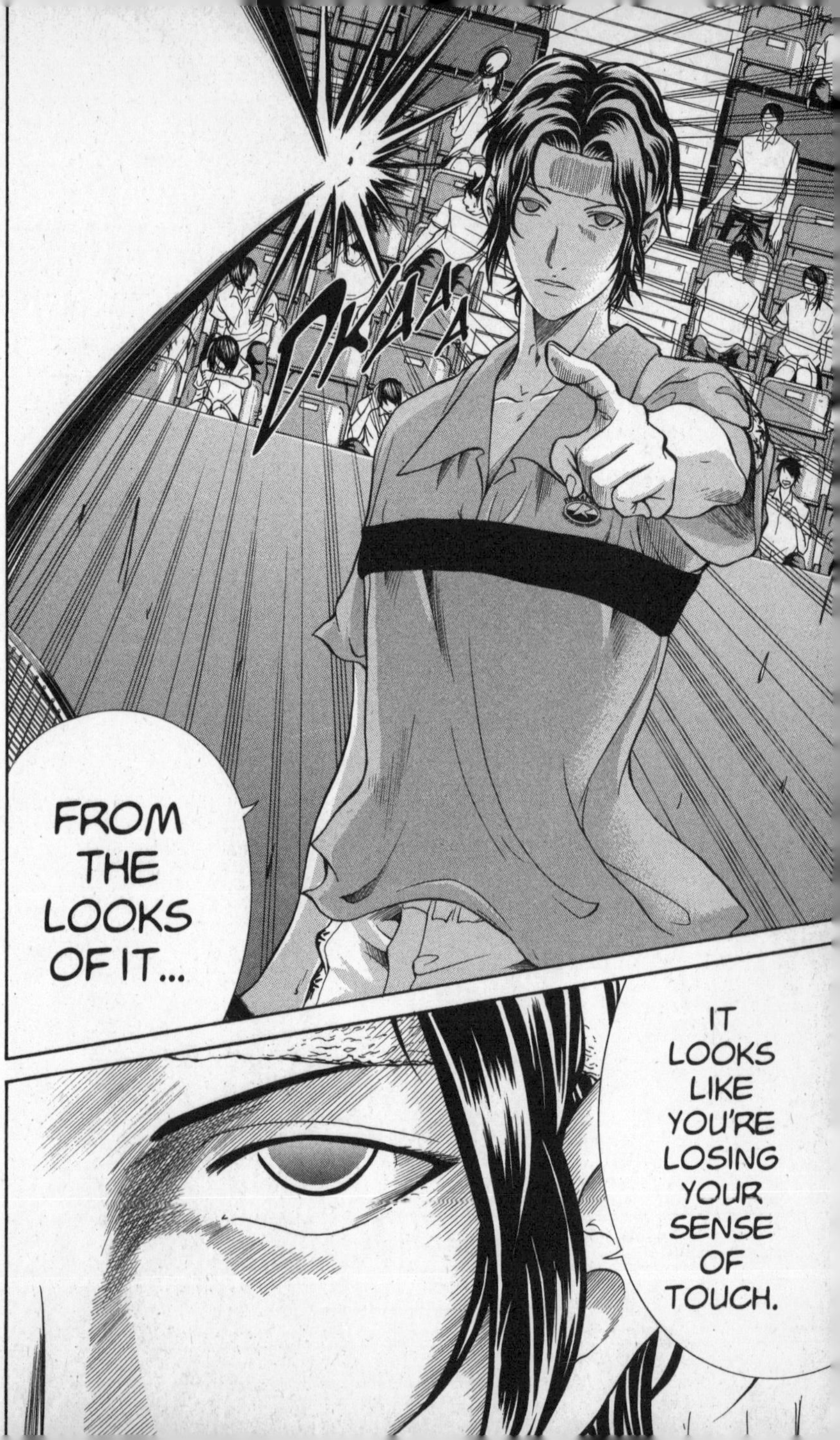
FROM THE LOOKS OF IT...
IT LOOKS LIKE YOU'RE LOSING YOUR SENSE OF TOUCH.

GENIUS 375:
FINAL SHOWDOWN! THE PRINCE VS. THE CHILD OF THE GODS, PART 5

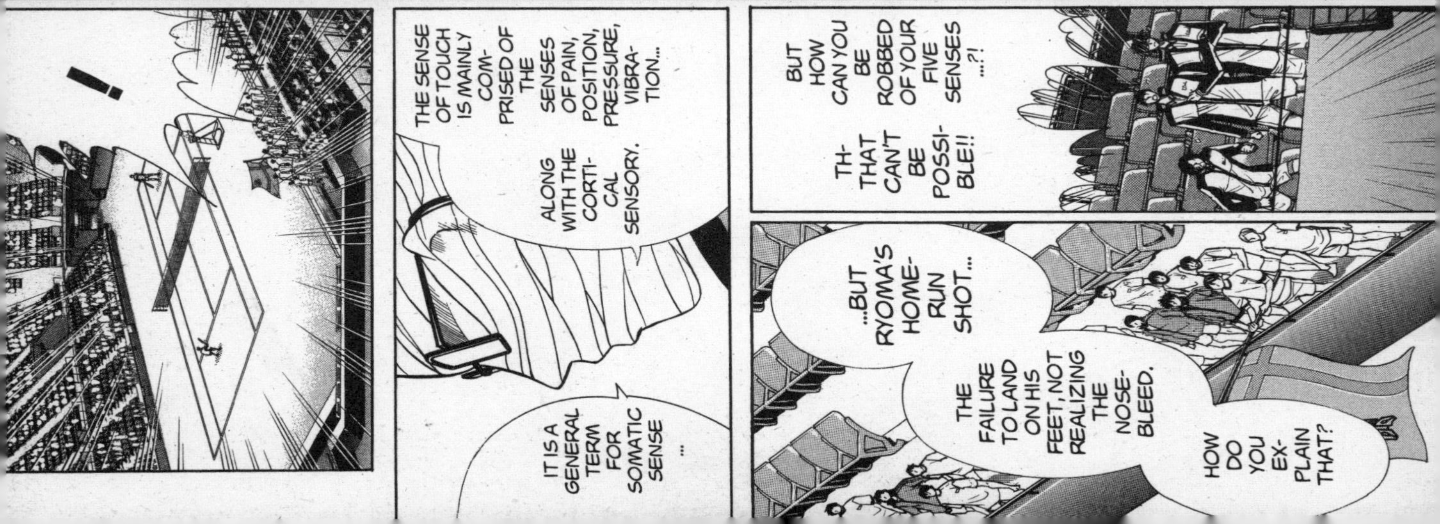
!
THE SENSE OF TOUCH IS MAINLY COM-PRISED OF THE SENSES OF PAIN, POSITION, PRESSURE, VIBRA-TION...
ALONG WITH THE CORTI-CAL SENSORY.
IT IS A GENERAL TERM FOR SOMATIC SENSE ...
BUT HOW CAN YOU BE ROBBED OF YOUR FIVE SENSES ...?!
TH-THAT CAN'T BE POSSI-BLE!!
...BUT RYOMA'S HOME-RUN SHOT...
THE FAILURE TO LAND ON HIS FEET, NOT REALIZING THE NOSE-BLEED.
HOW DO YOU EX-PLAIN THAT?

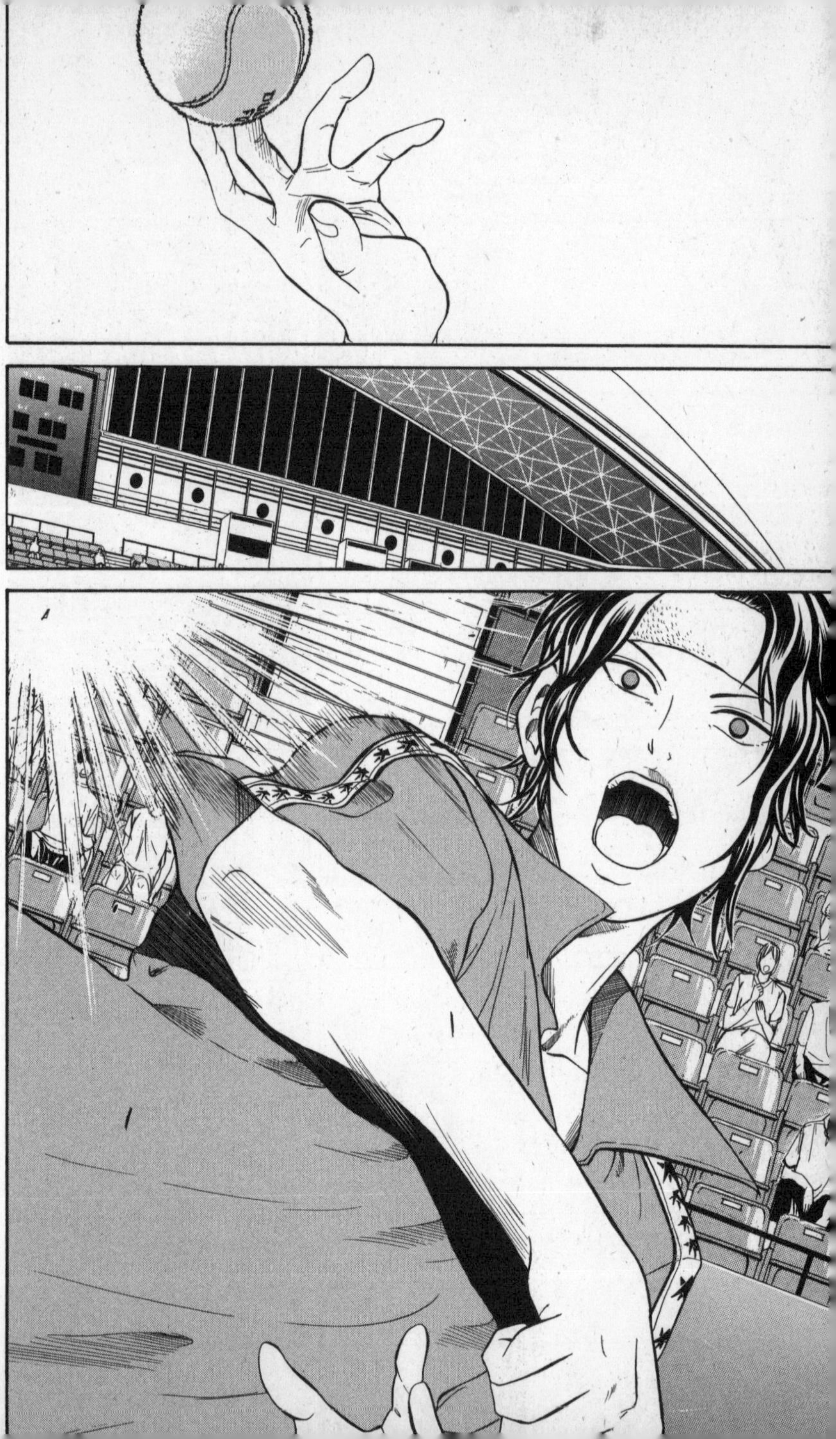

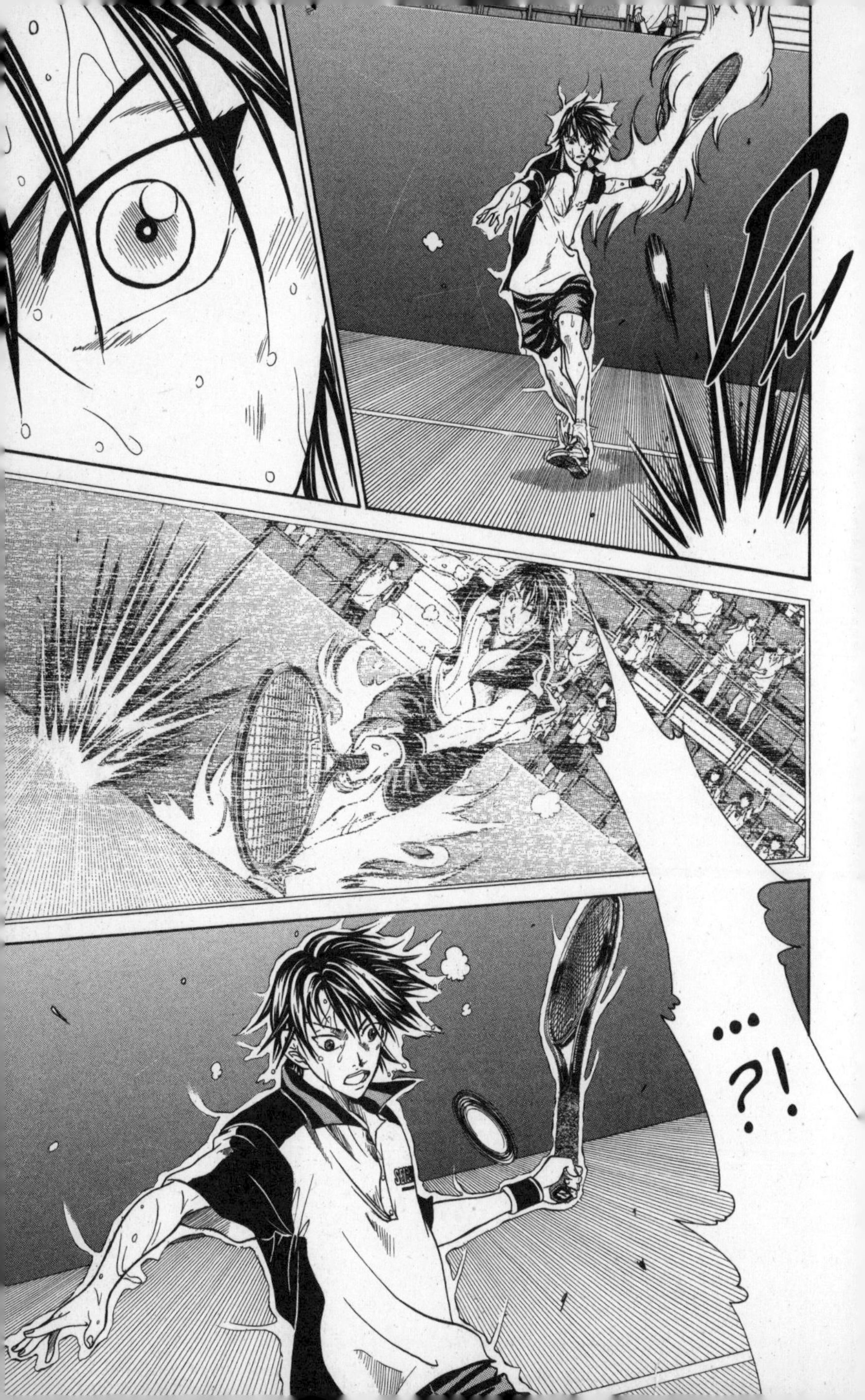
...?!

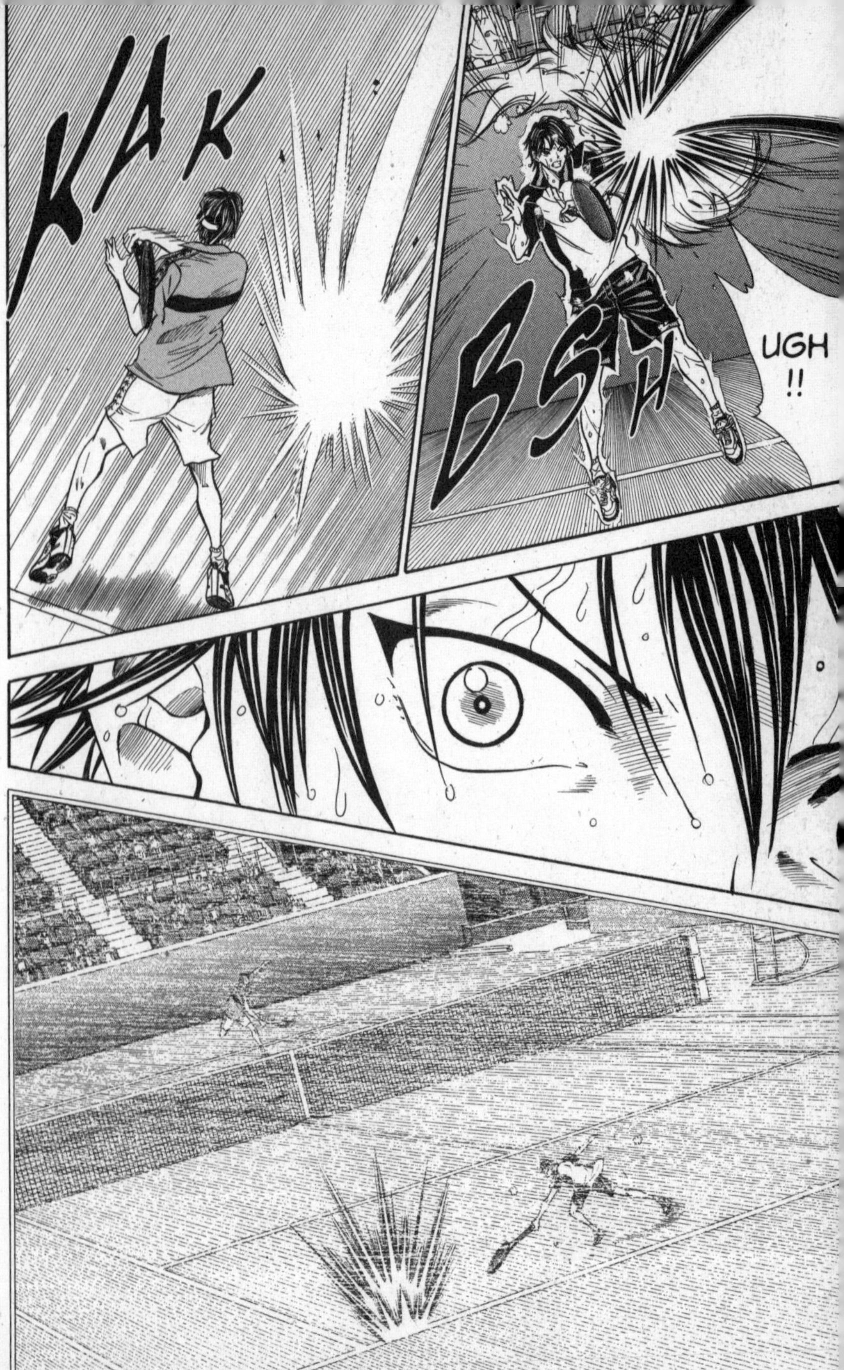
BSH
UGH !!
KAK

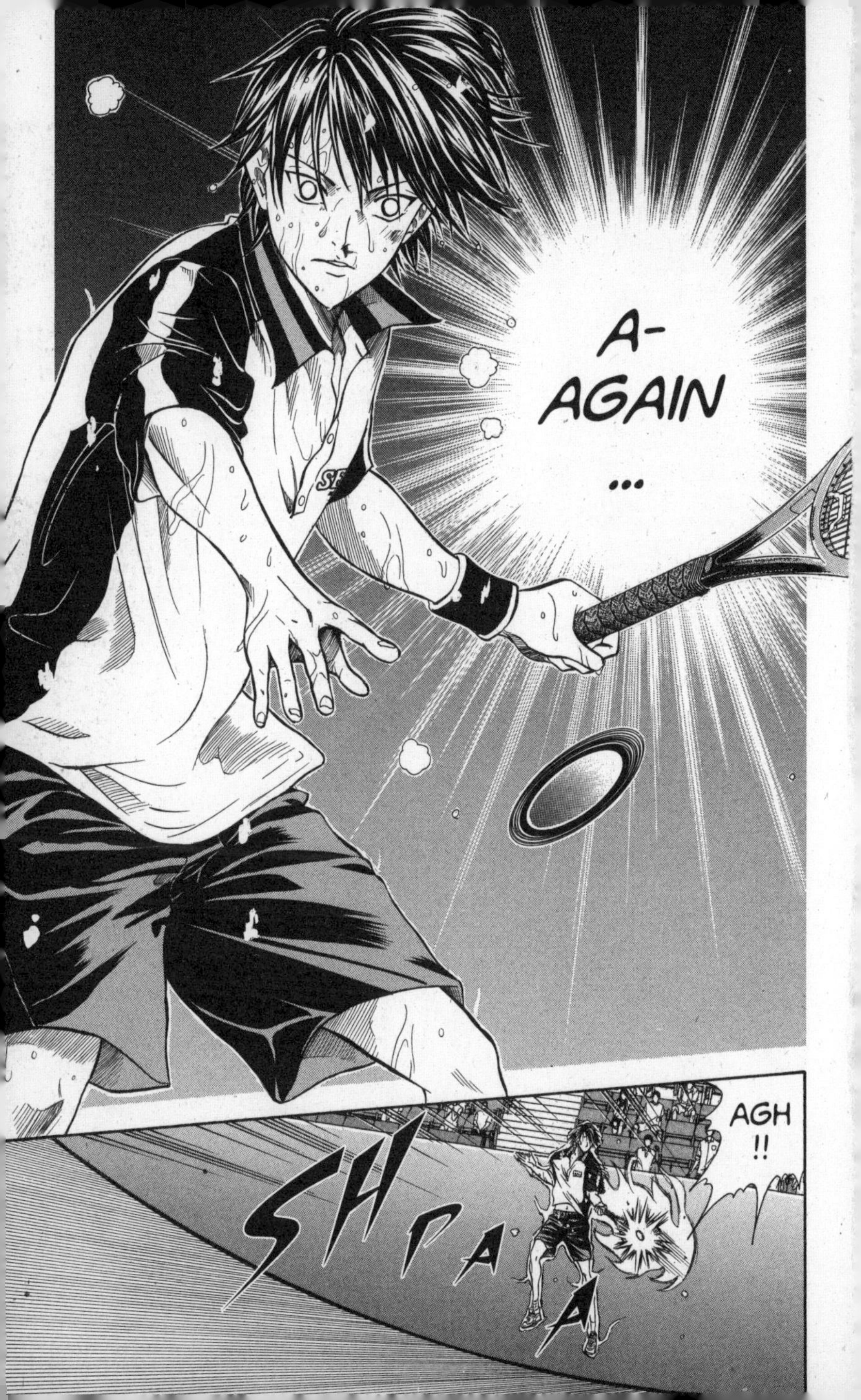
A- AGAIN ...
AGH !!
SHPAA

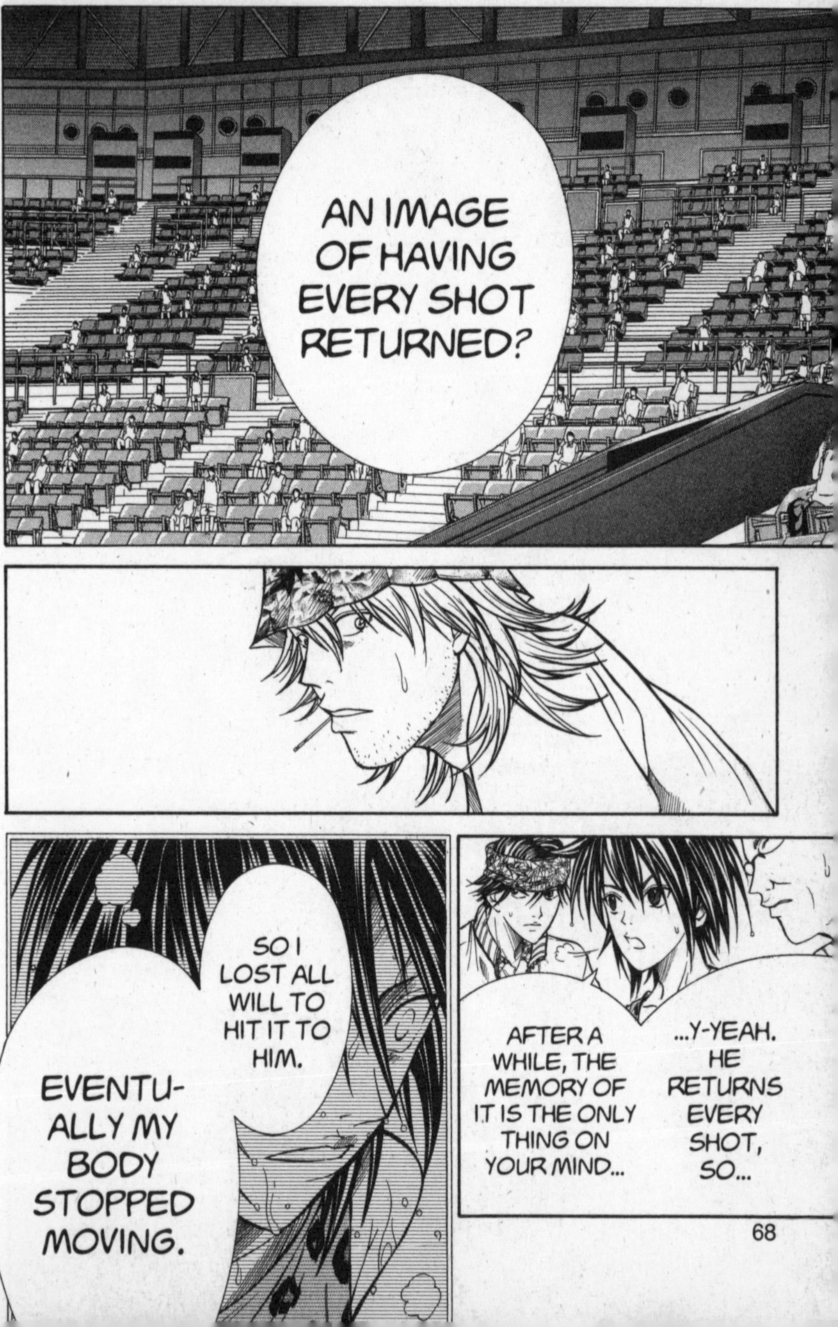
AN IMAGE OF HAVING EVERY SHOT RETURNED?
...Y-YEAH. HE RETURNS EVERY SHOT, SO...
AFTER A WHILE, THE MEMORY OF IT IS THE ONLY THING ON YOUR MIND...
SO I LOST ALL WILL TO HIT IT TO HIM.
EVENTU-ALLY MY BODY STOPPED MOVING.

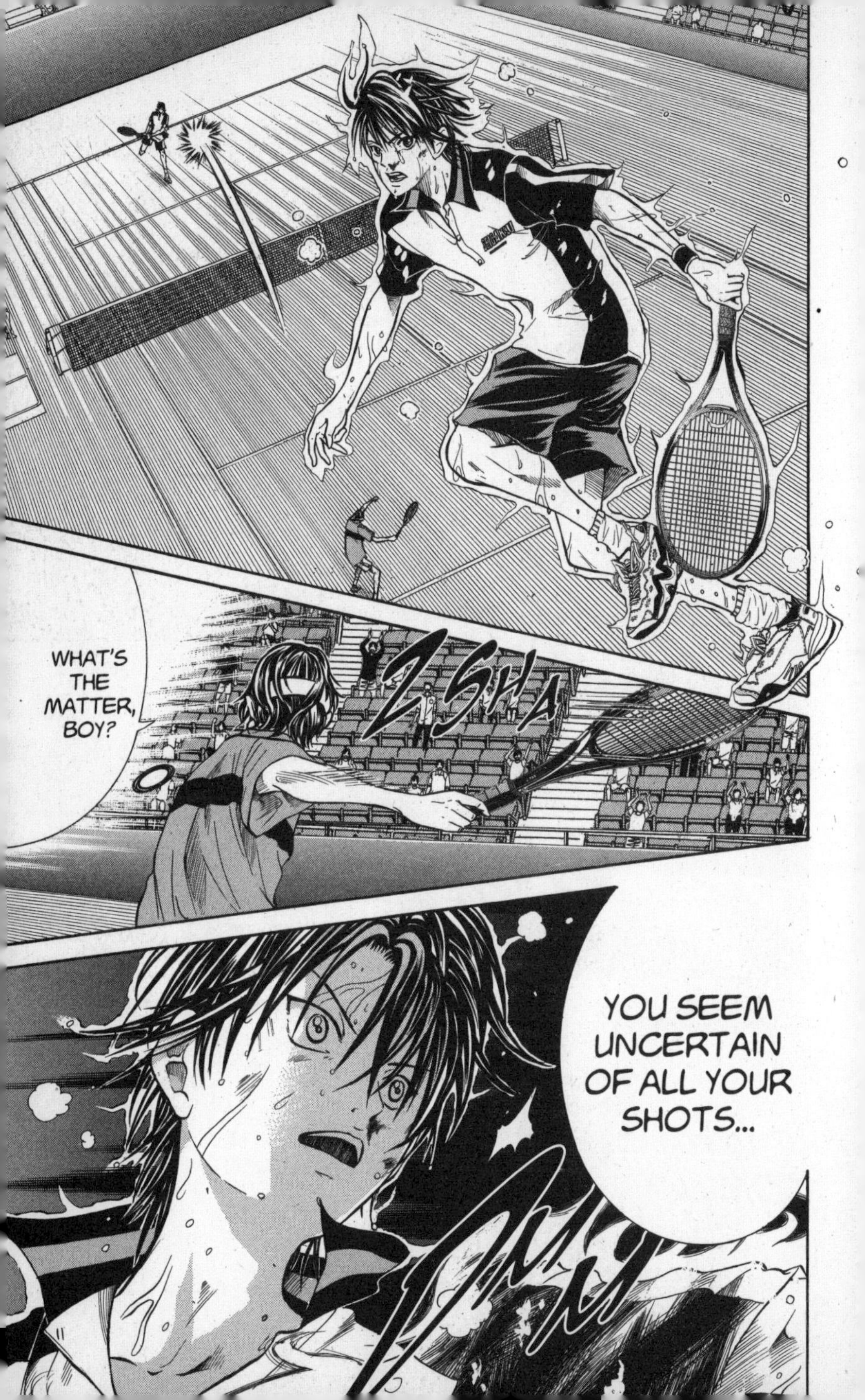
ZSHA
WHAT'S THE MATTER, BOY?
YOU SEEM UNCERTAIN OF ALL YOUR SHOTS...

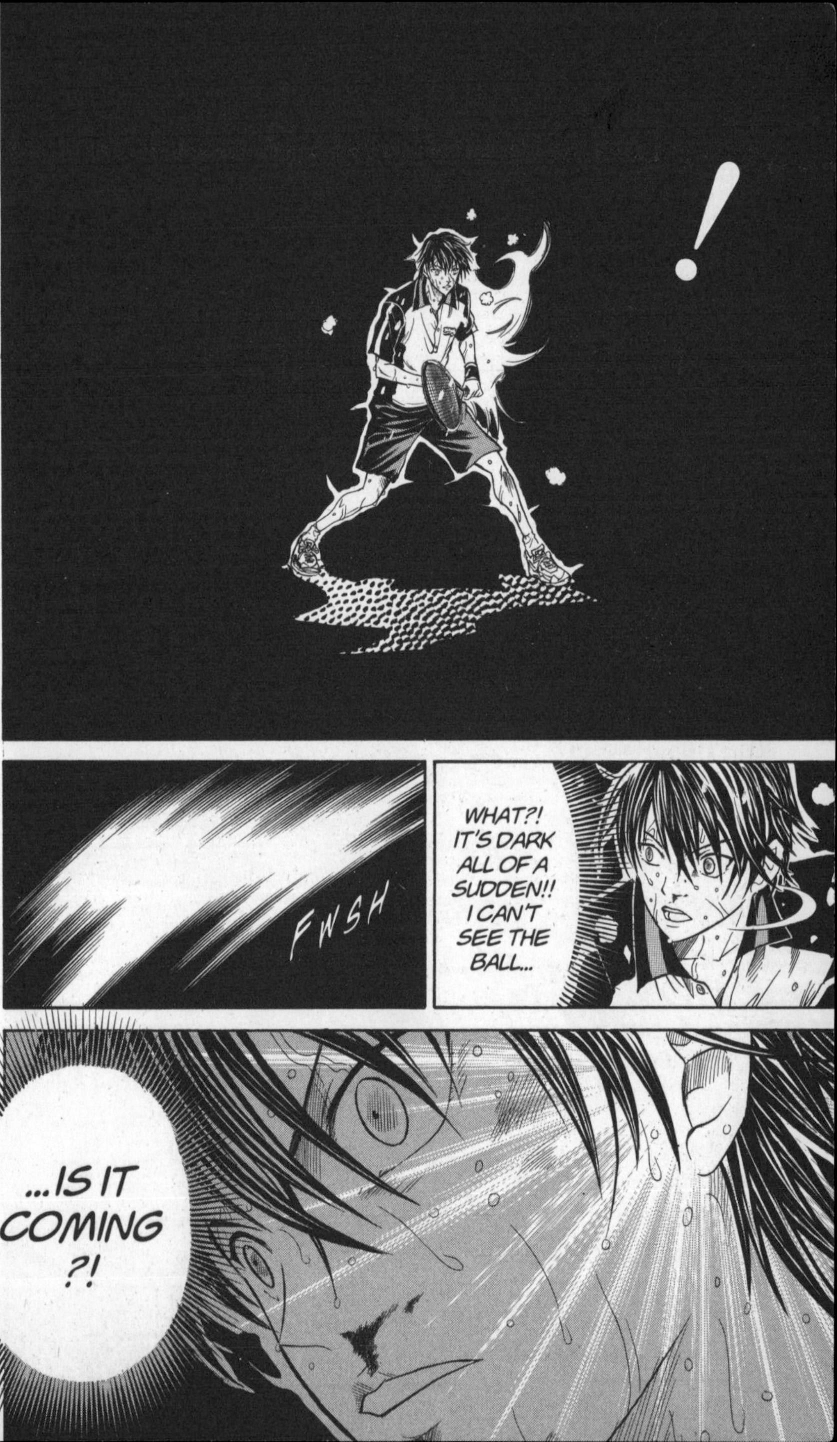
!
WHAT?! IT'S DARK ALL OF A SUDDEN!! I CAN'T SEE THE BALL...
FWSH
...IS IT COMING ?!

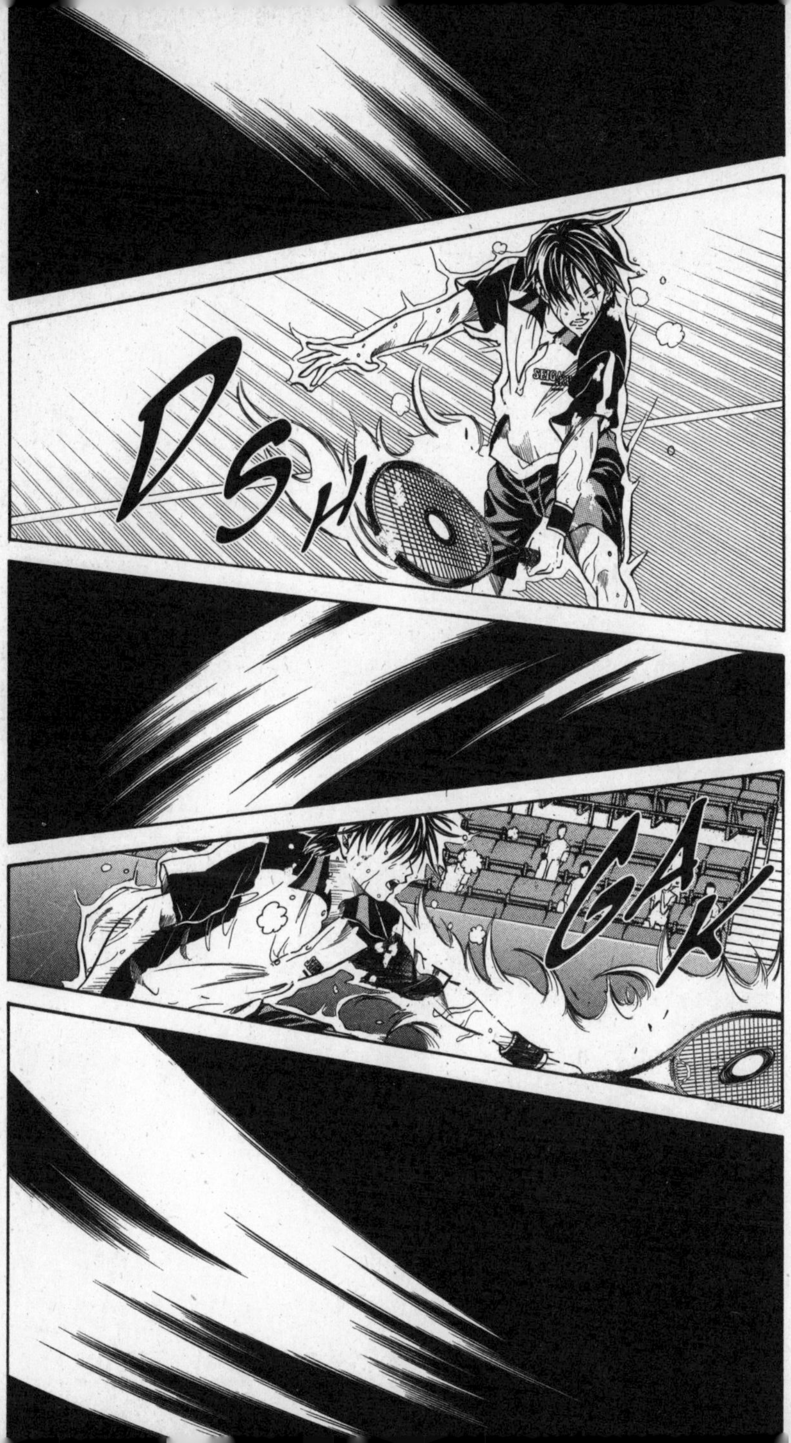
DSH
GAK

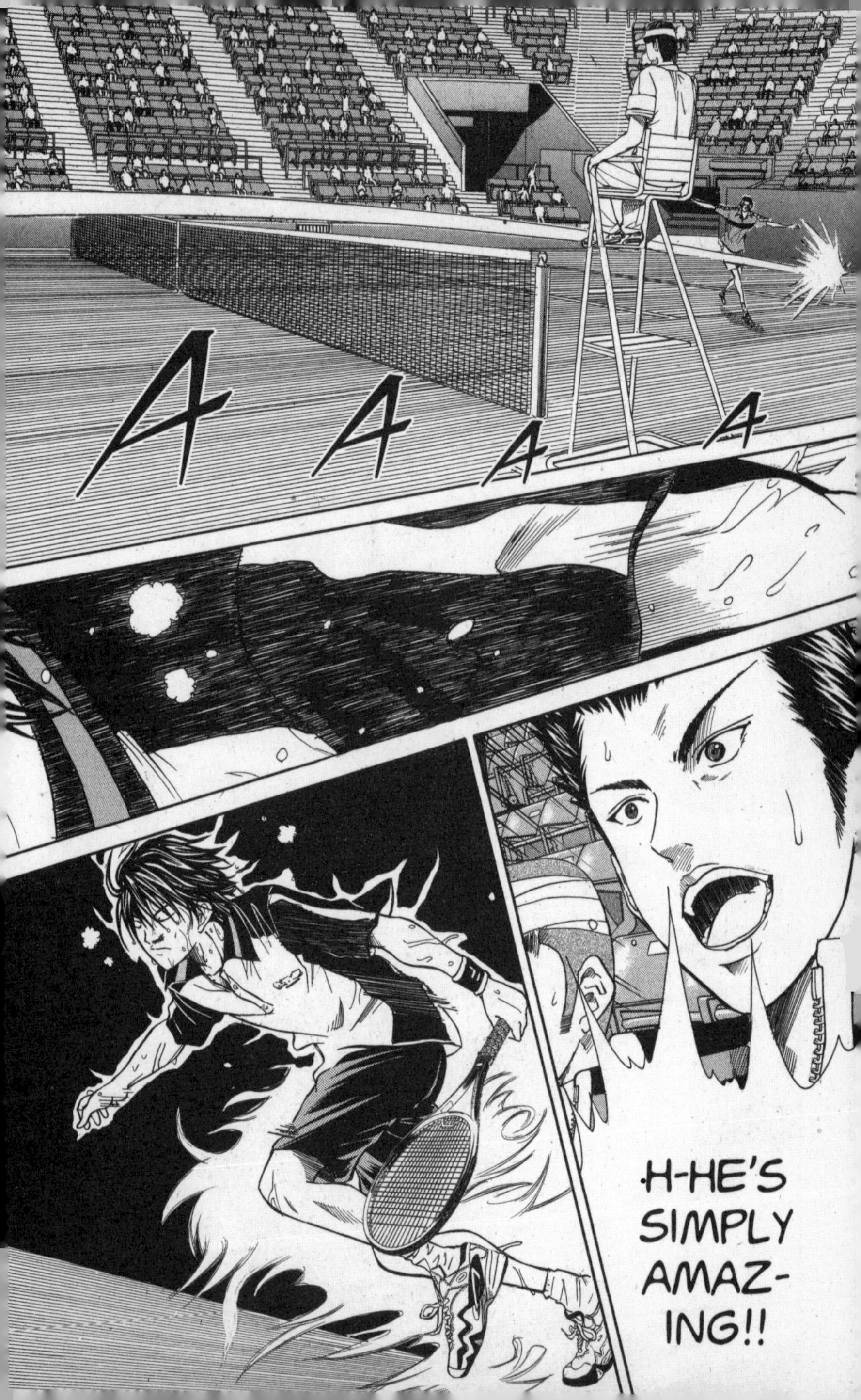
A A A A
H-HE'S SIMPLY AMAZ-ING!!

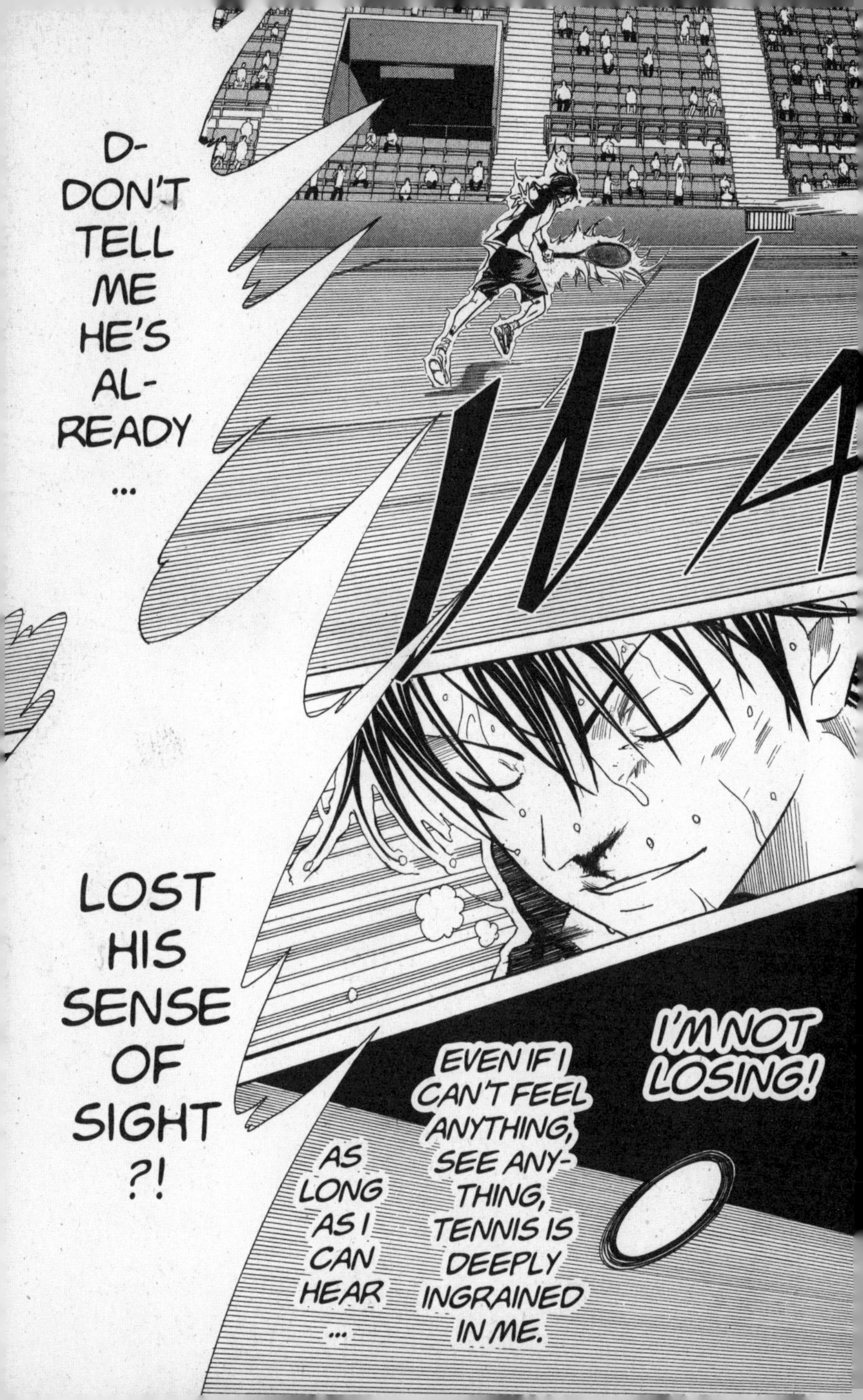

D-DON'T TELL ME HE'S AL-READY ...
LOST HIS SENSE OF SIGHT ?!
I'M NOT LOSING!
EVEN IF I CAN'T FEEL ANYTHING, SEE ANY-THING, TENNIS IS DEEPLY INGRAINED IN ME.
AS LONG AS I CAN HEAR ...

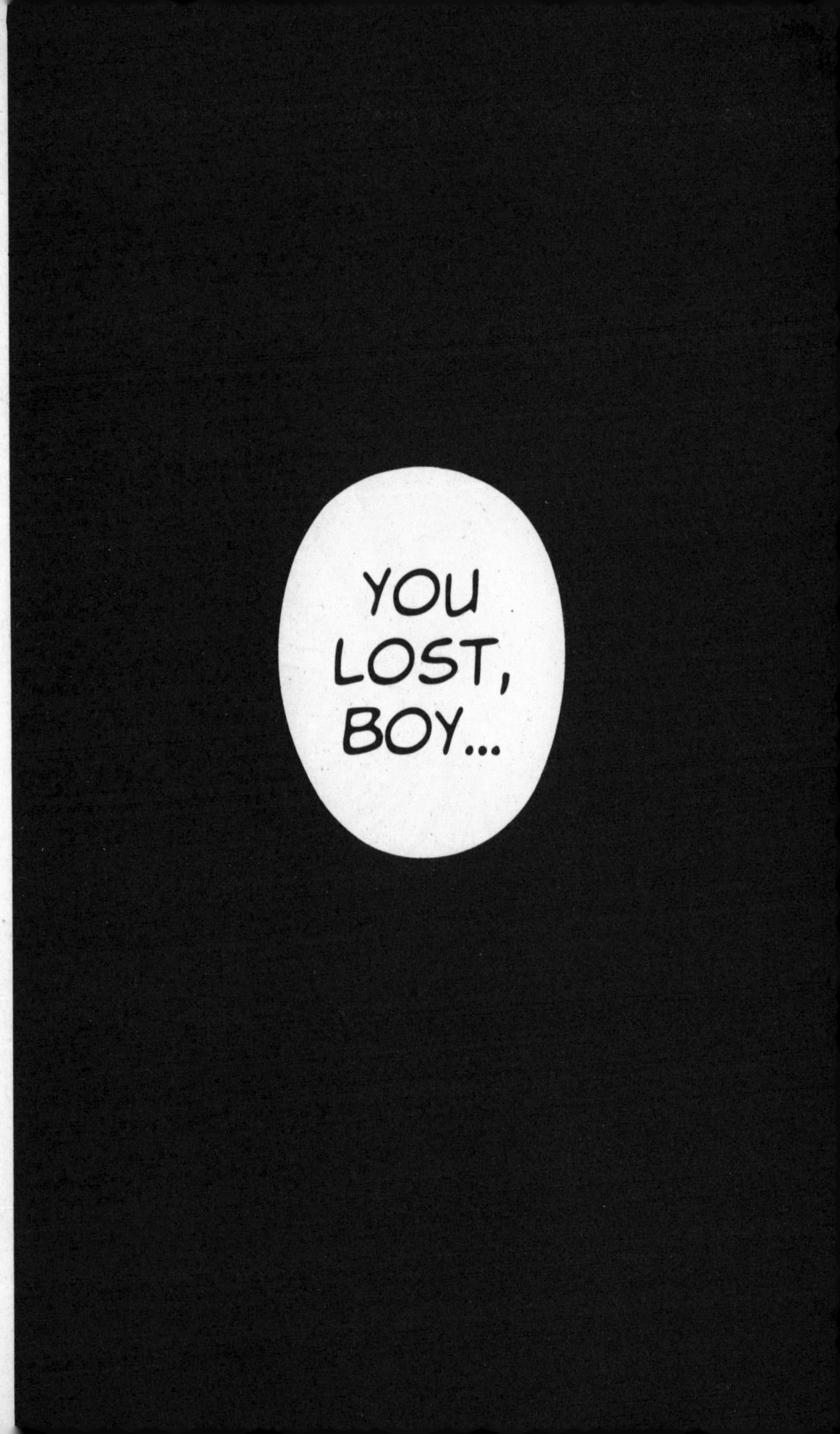
YOU LOST, BOY...

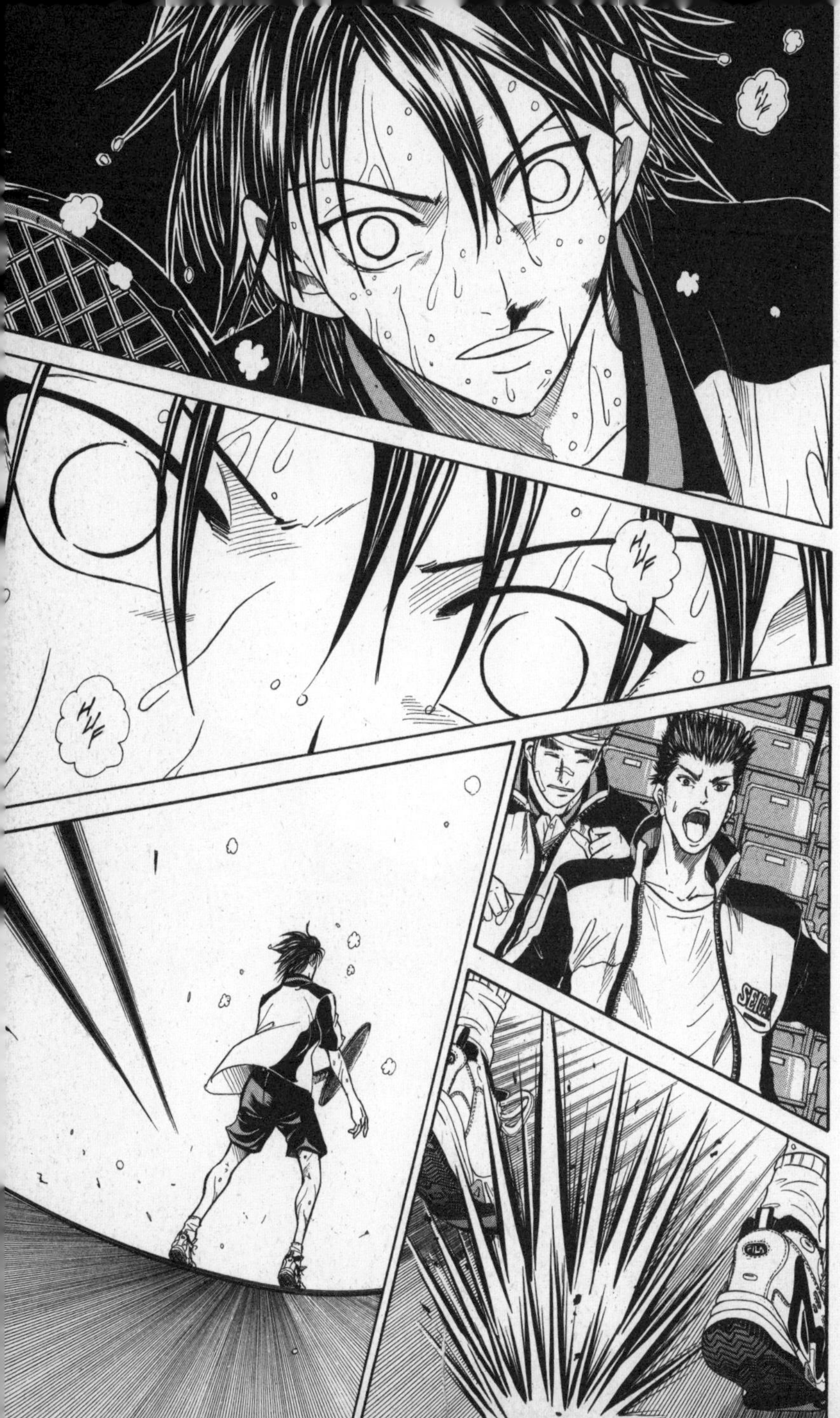
HUF
HUF
HUF

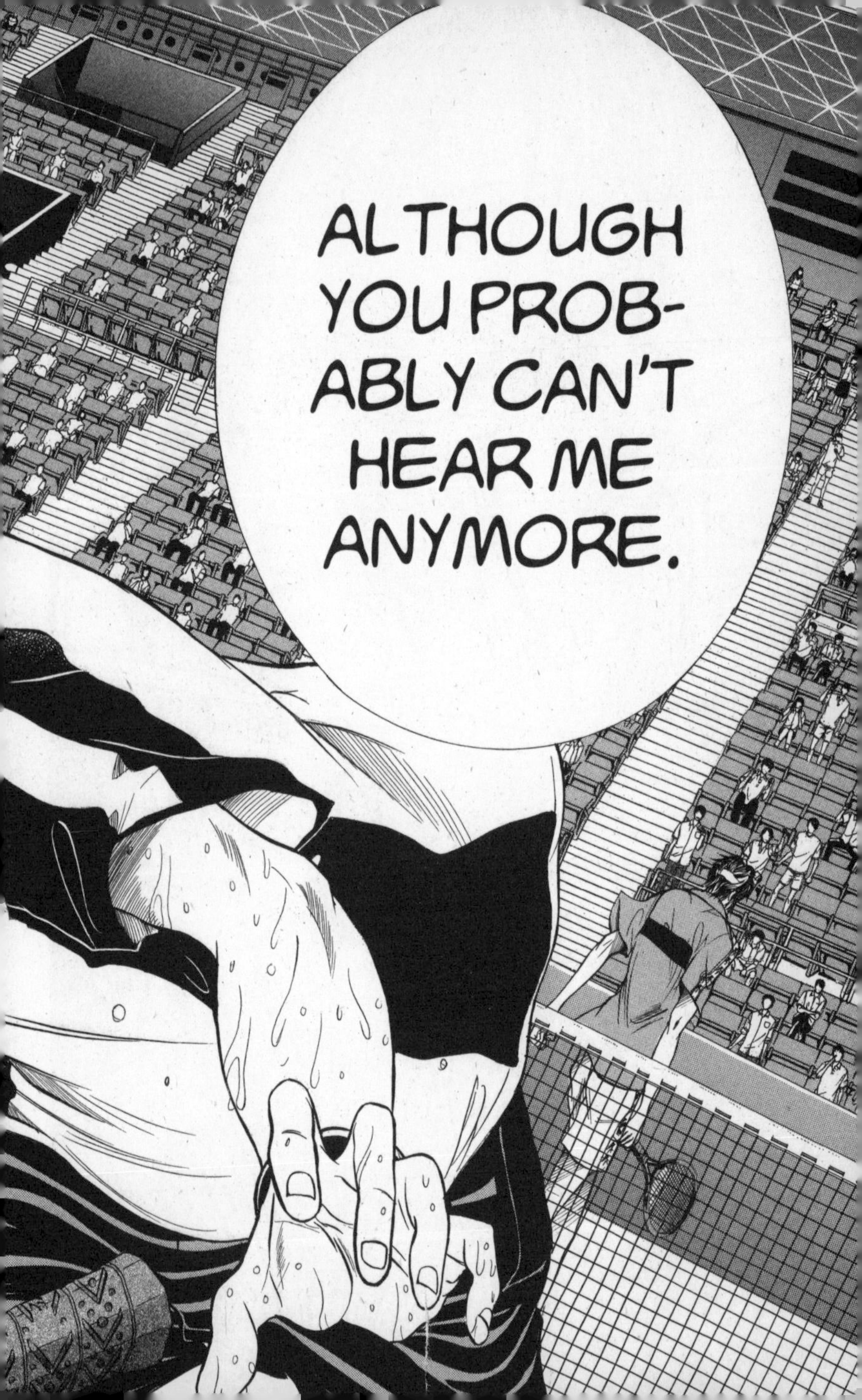
ALTHOUGH YOU PROB-ABLY CAN'T HEAR ME ANYMORE.

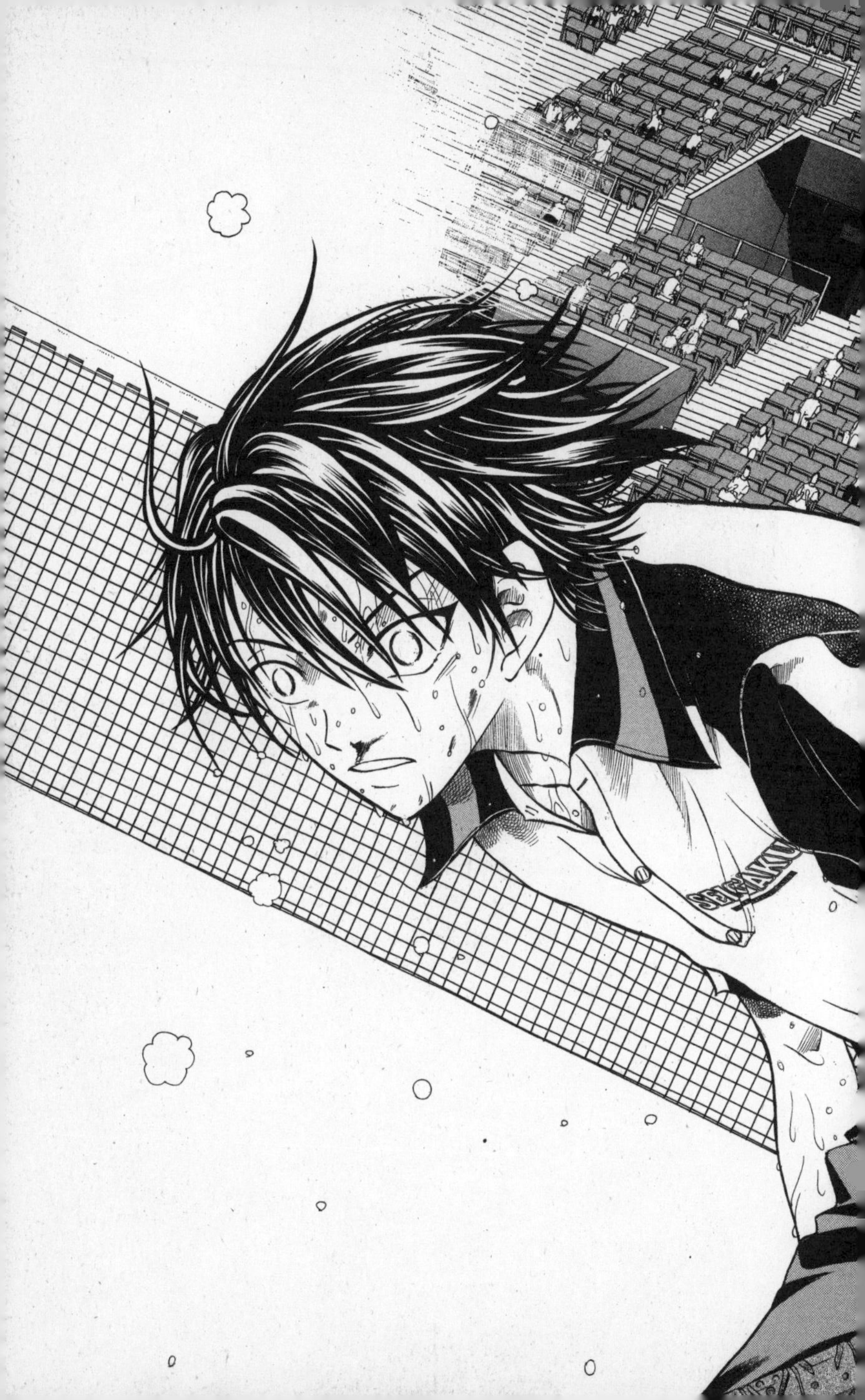

2008 Valentine's Day Results!! ③

31st KINTARO TOYAMA 8

31st AKIRA KAMIO 8

31st HAJIME MIZUKI 8

31st TORAJIRO SAEKI 8

35th MUNEHIRO KABAJI 7

36th KEI TANISHI 6

36th HIROSHI CHINEN 6

36th SHINJI IBU 6

36th ATSUSHI KISARAZU 6

40th HIKARU AMANE 5

40th YUJI HITOUJI 5

40th KOHARU KONJIKI 5

43rd HARUKAZE KUROBANE 4

43rd KIPPEI TACHIBANA 4

43rd SENRI CHITOSE 4

43rd JIN AKUTSU 4

43rd KENTARO AOI 4

48th KACHIRO KATO, SATOSHI HORIO, KATSUO MIZUNO (TRIO) 3

48th NANJIRO ECHIZEN 3

50th LILIADENT KRAUSER 2

50th HAGINOSUKE TAKI 2

50th KALPIN 2

(Rest of results omitted)

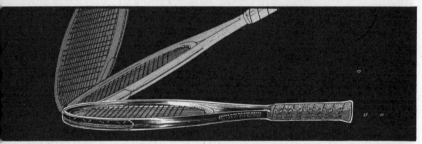

GENIUS 376:
FINAL SHOWDOWN! THE PRINCE VS. THE CHILD OF THE GODS, PART 6

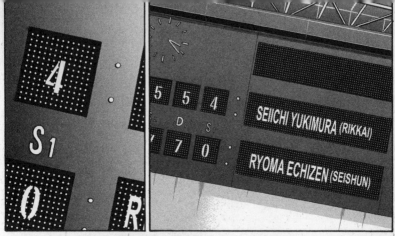

SEIICHI YUKIMURA (RIKKAI)

RYOMA ECHIZEN (SEISHUN)

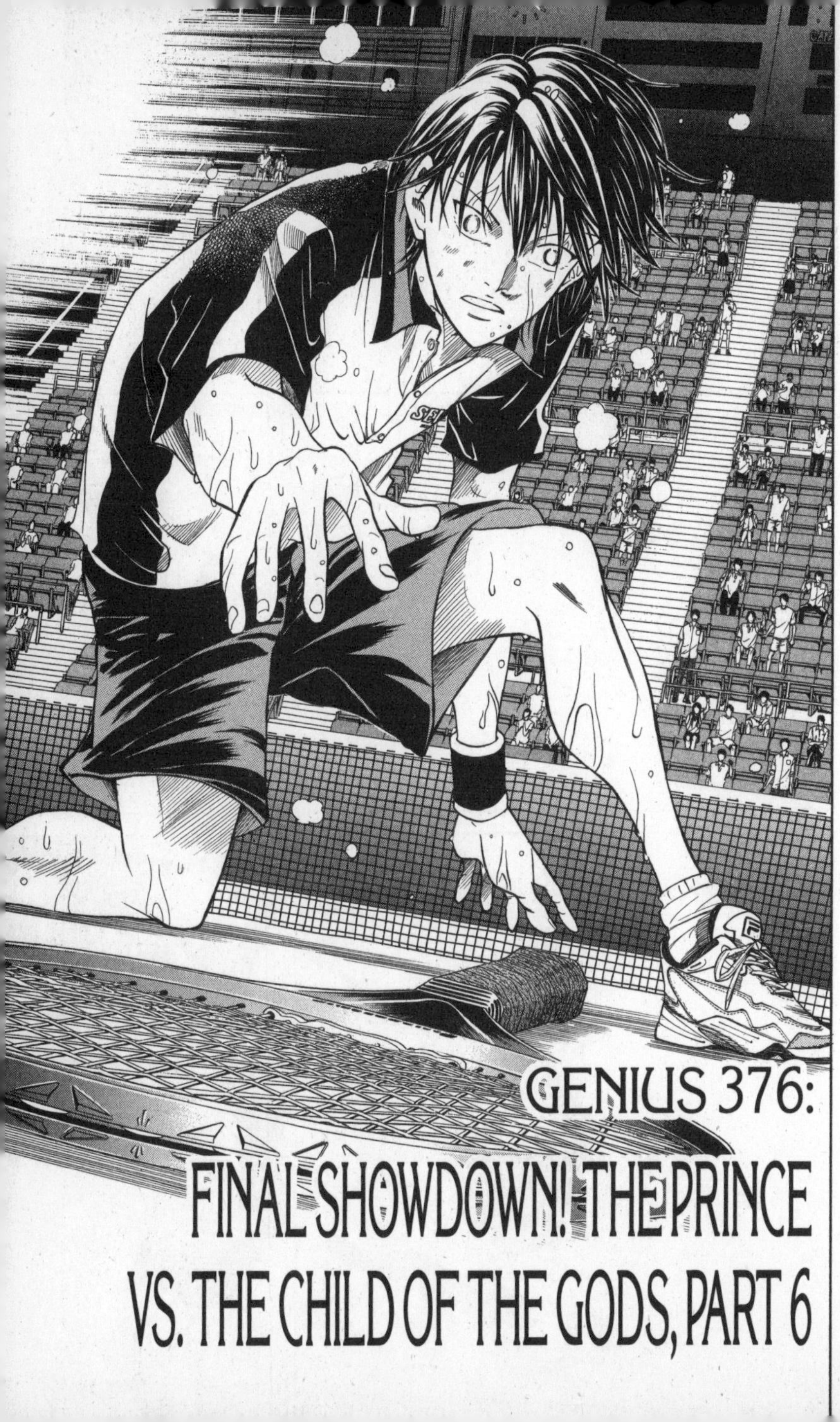
GENIUS 376:
FINAL SHOWDOWN! THE PRINCE
VS. THE CHILD OF THE GODS, PART 6

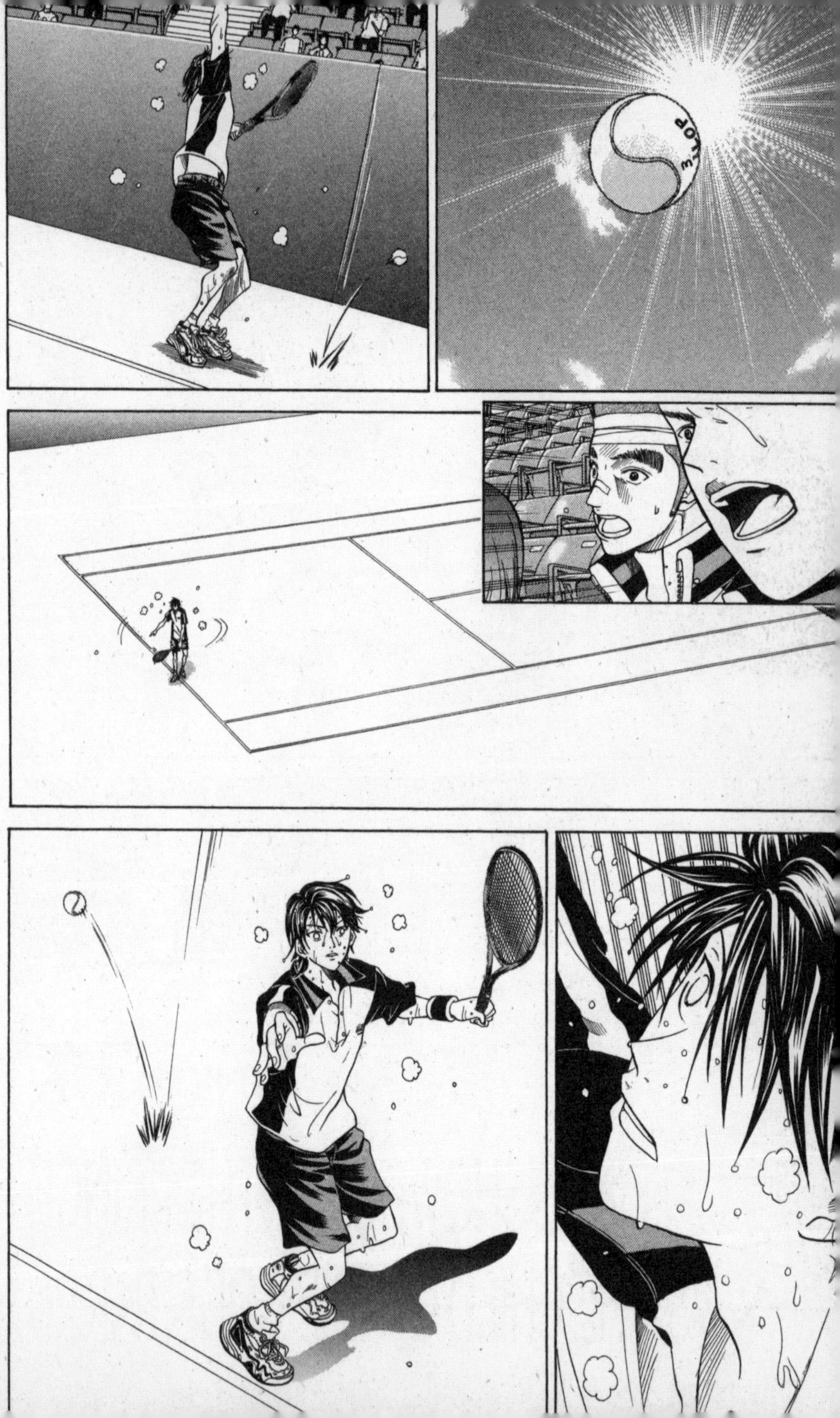

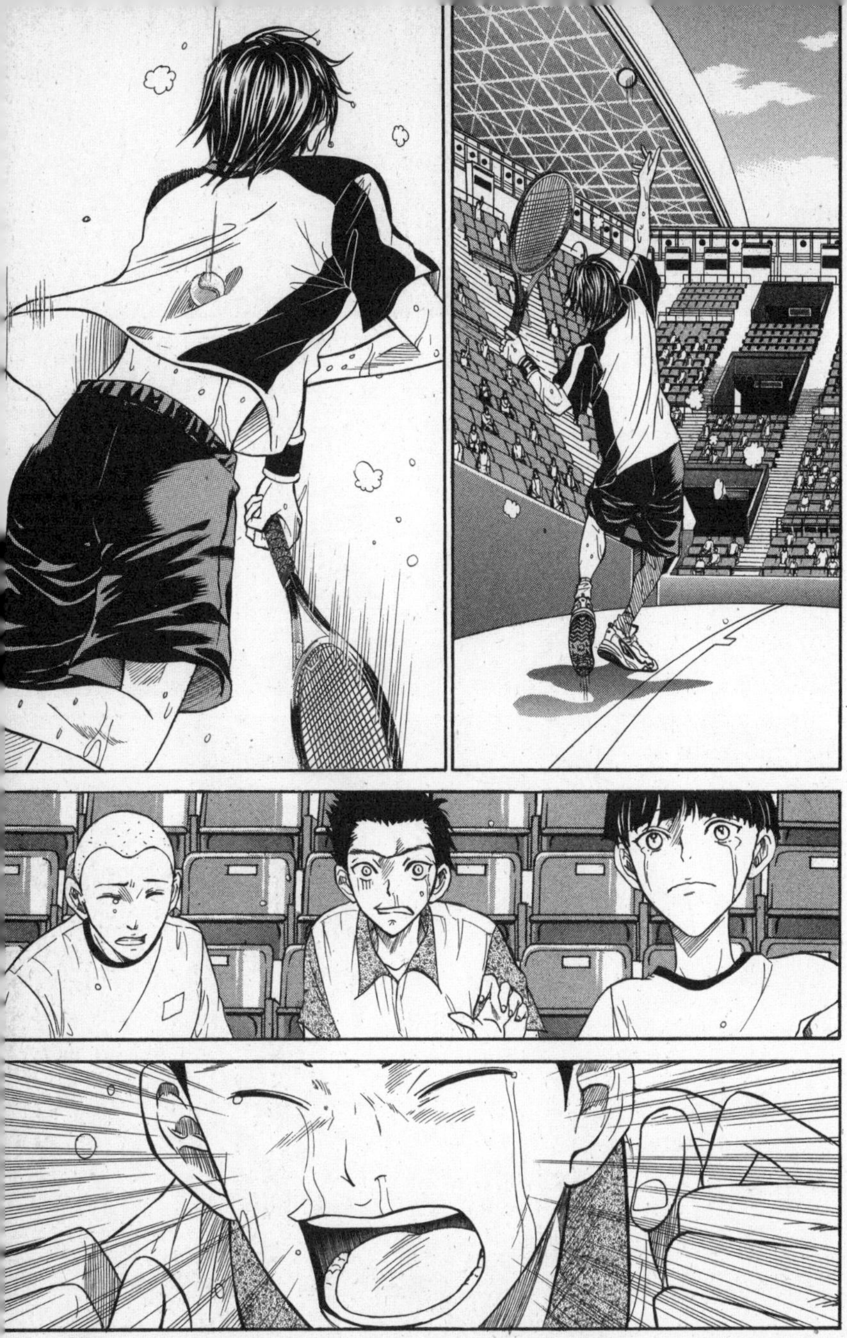

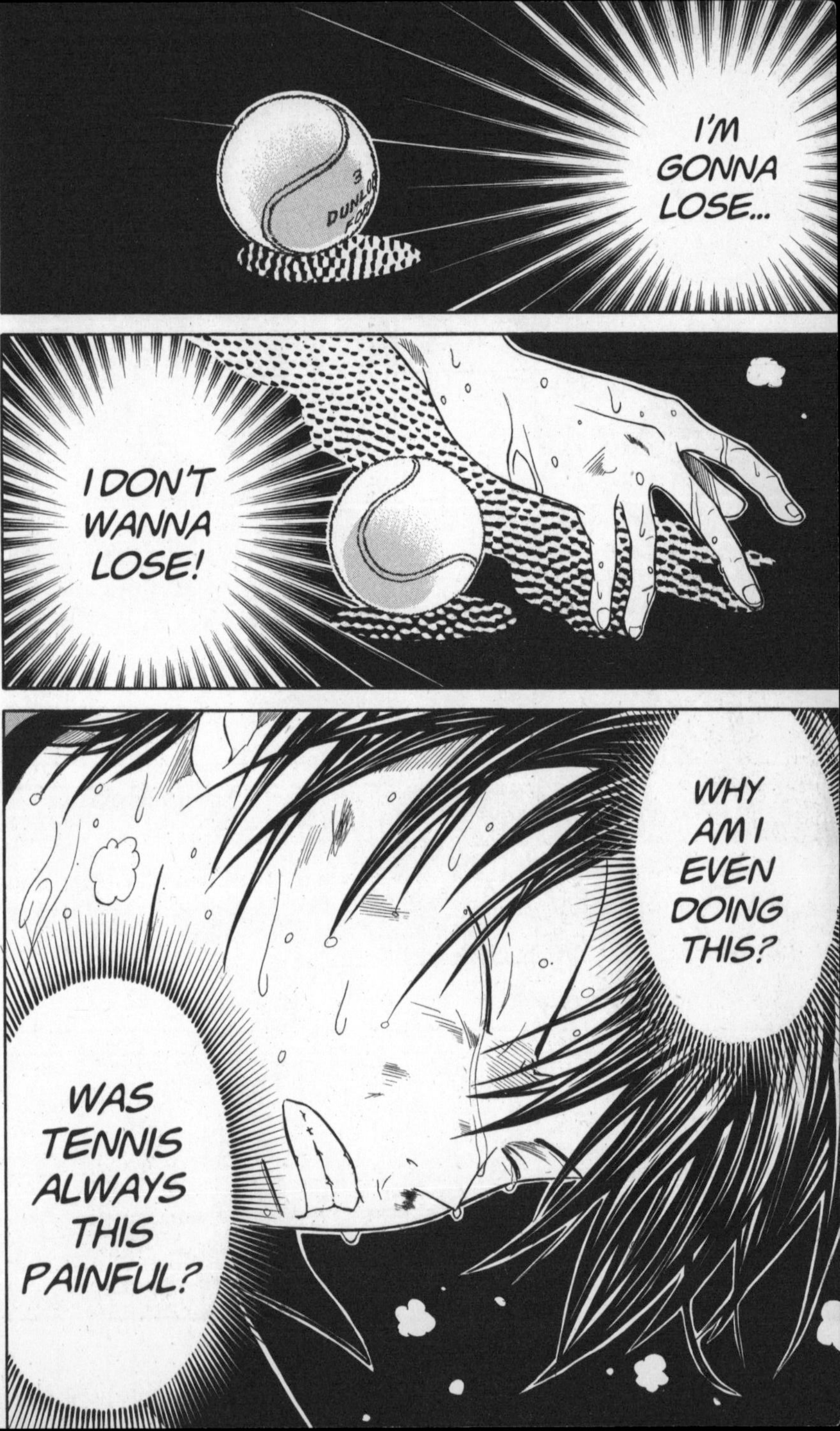
I'M GONNA LOSE...
I DON'T WANNA LOSE!
WHY AM I EVEN DOING THIS?
WAS TENNIS ALWAYS THIS PAINFUL?

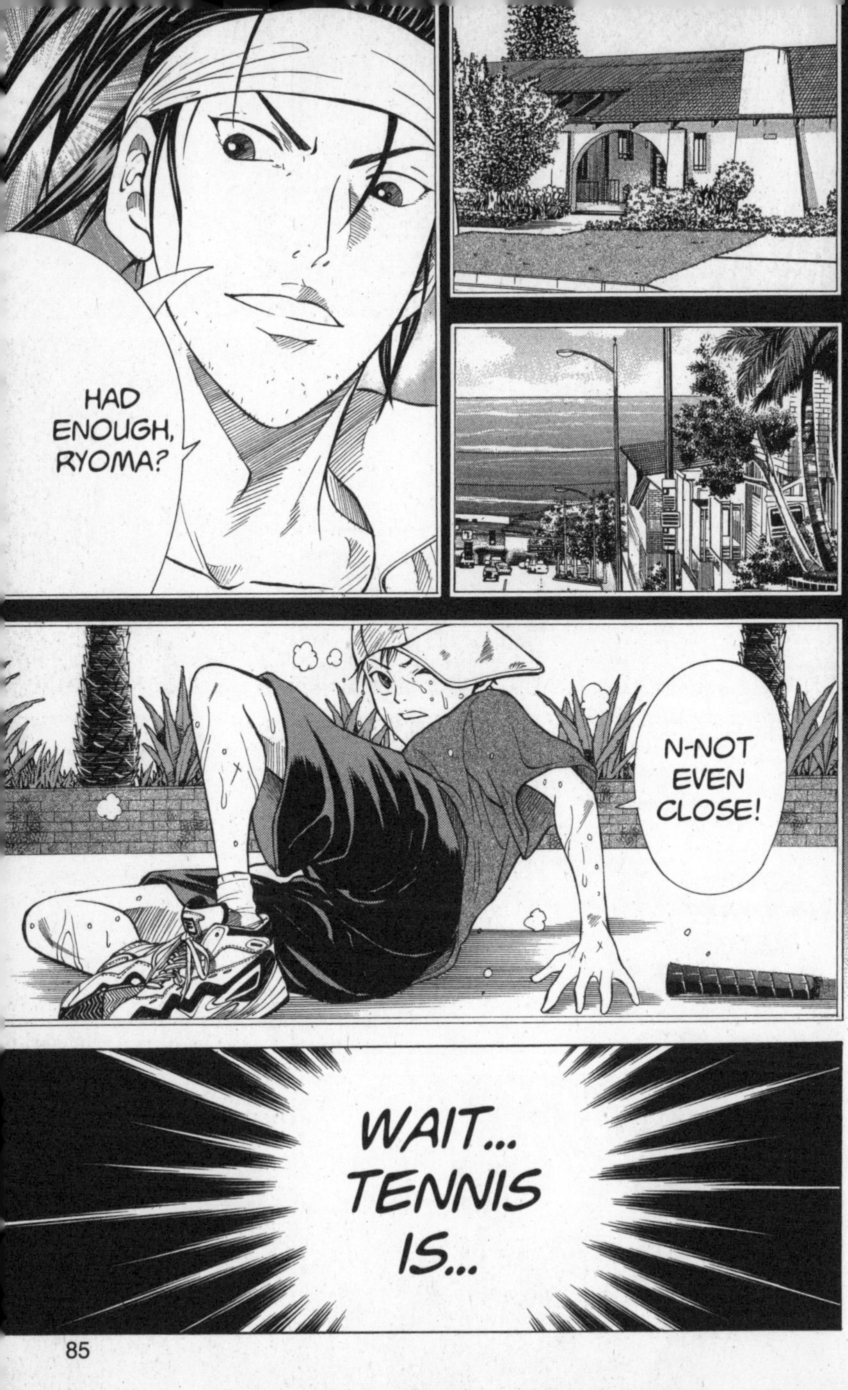
HAD ENOUGH, RYOMA?
N-NOT EVEN CLOSE!
WAIT... TENNIS IS...

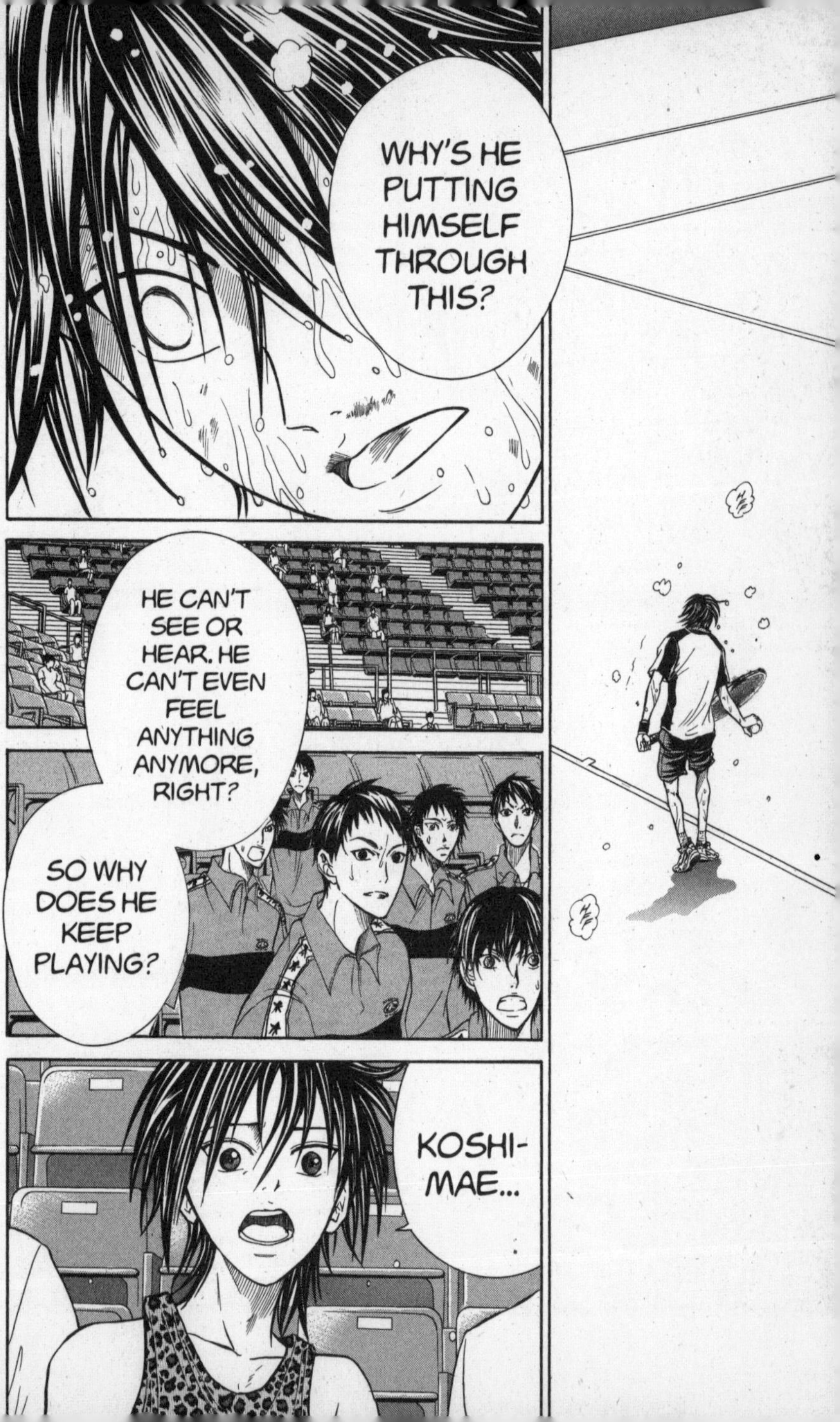
WHY'S HE PUTTING HIMSELF THROUGH THIS?
HE CAN'T SEE OR HEAR. HE CAN'T EVEN FEEL ANYTHING ANYMORE, RIGHT?
SO WHY DOES HE KEEP PLAYING?
KOSHI-MAE...

COACH RYU-ZAKI!

NOO...

I'M SORRY, RYOMA...!

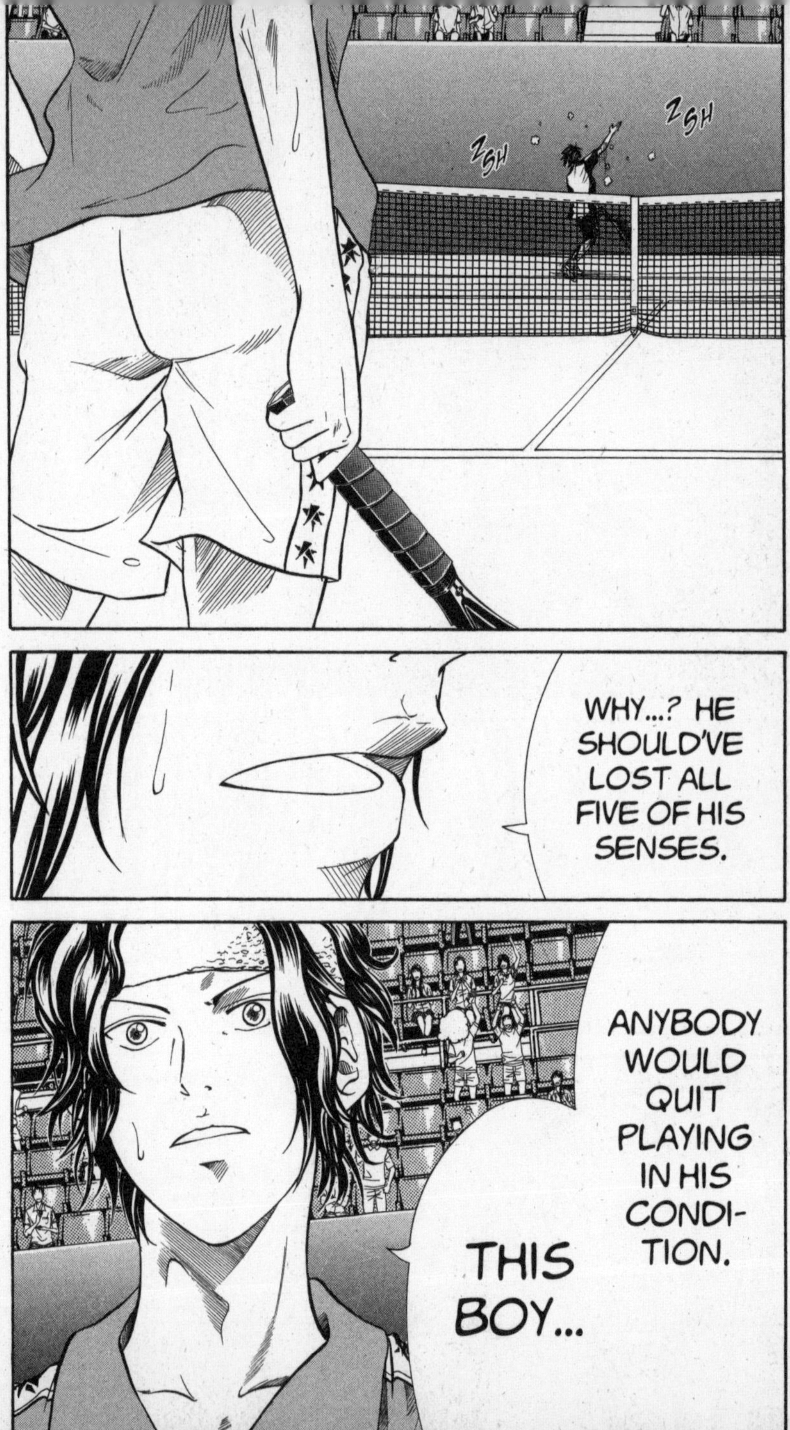
ZSH
ZSH
WHY...? HE SHOULD'VE LOST ALL FIVE OF HIS SENSES.
ANYBODY WOULD QUIT PLAYING IN HIS CONDI-TION.
THIS BOY...

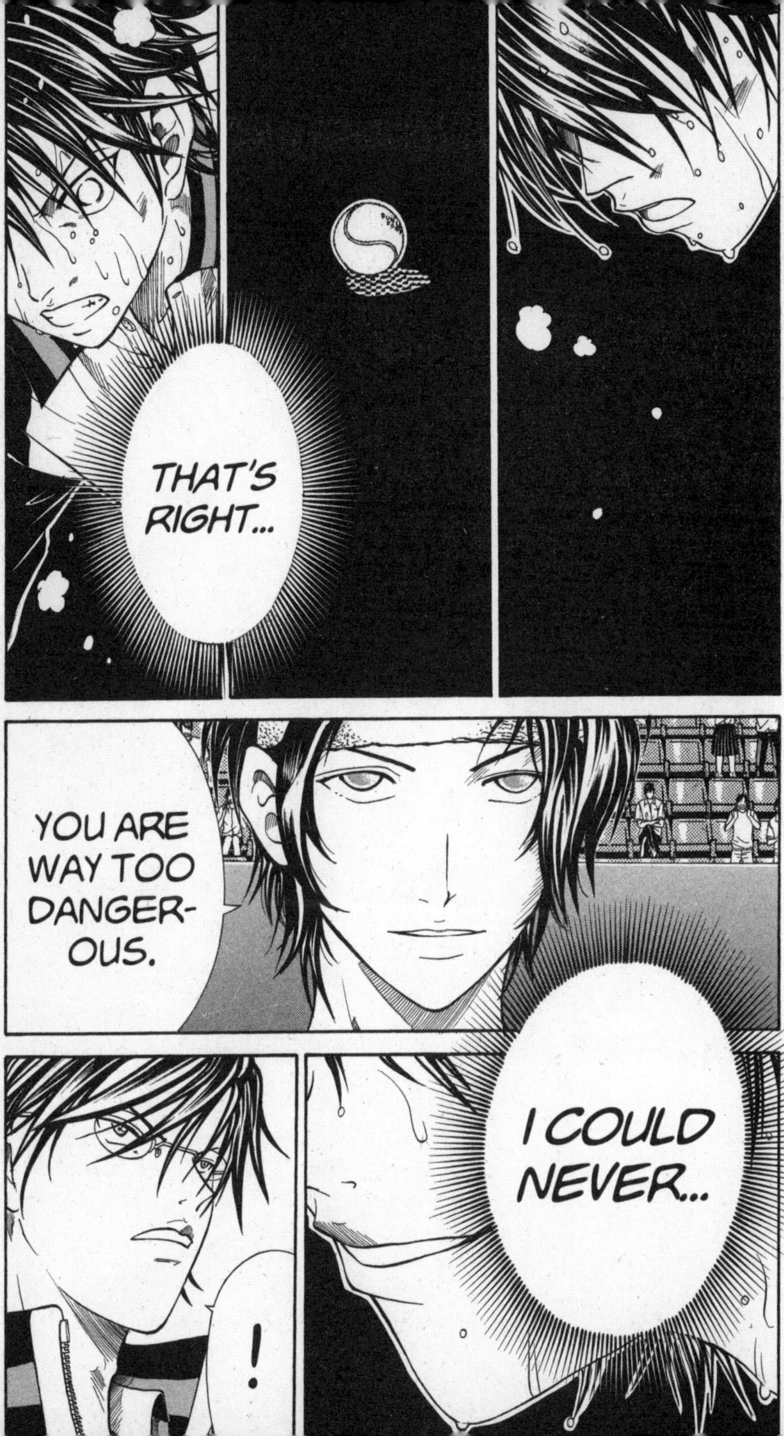
THAT'S RIGHT...
YOU ARE WAY TOO DANGER-OUS.
I COULD NEVER...
!

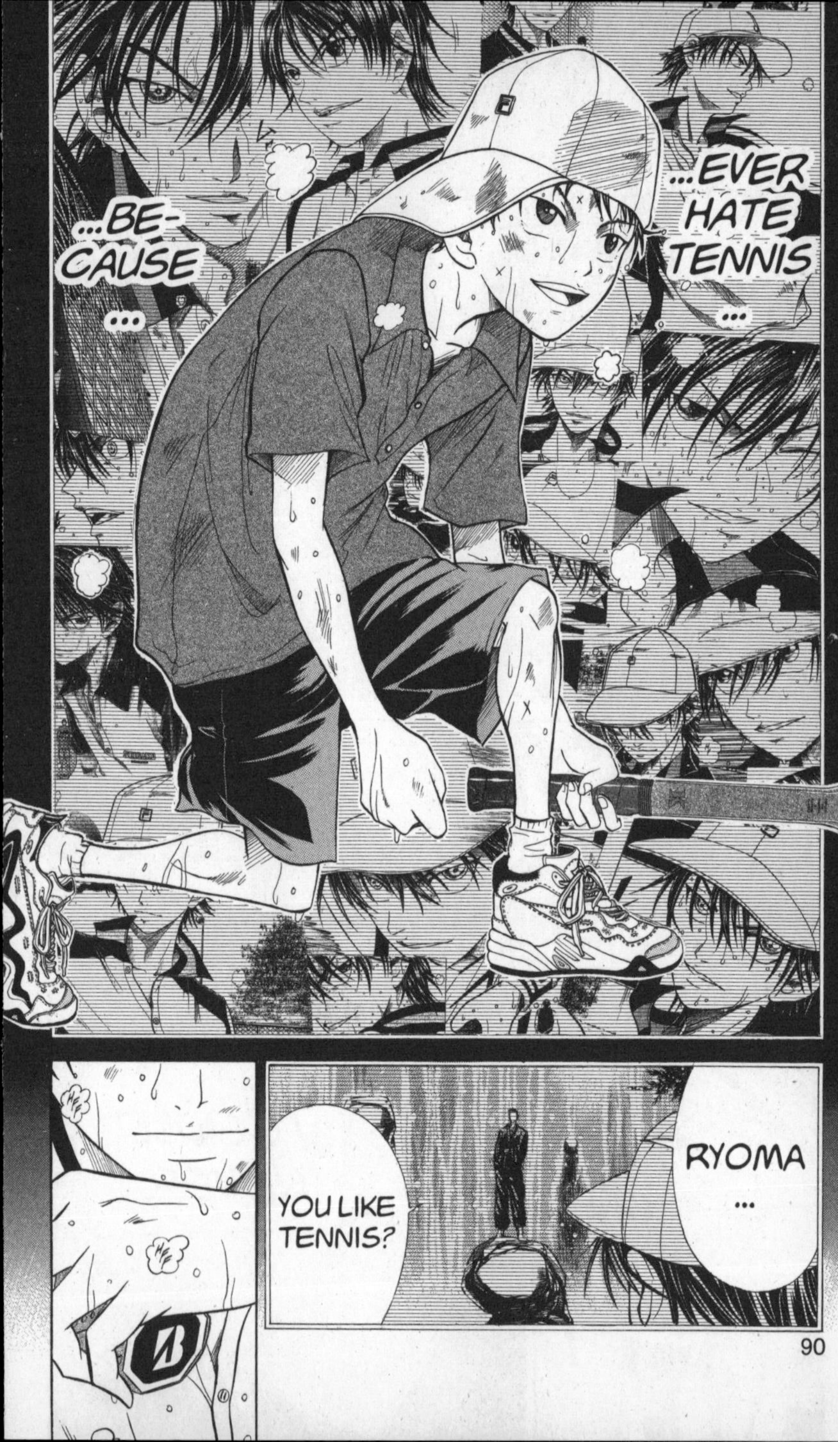
...EVER HATE TENNIS ...
...BE-CAUSE ...
RYOMA ...
YOU LIKE TENNIS?
HFF
HFF

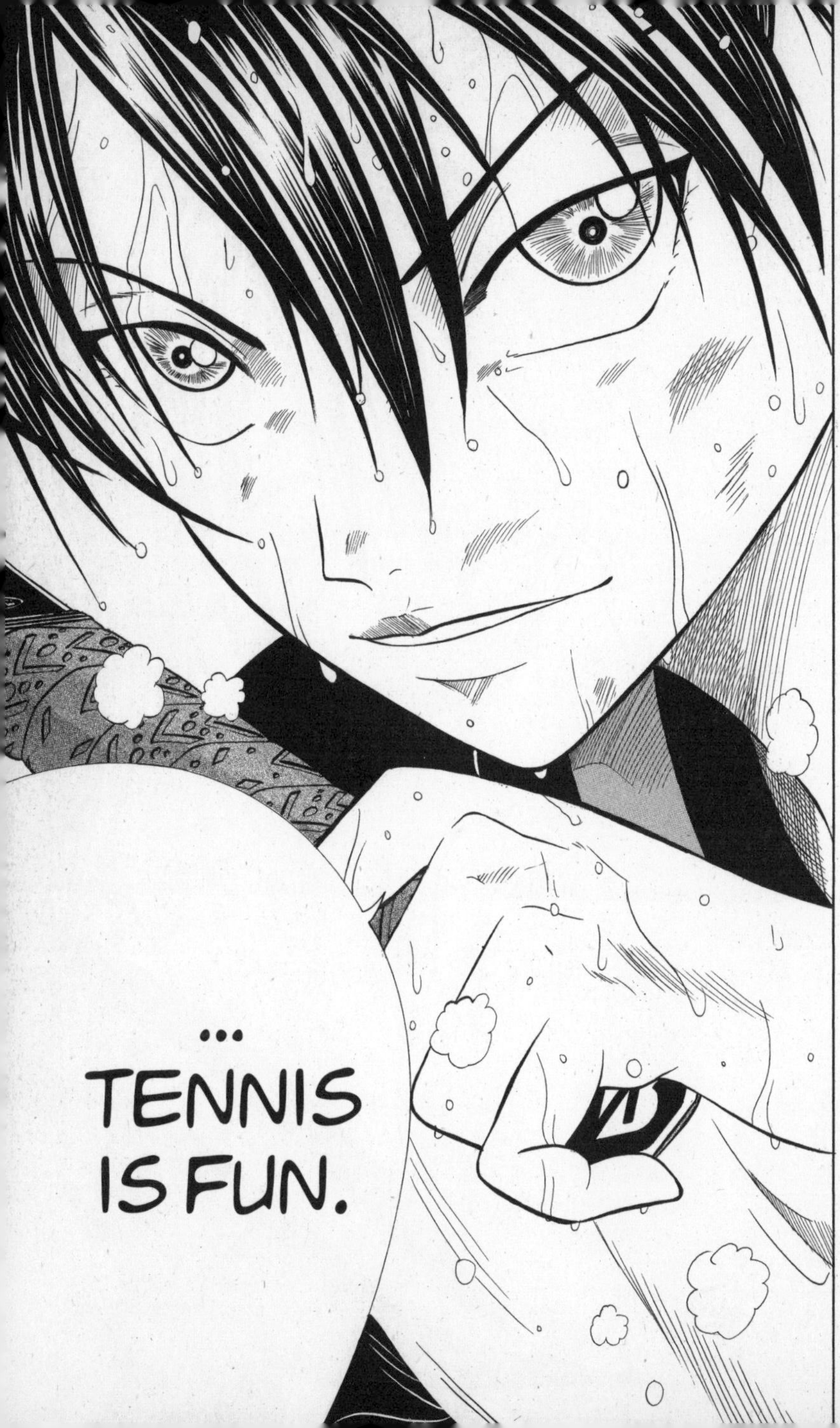
... TENNIS IS FUN.

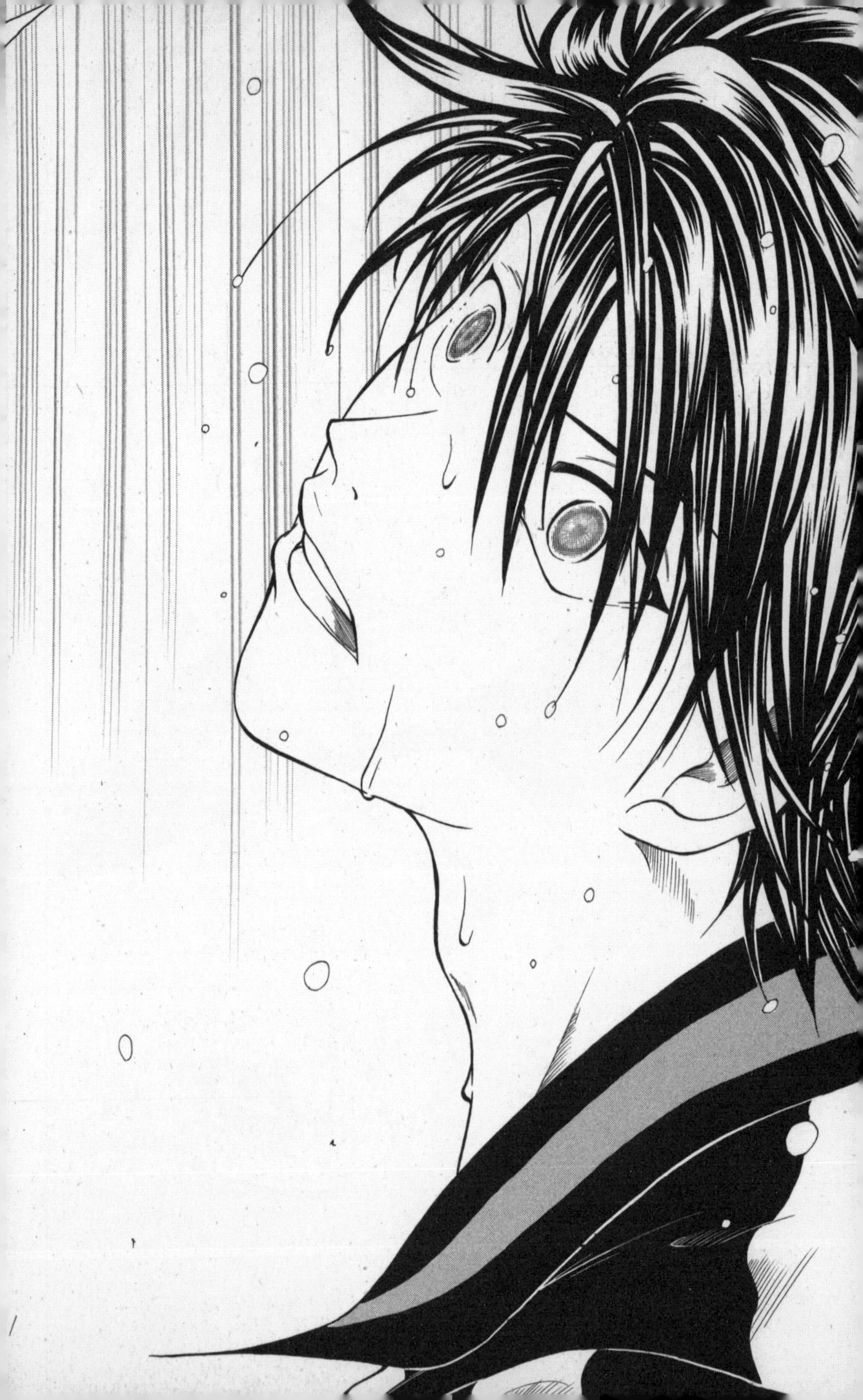

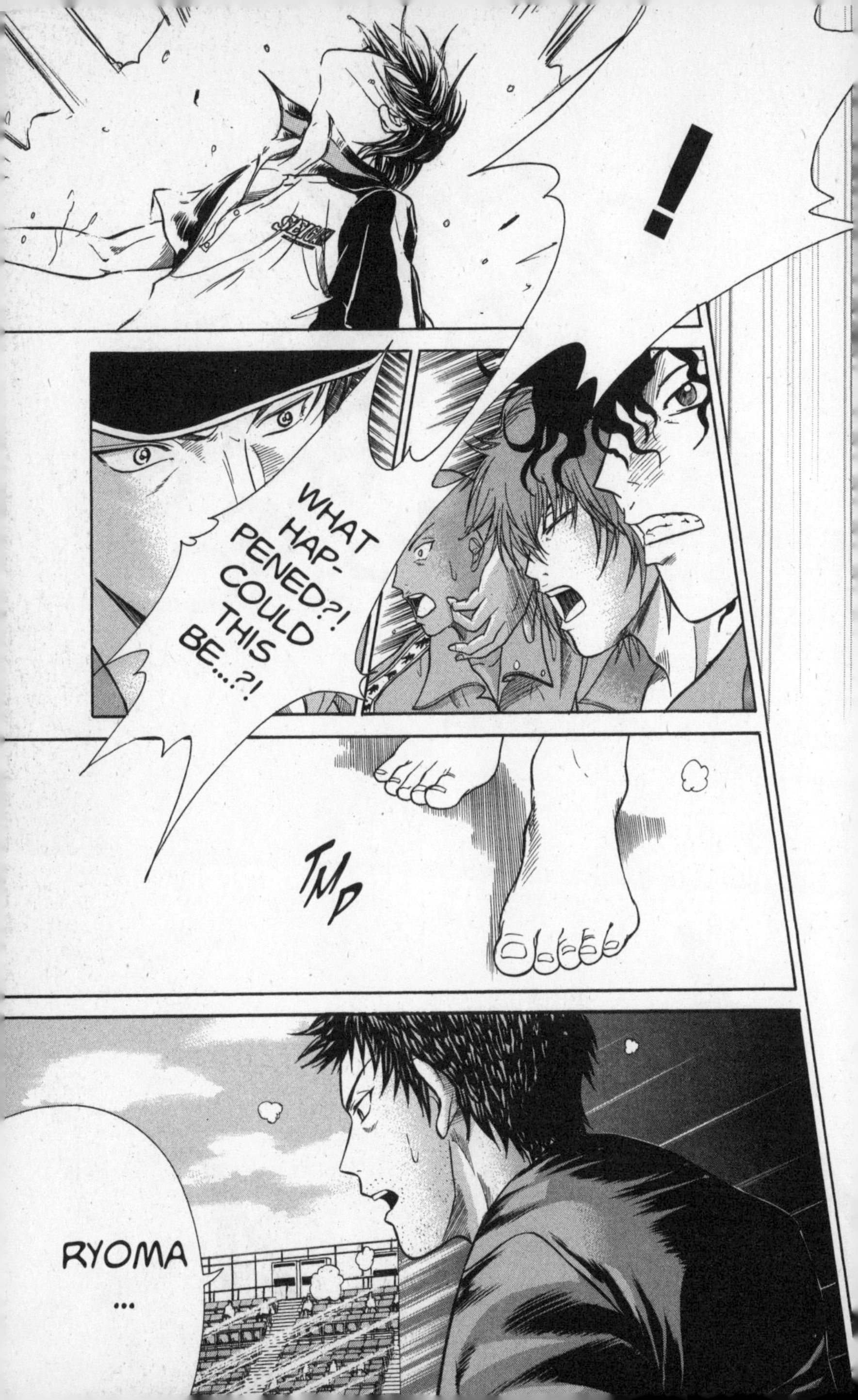
!
WHAT HAP-PENED?! COULD THIS BE...?!
TMP
RYOMA ...

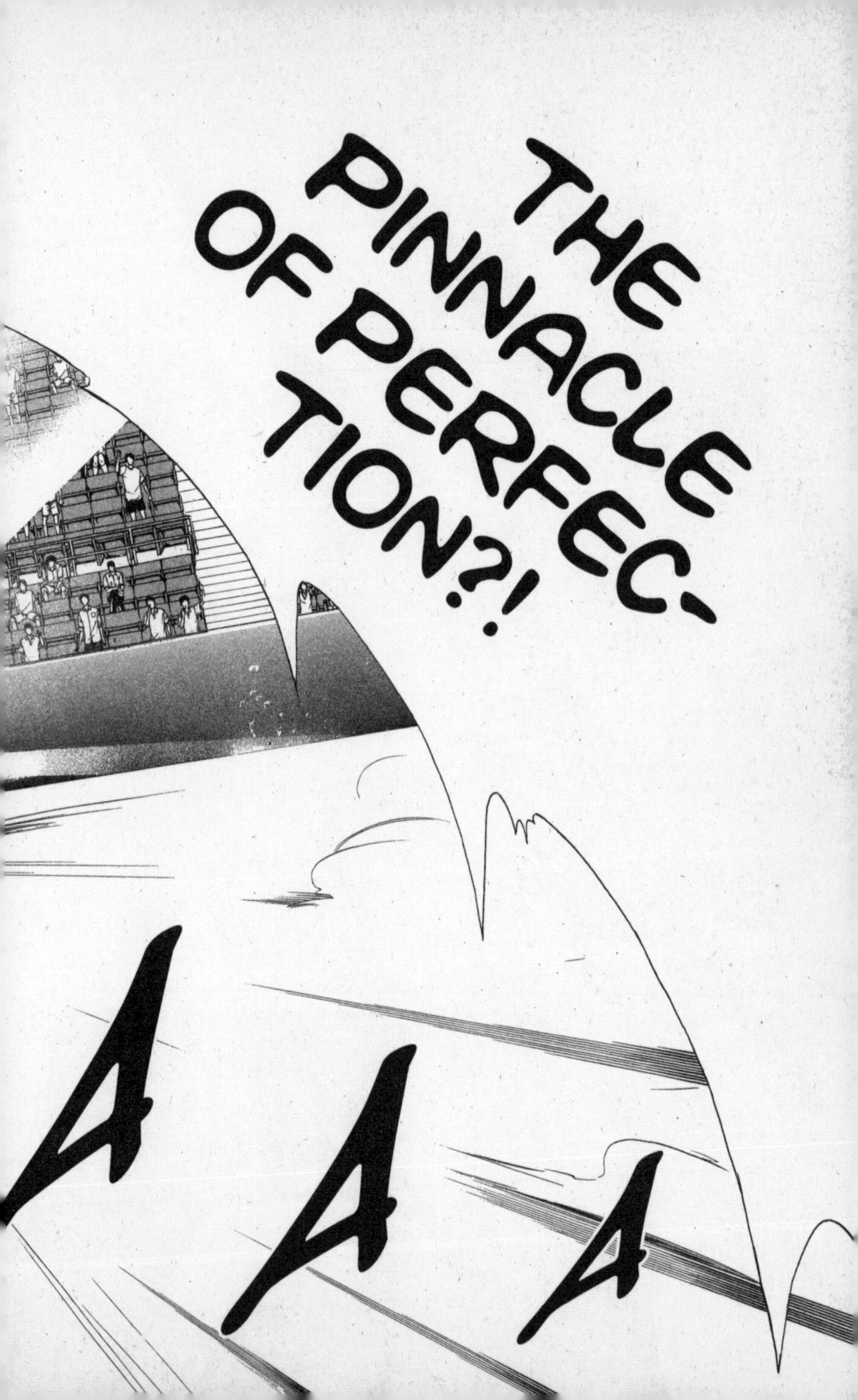
THE PINNACLE OF PERFEC-TION?!
AAA

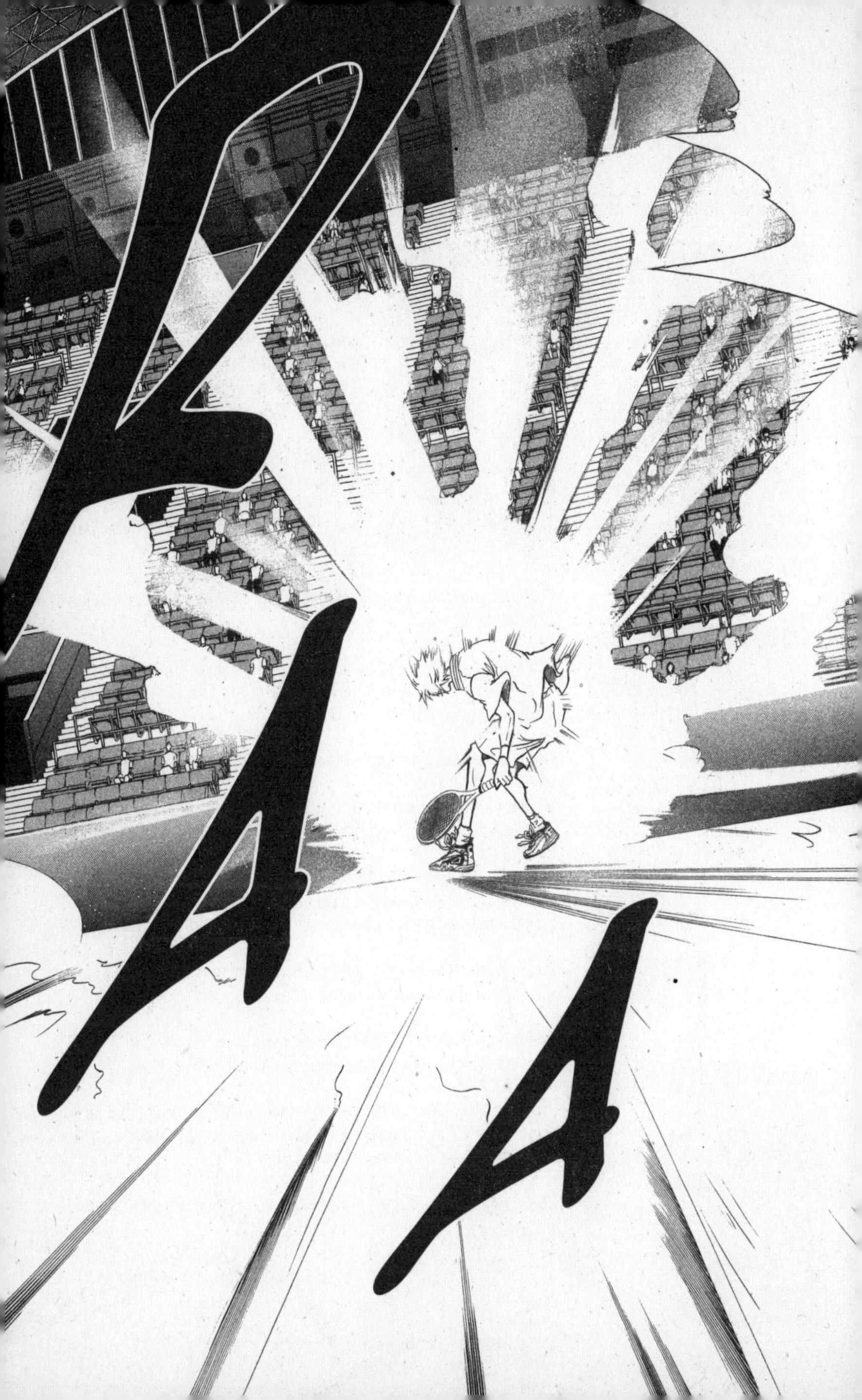

Prince of Tennis Serialization Completion Memorial Party Report

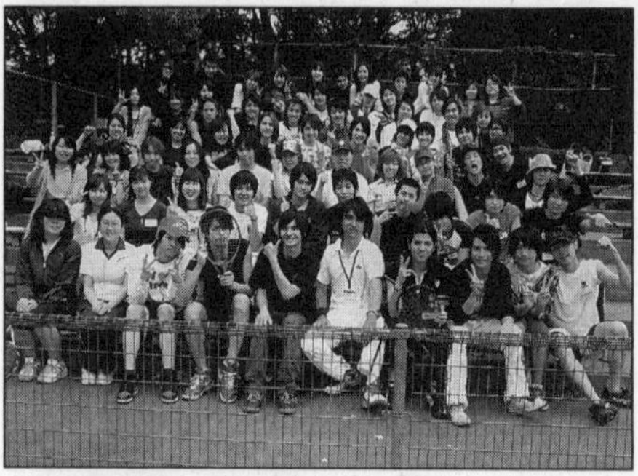
A shot before the party capturing everybody's high spirits.

The Prince of Tennis, which was published in *Weekly Shonen Jump*, ended its serialization on March 3.

And on May 9, the Prince of Tennis Serialization Completion Memorial Party – Daytime Portion was held at Ariake Tennis no Mori.

Close to a hundred guests gathered, including cast members from the musical, voice actors, various staff members, and TK Works staff, as well as seven fan representatives.

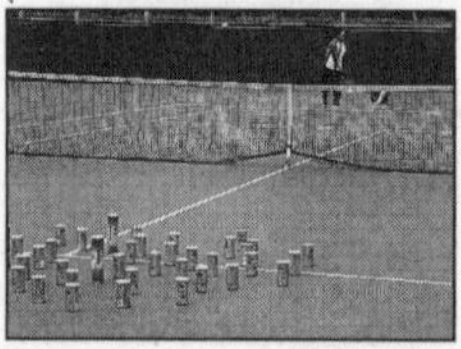
Things not going as well as they did for Ryoma? Ms. Minagawa playing Ryoma in the anime.

Everybody was excited even before creator Takeshi Konomi made his opening remarks.

Following the opening remarks and the ceremonial photo session, the "Can Hitting Game," the game made famous in *The Prince of Tennis* volume 1, was held!

Each participant was given seven shots with fifty cans placed on the court.

But nobody could hit them! Inside the cans were cards with prizes written on them, so everybody's motivation was high, but nobody could hit them.

Now we know how good Ryoma is. You would have to be extremely confident to say "If I hit it a hundred times will you give me a million yen?!"

After a while, it wasn't the musical cast members or the voice actors, it was staff that began hitting the cans.

Comments like "Do the Laser Beam" and "Show Us a Grand Smash" from the spectators may have worked against them…

Then it was Konomi's turn. It was on the author's third shot that he struck a can. The crowd cheered, and he quickly checked the card in the can, and out came Inui's Special Drink card!!

That's right! This is *Prince of Tennis* after all! Not every can included prizes!

The author braced himself and graciously drank up the suspicious black liquid.

What followed can be seen in the photos to the left.

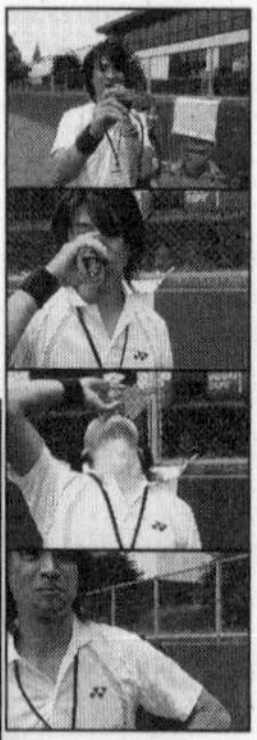
Creator Konomi chugging it. His expression of anguish and…

Thud…

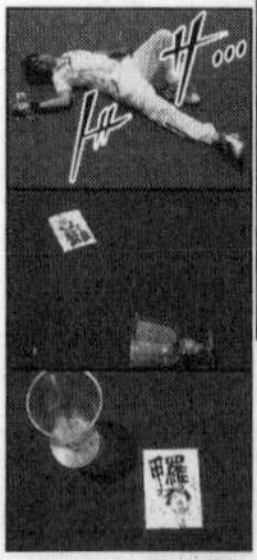
Shell Cola

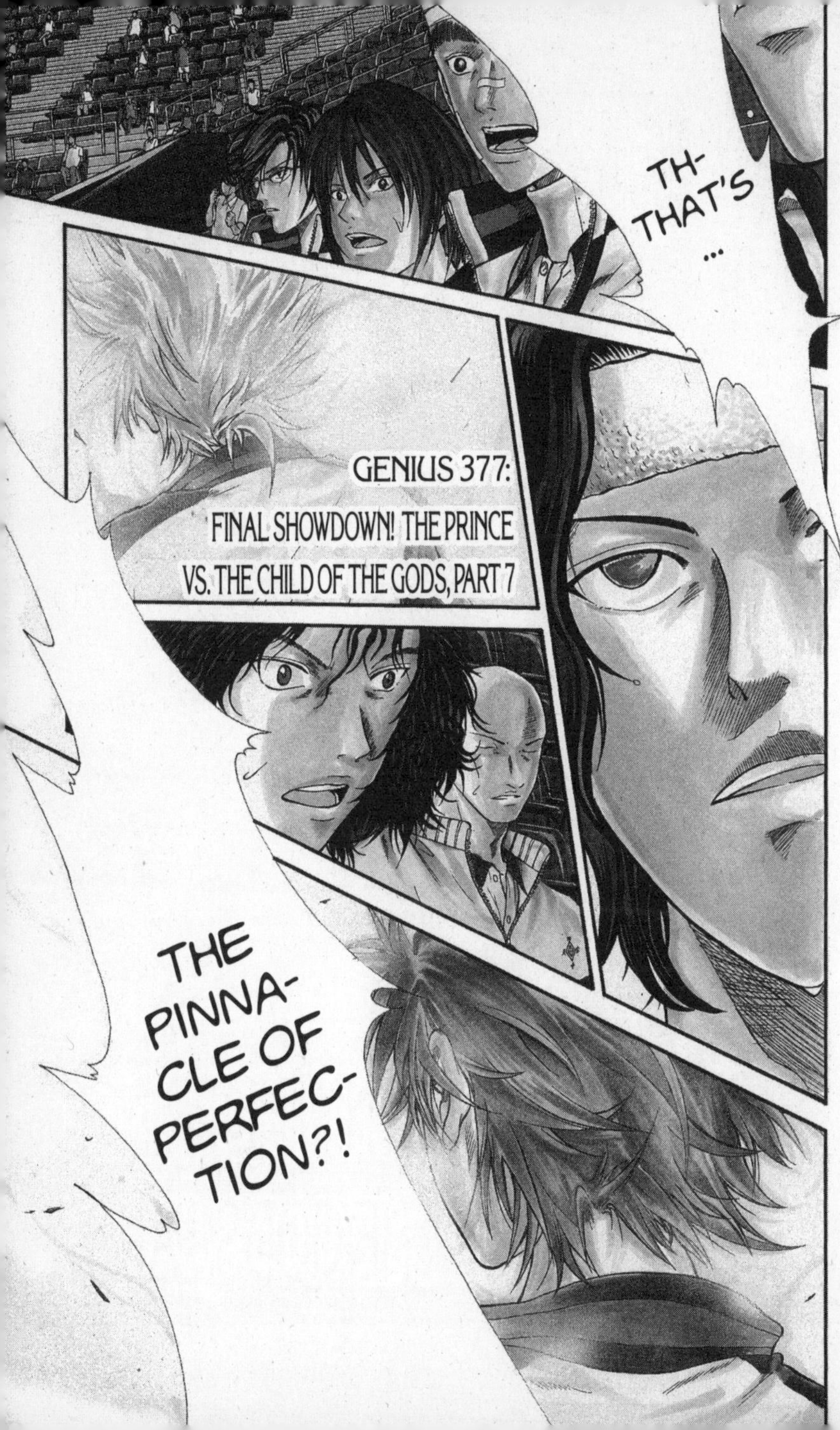
TH- THAT'S ...
GENIUS 377:
FINAL SHOWDOWN! THE PRINCE VS. THE CHILD OF THE GODS, PART 7
THE PINNA-CLE OF PERFEC-TION?!

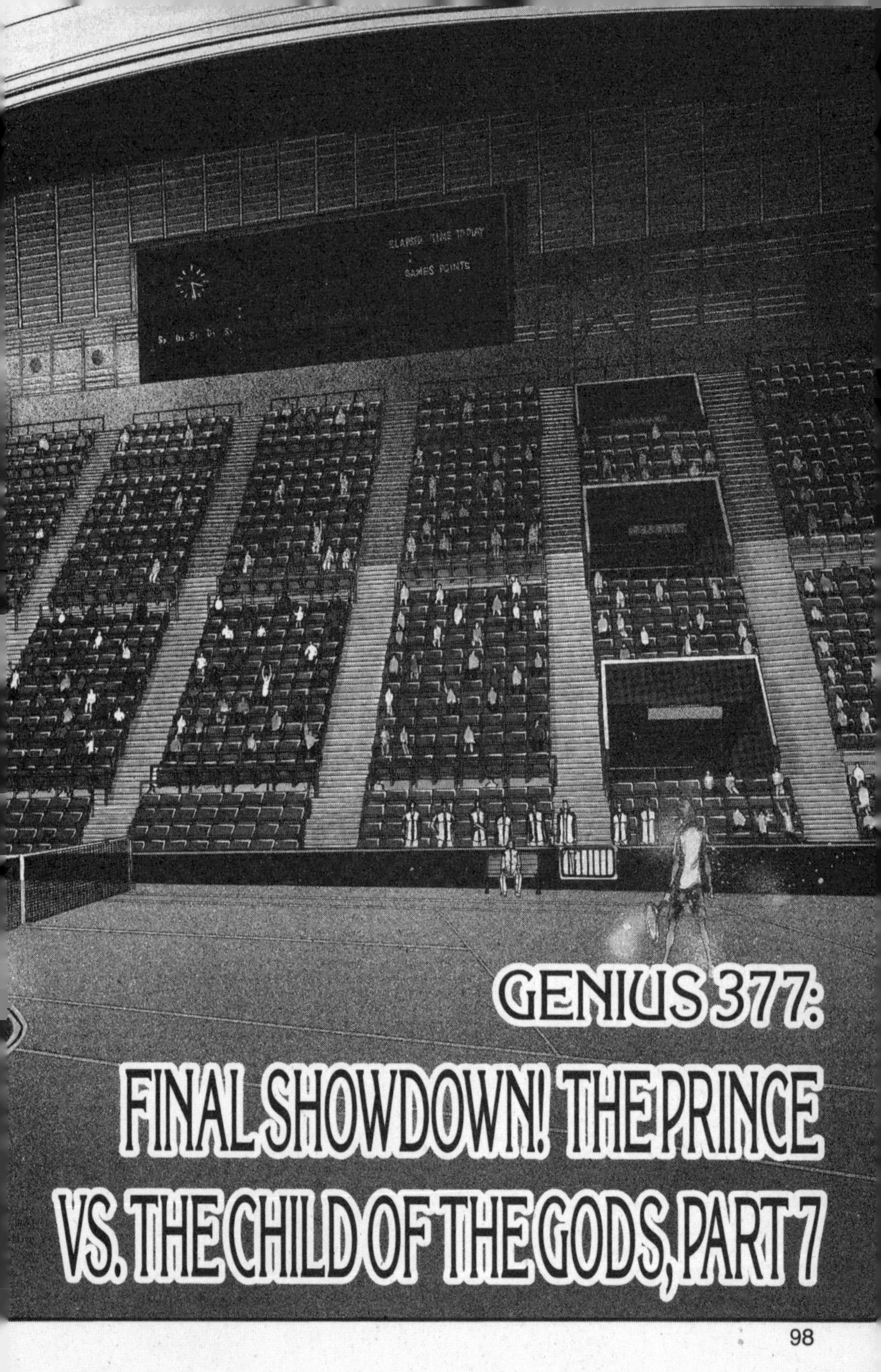
ELAPSED TIME TODAY
GAMES POINTS
GENIUS 377:
FINAL SHOWDOWN! THE PRINCE VS. THE CHILD OF THE GODS, PART 7

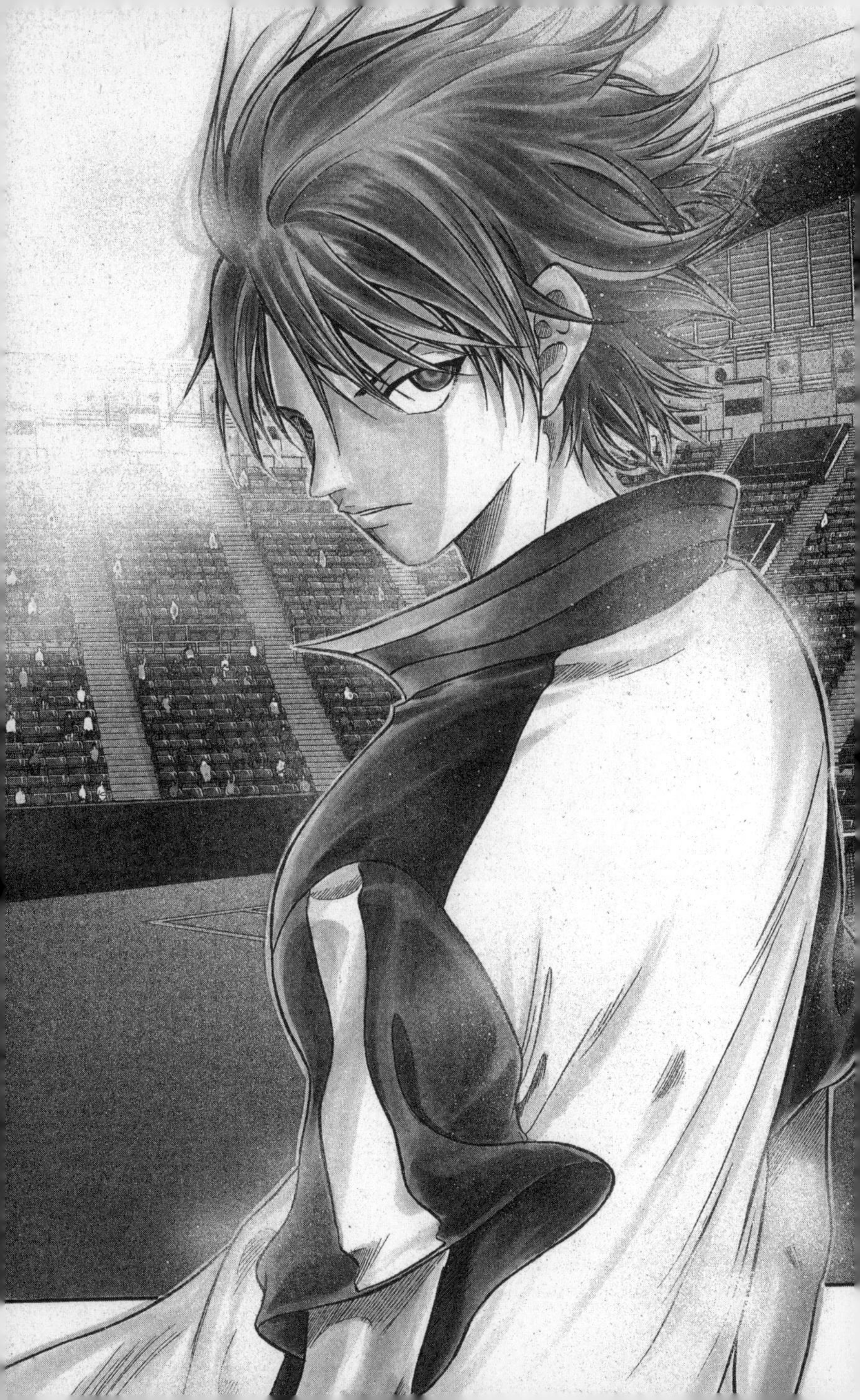

テニスの王子様

THE PRINCE OF TENNIS

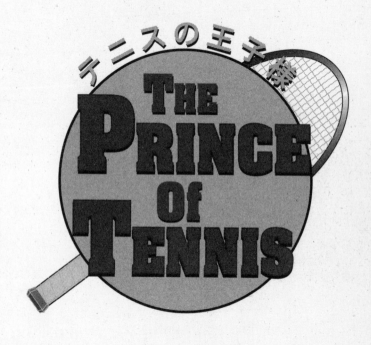

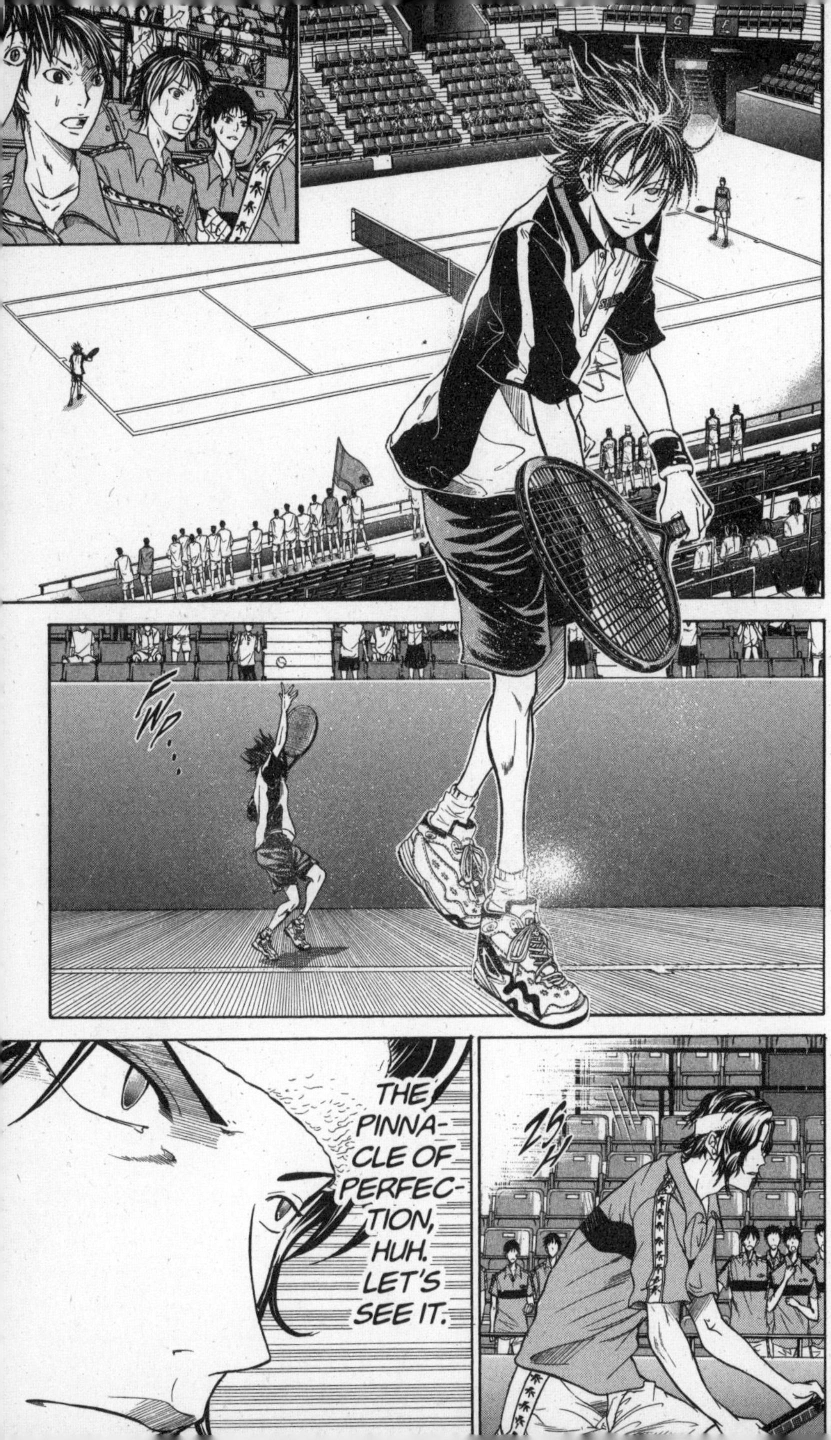
FWP...
THE PINNACLE OF PERFECTION, HUH. LET'S SEE IT.
ZSSH

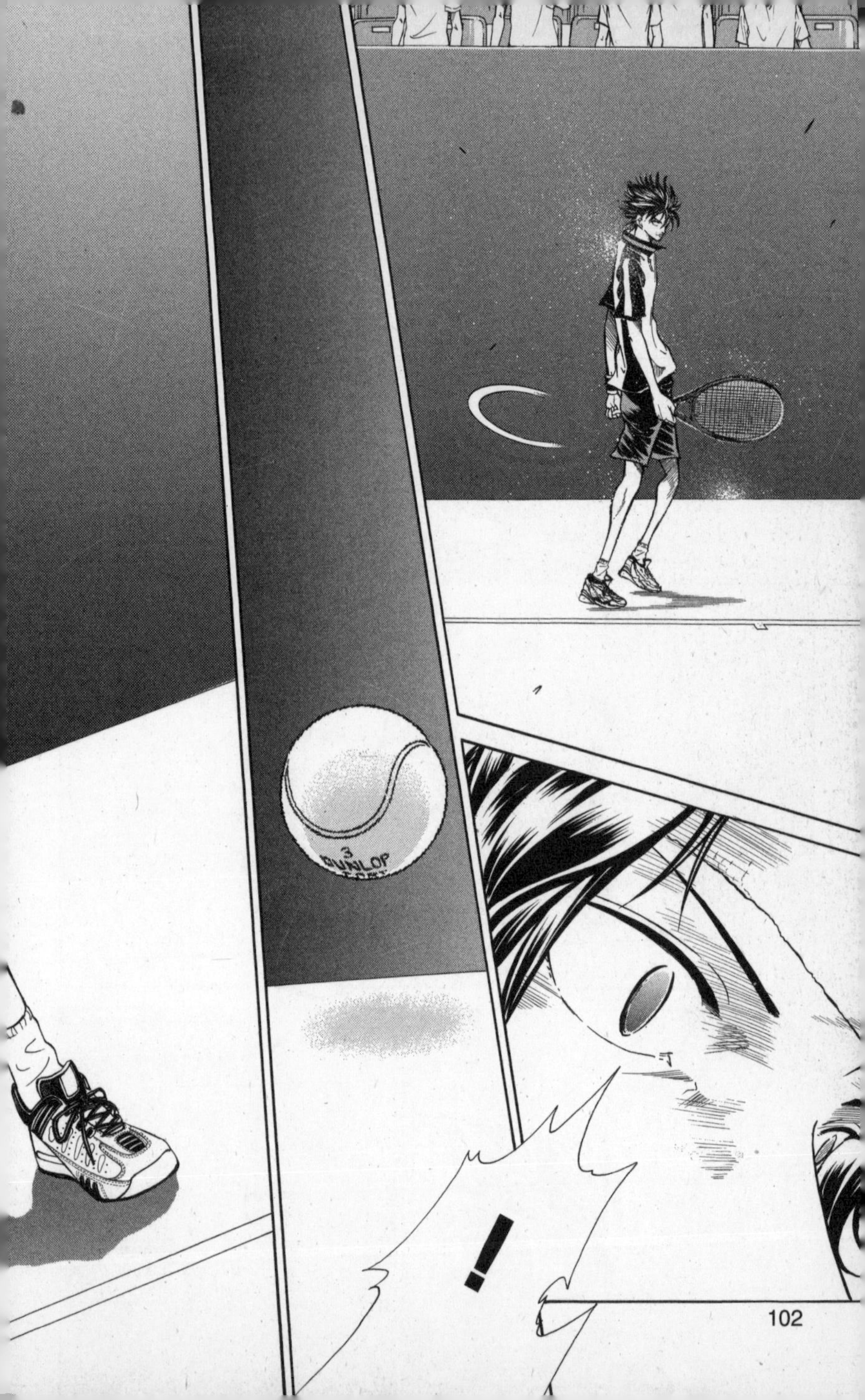
3
DUNLOP
!

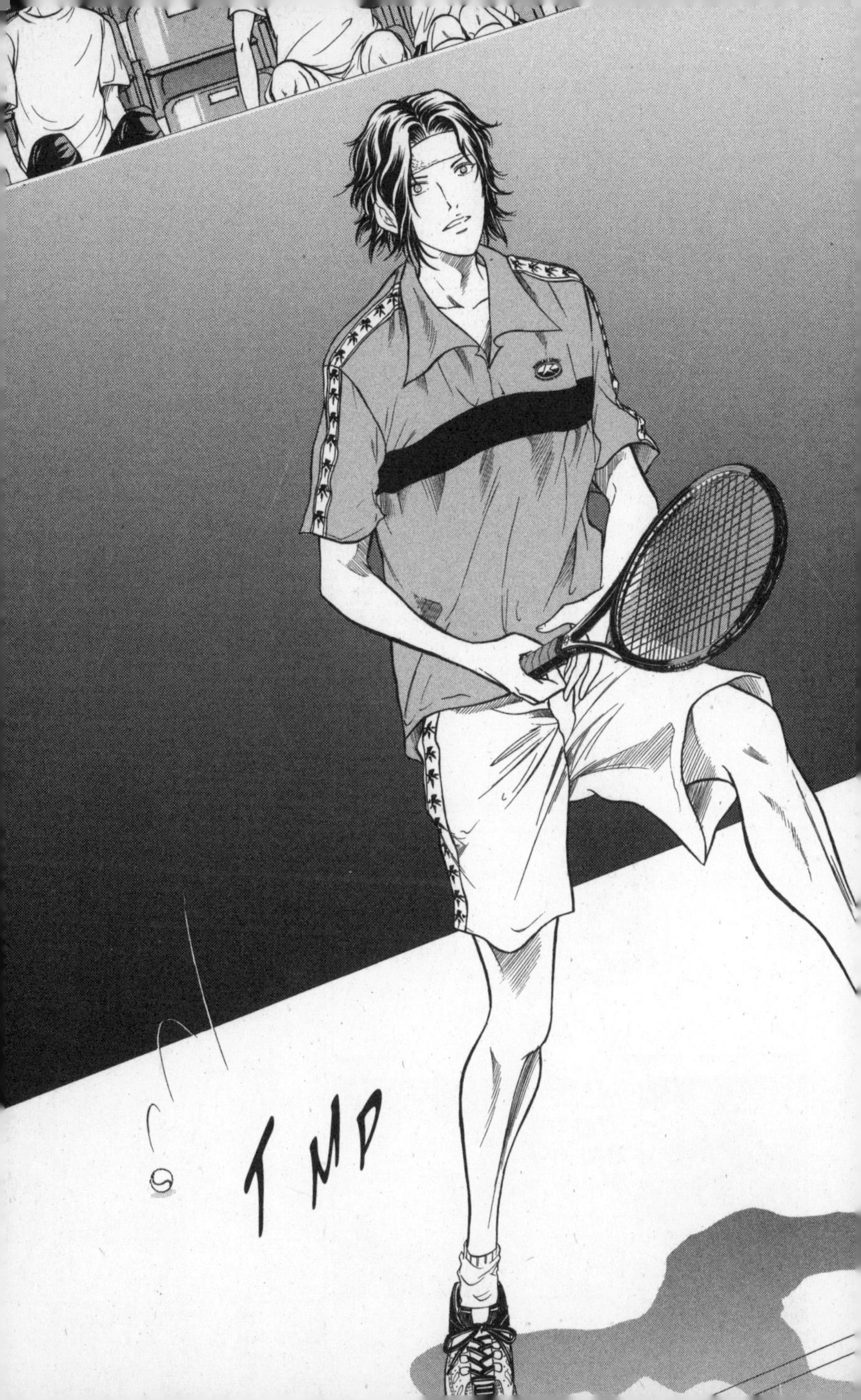
TMP

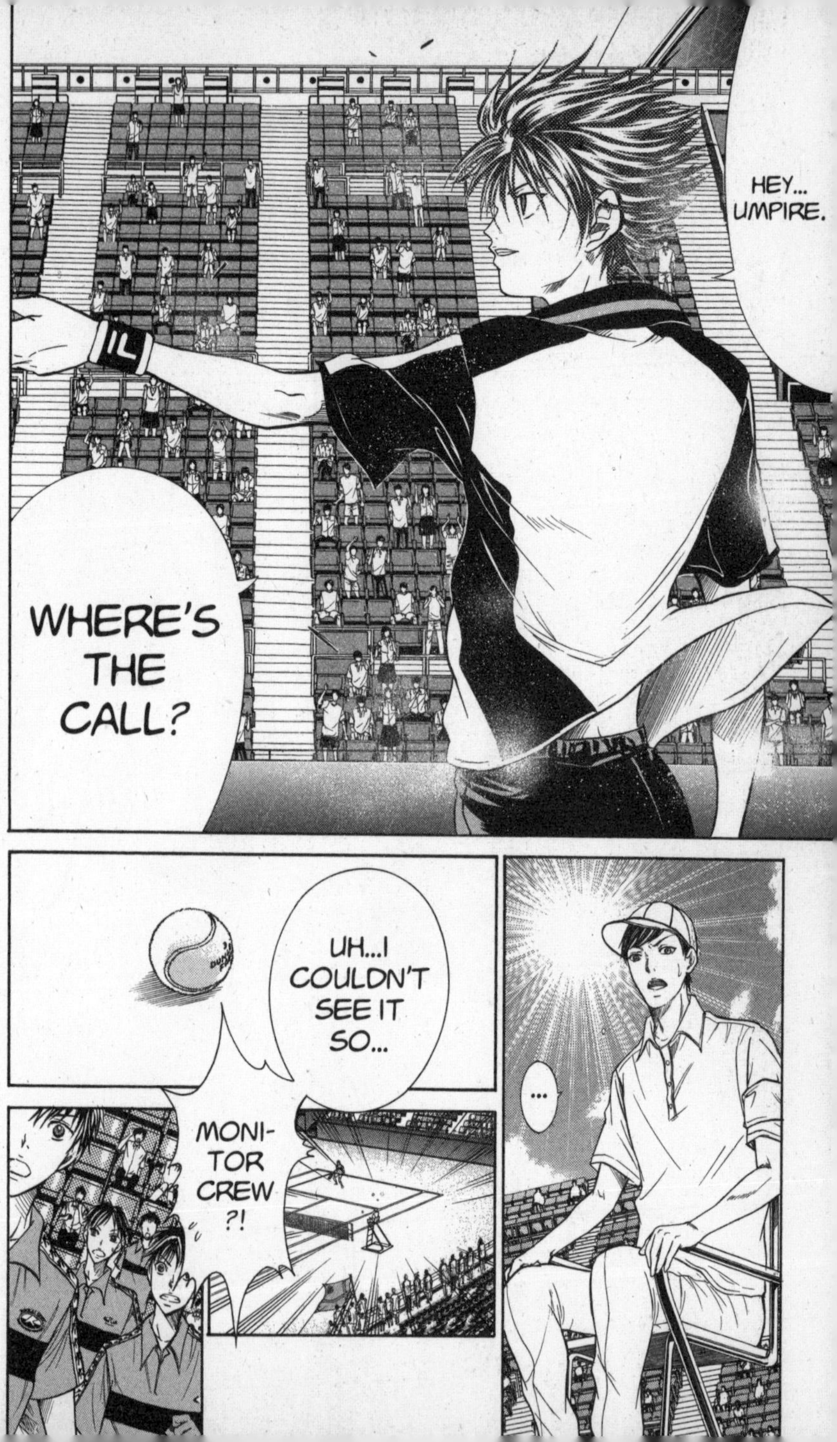
HEY... UMPIRE.
WHERE'S THE CALL?
...
UH...I COULDN'T SEE IT SO...
MONI-TOR CREW?!

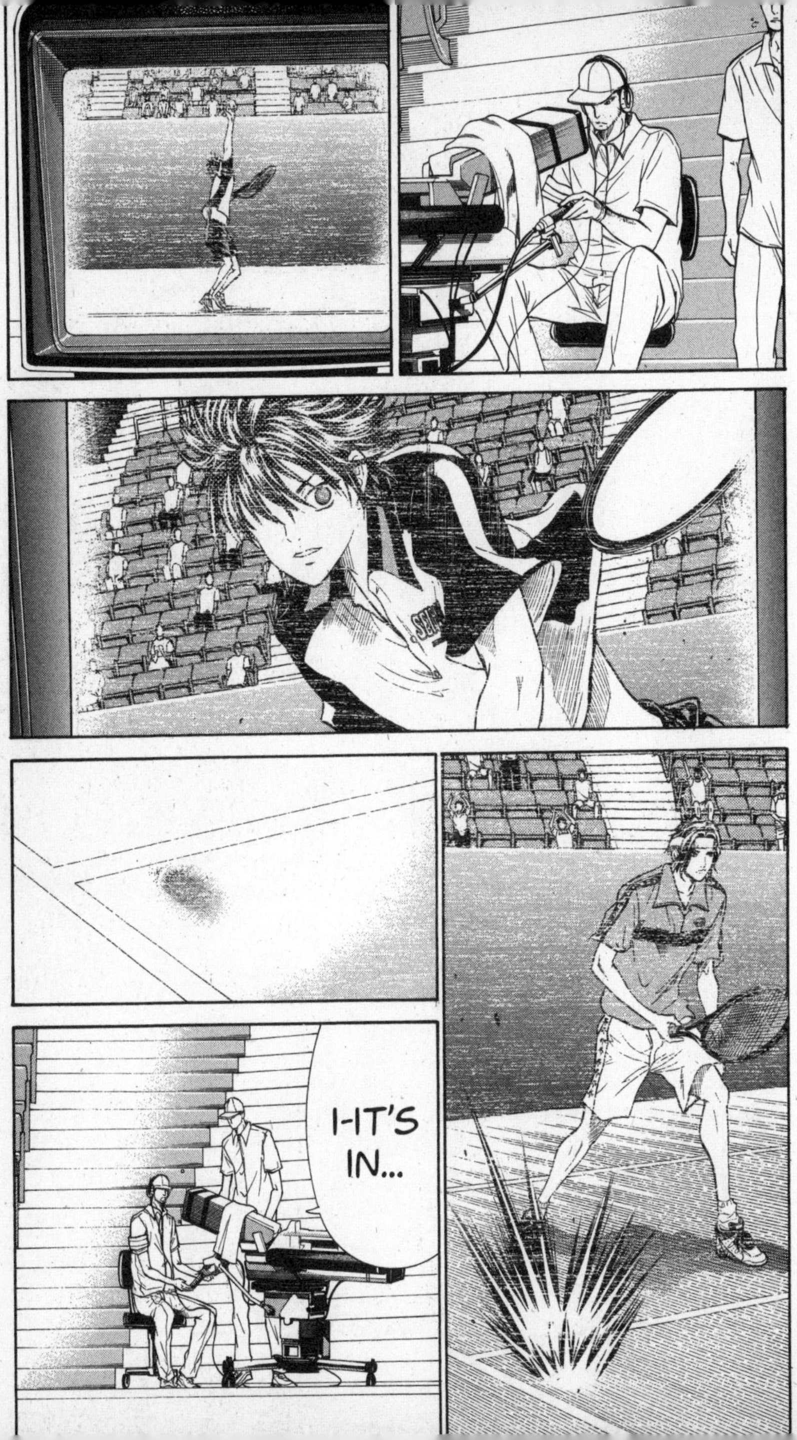
I-IT'S IN...

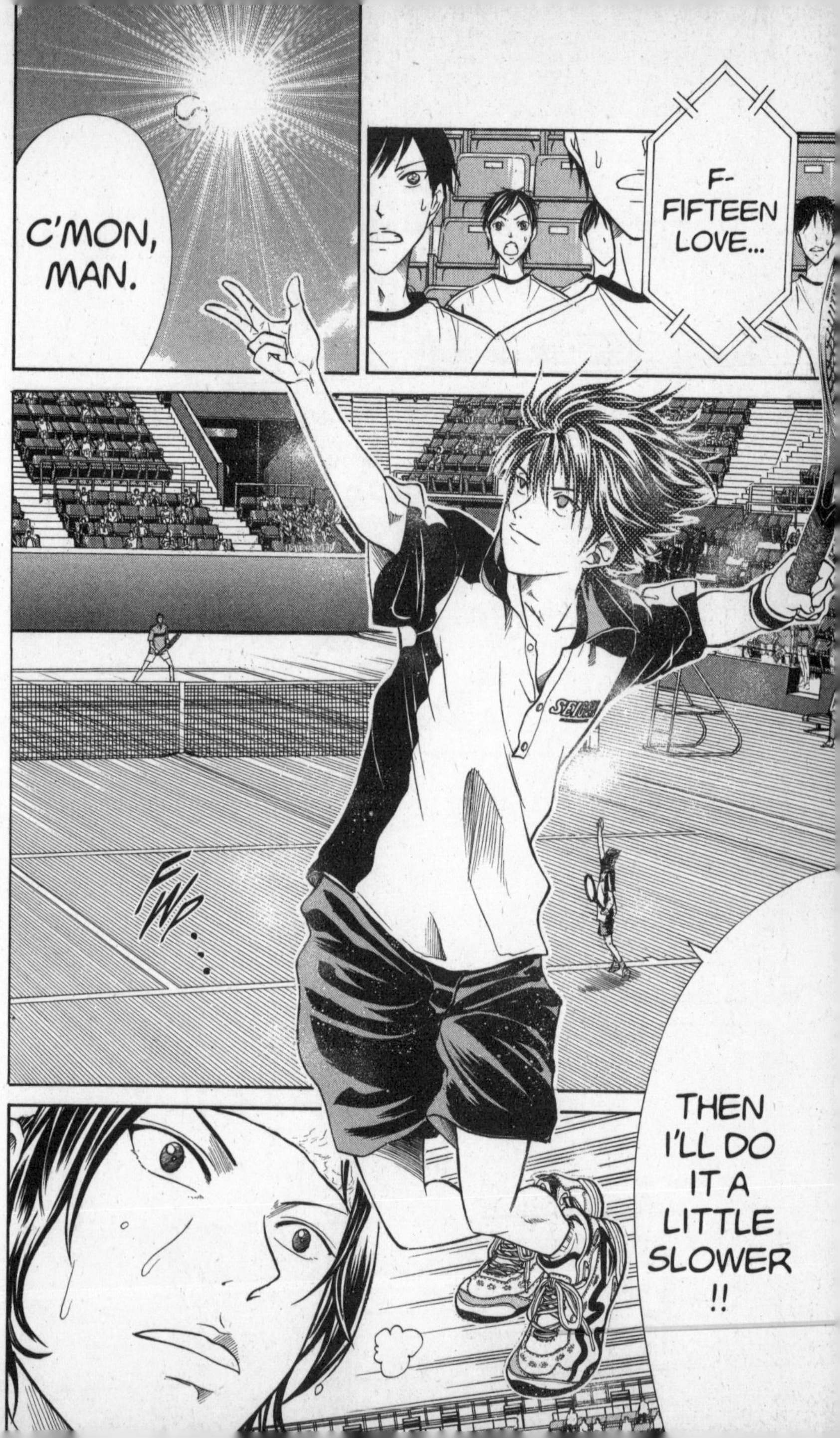
F- FIFTEEN LOVE...
C'MON, MAN.
FWP...
THEN I'LL DO IT A LITTLE SLOWER !!

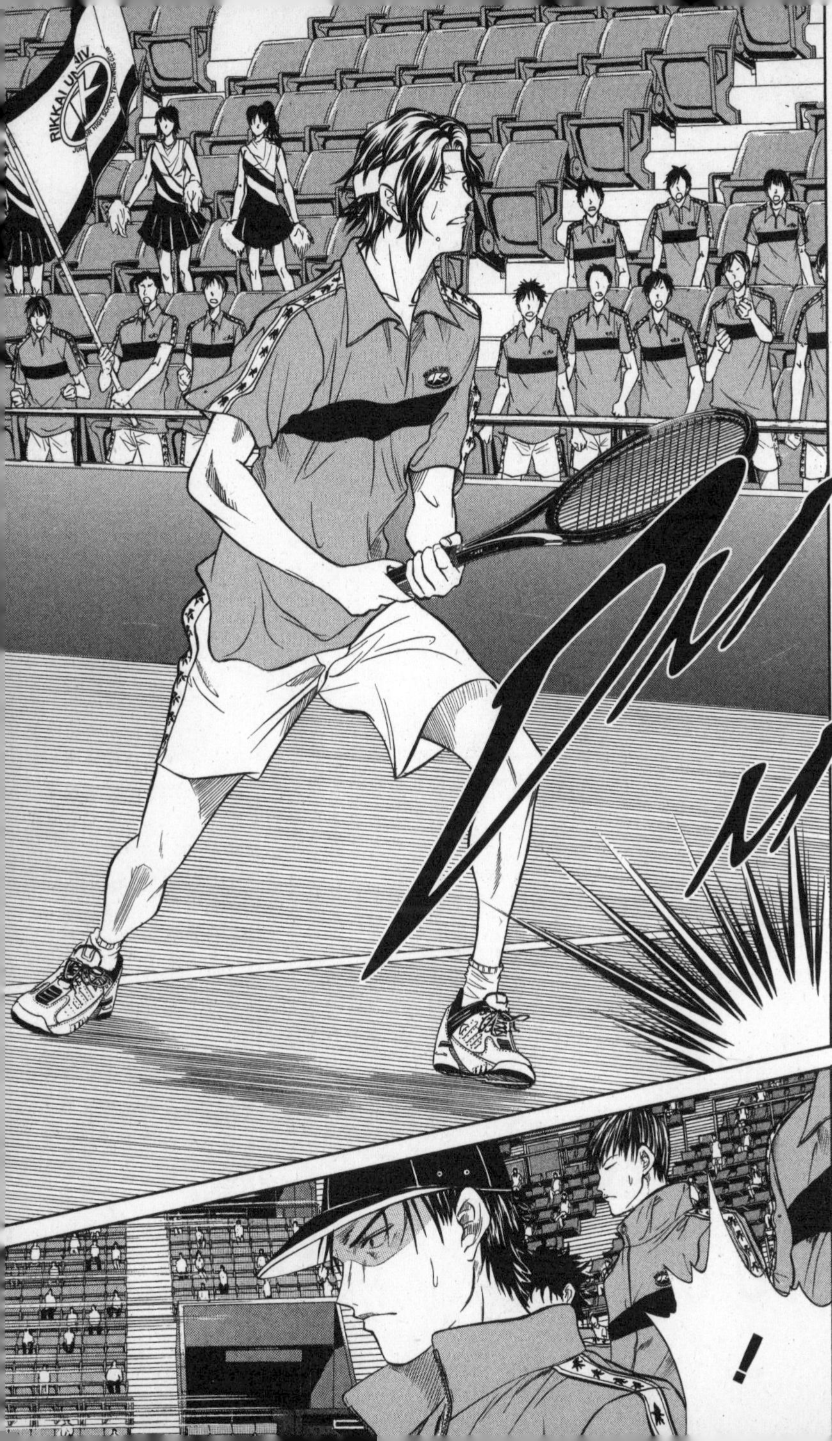
RIKKAI UNIV.
!

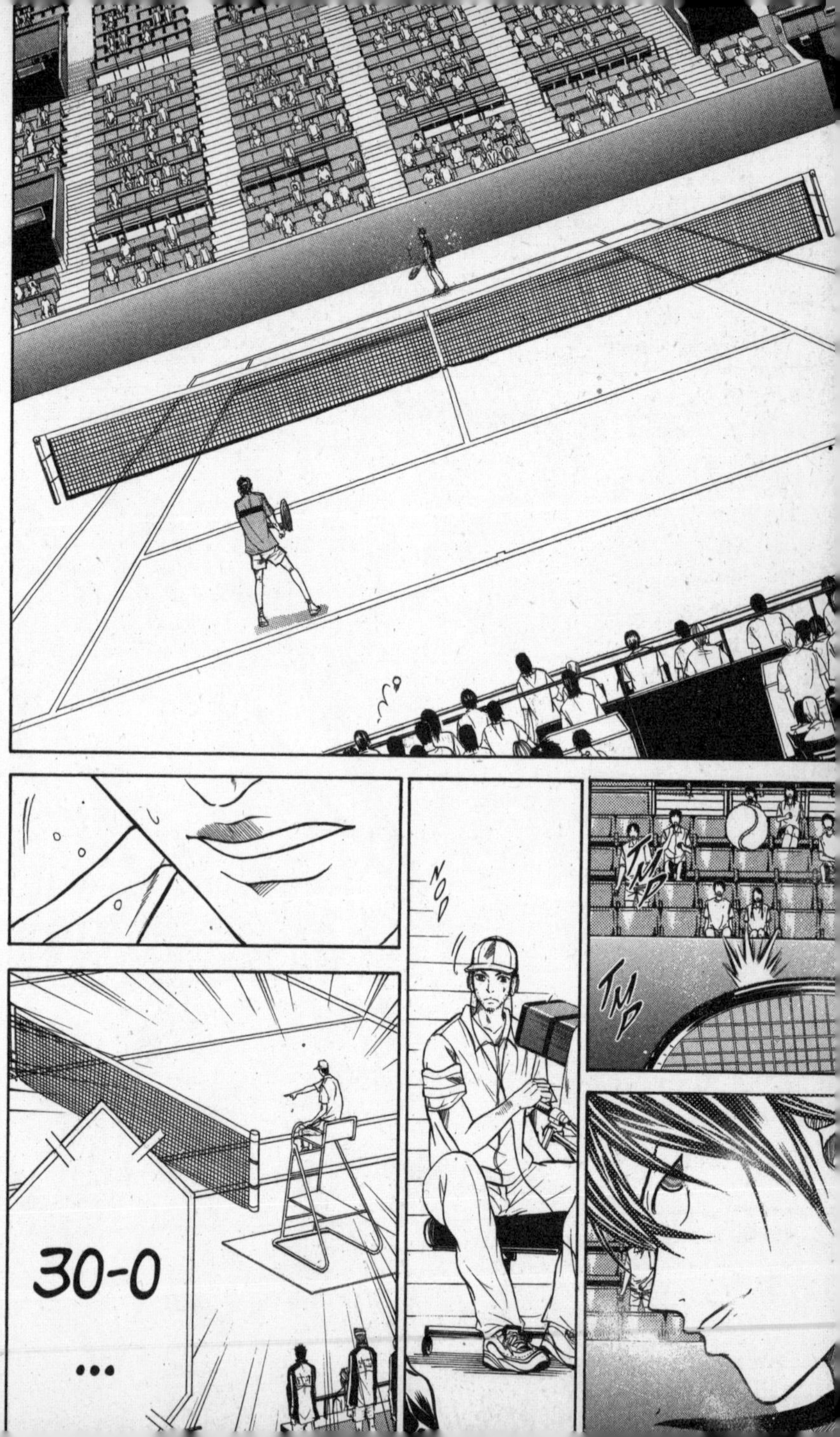
TMP
TMP
NOD
30-0
...

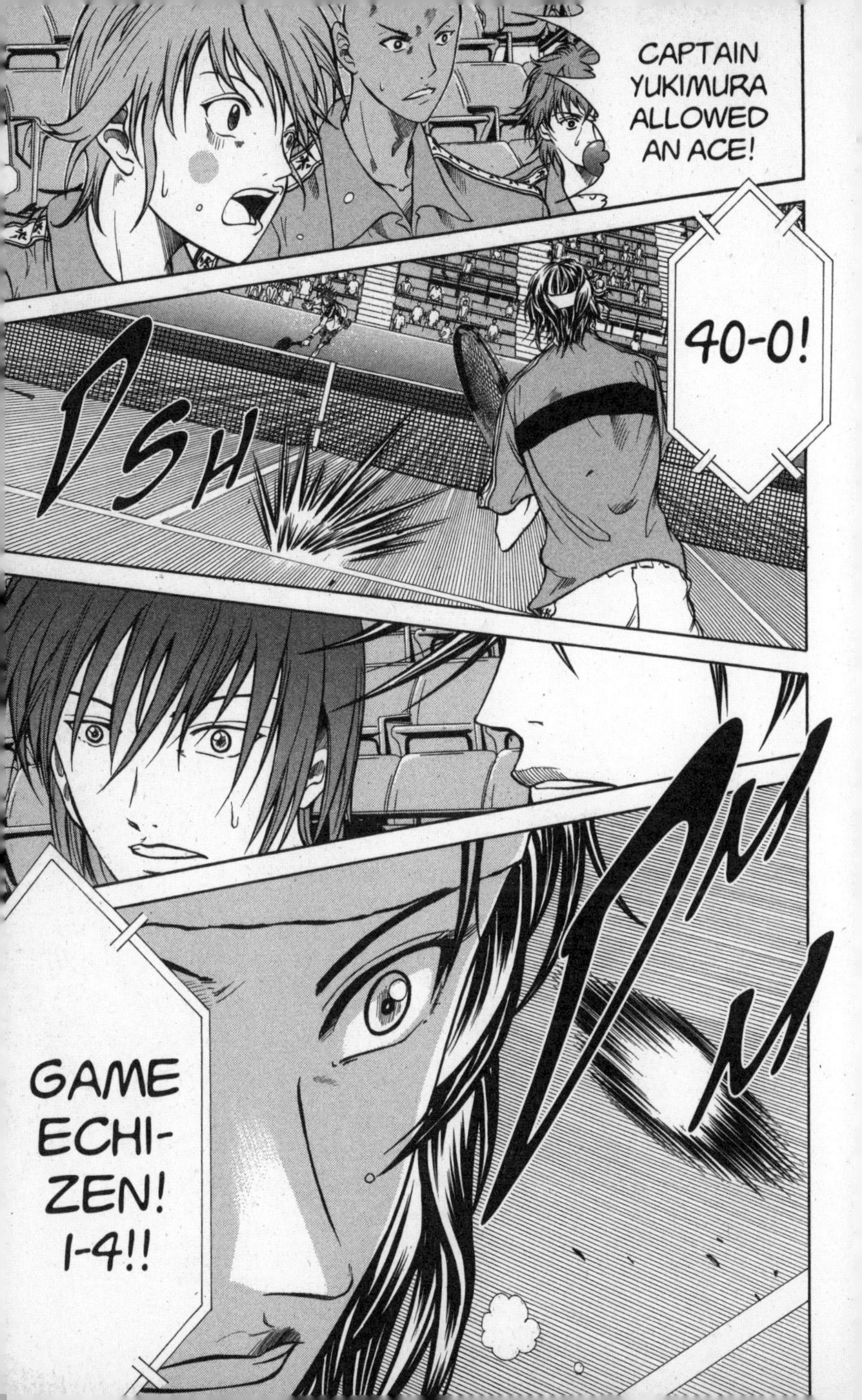
CAPTAIN YUKIMURA ALLOWED AN ACE!
40-0!
DSH
GAME ECHIZEN! 1-4!!

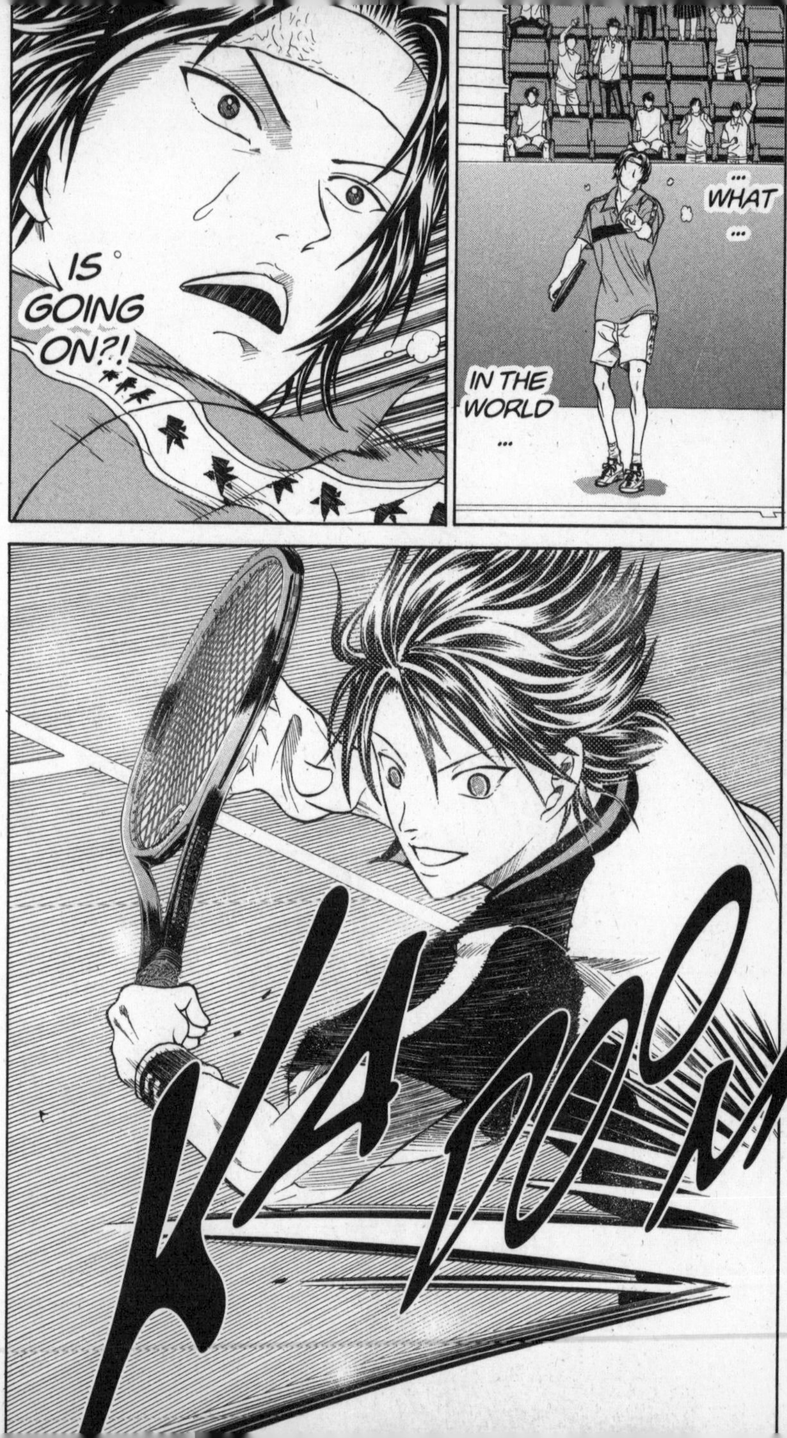

... WHAT ...
IN THE WORLD ...
IS GOING ON?!

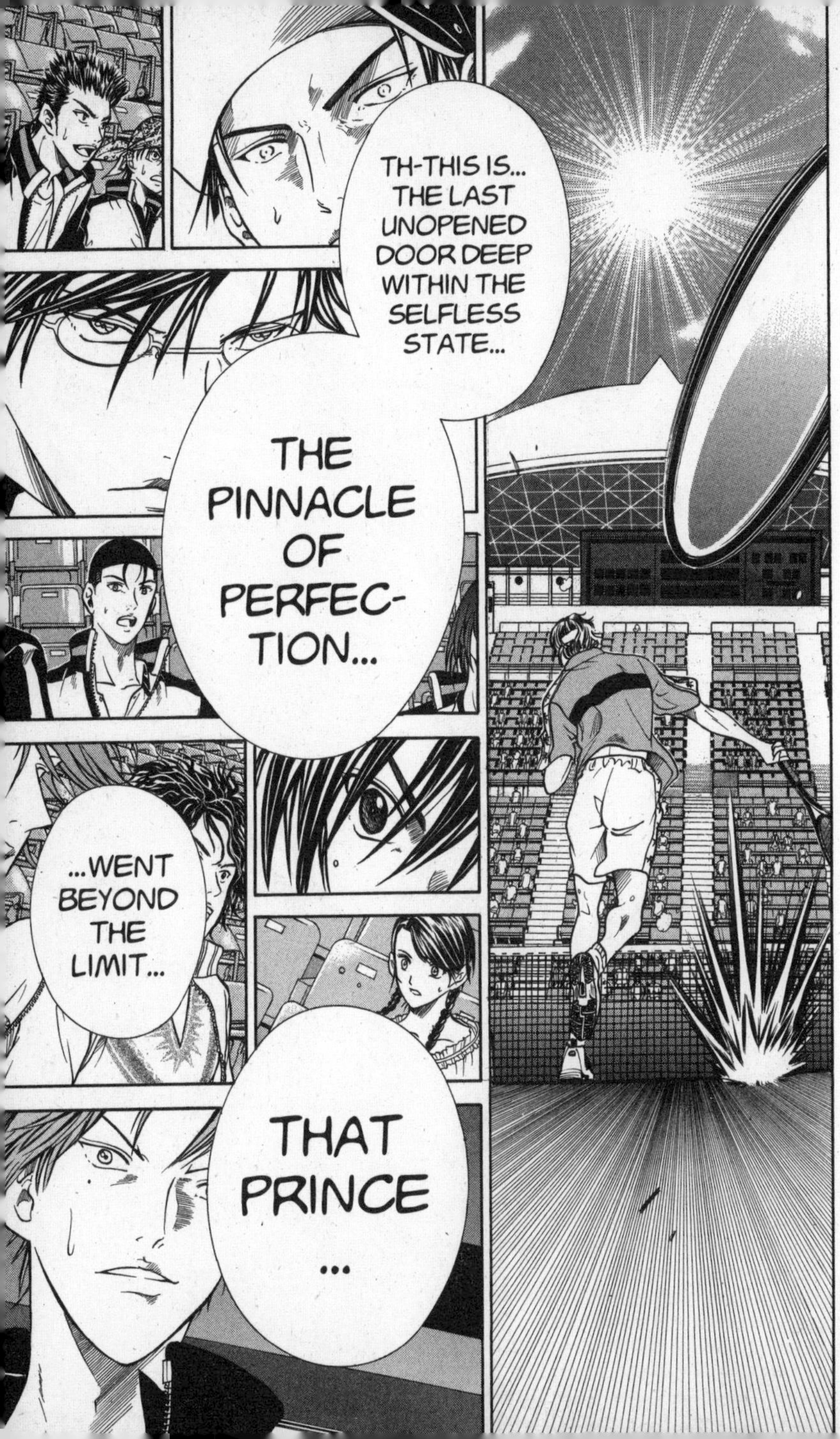
TH-THIS IS... THE LAST UNOPENED DOOR DEEP WITHIN THE SELFLESS STATE...
THE PINNACLE OF PERFECTION...
...WENT BEYOND THE LIMIT...
THAT PRINCE ...

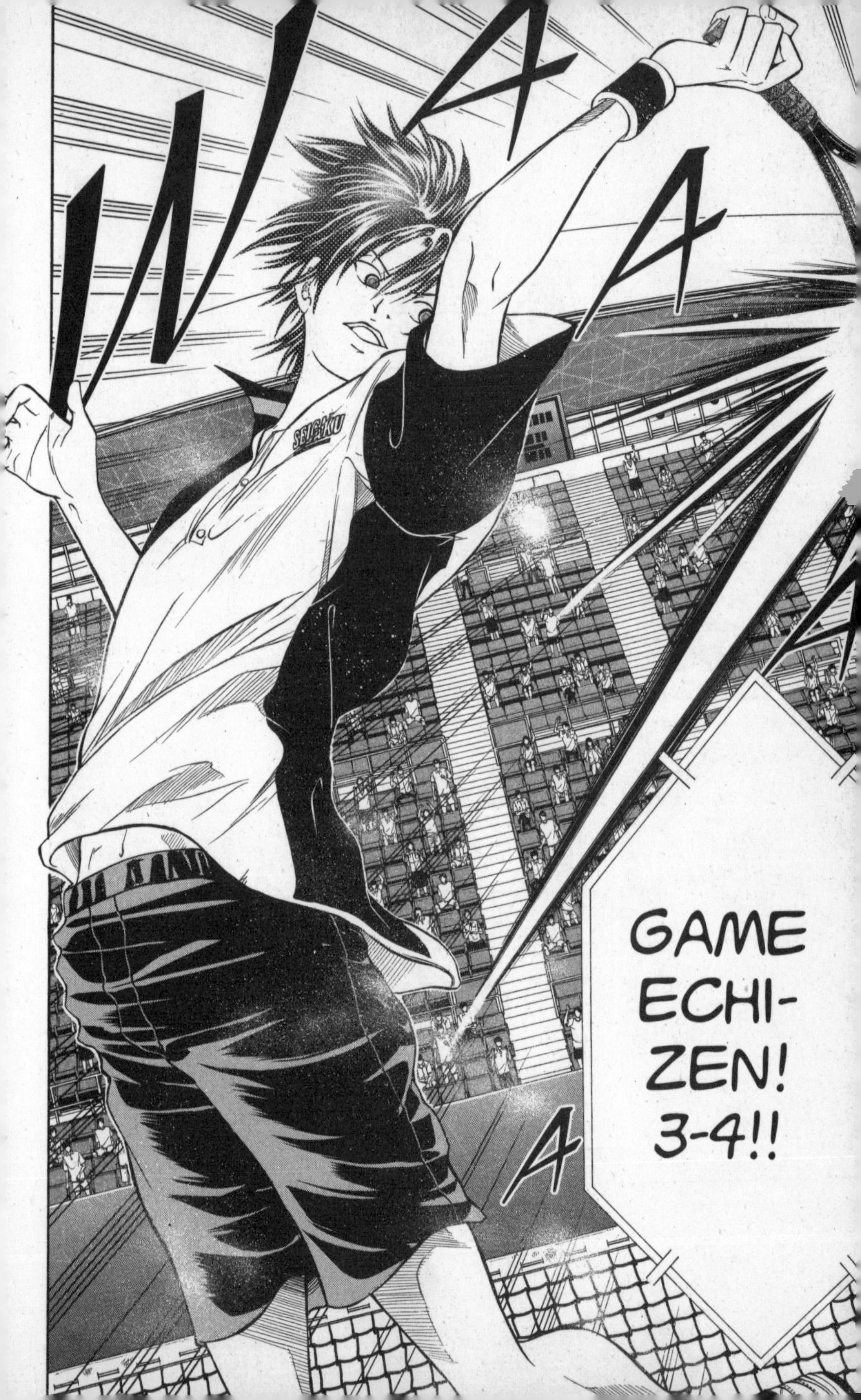
WAAAA
GAME ECHI-ZEN! 3-4!!

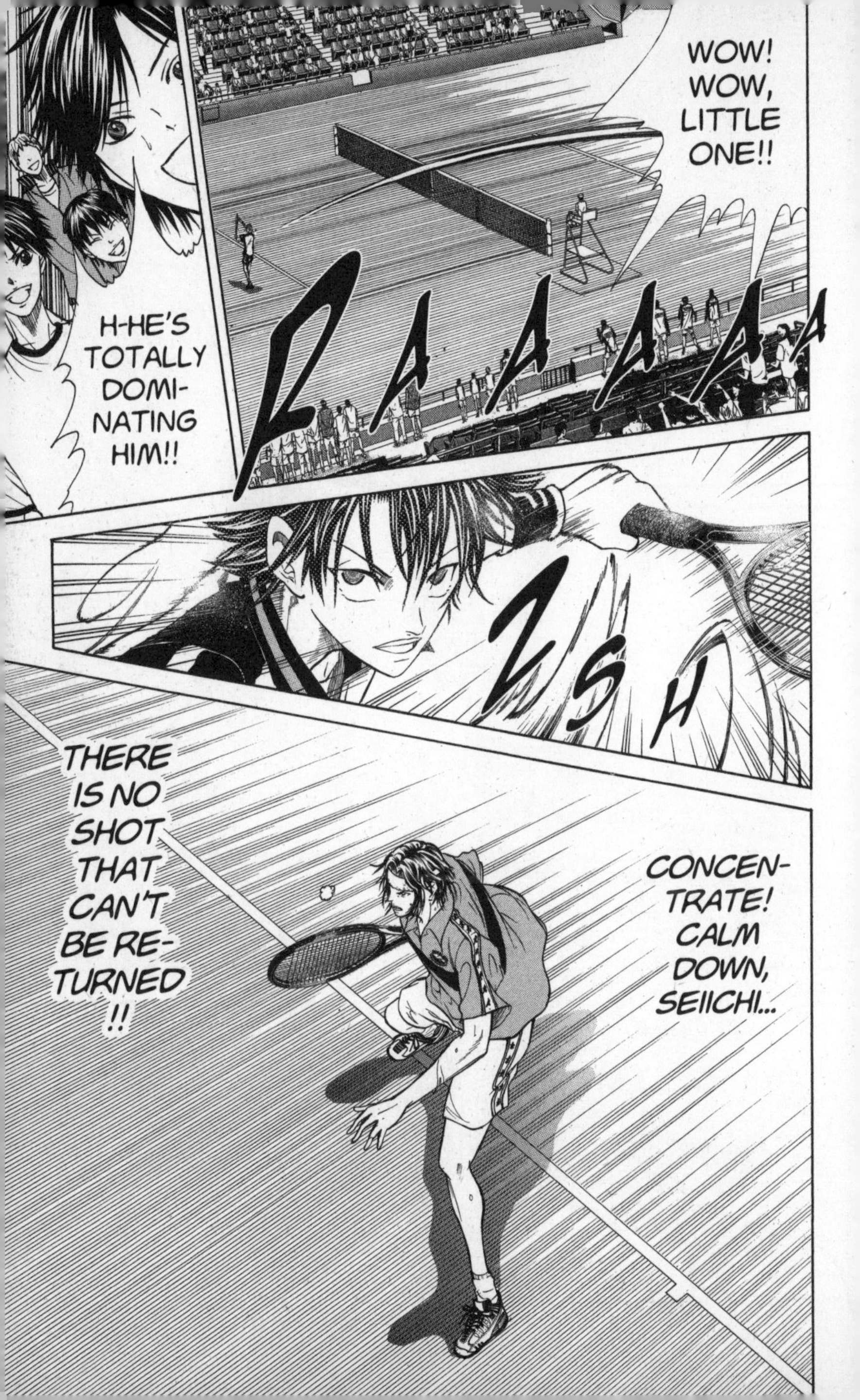
WOW! WOW, LITTLE ONE!!
H-HE'S TOTALLY DOMI-NATING HIM!!
RAAAAAA
ZSH
CONCEN-TRATE! CALM DOWN, SEIICHI...
THERE IS NO SHOT THAT CAN'T BE RE-TURNED!!

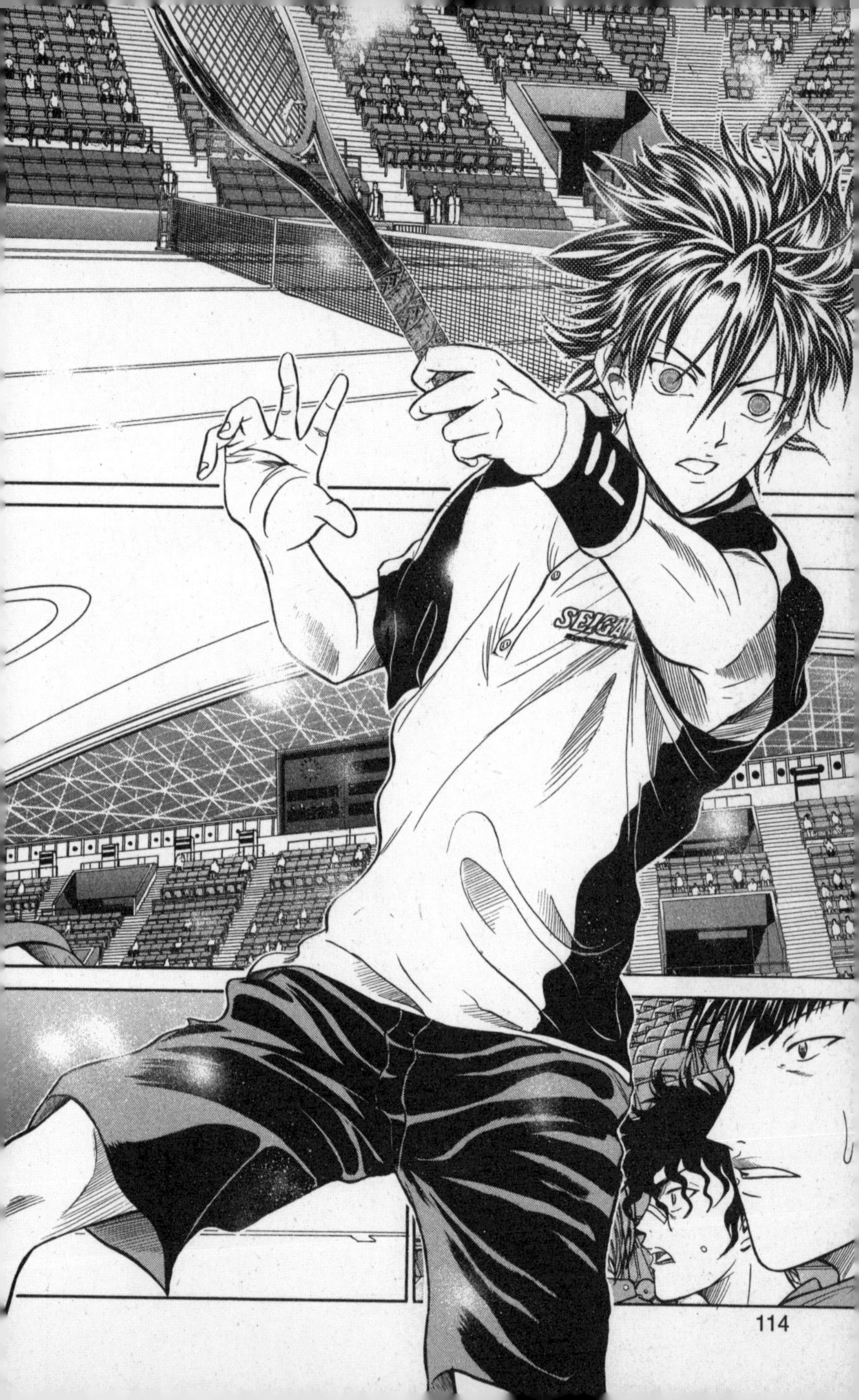

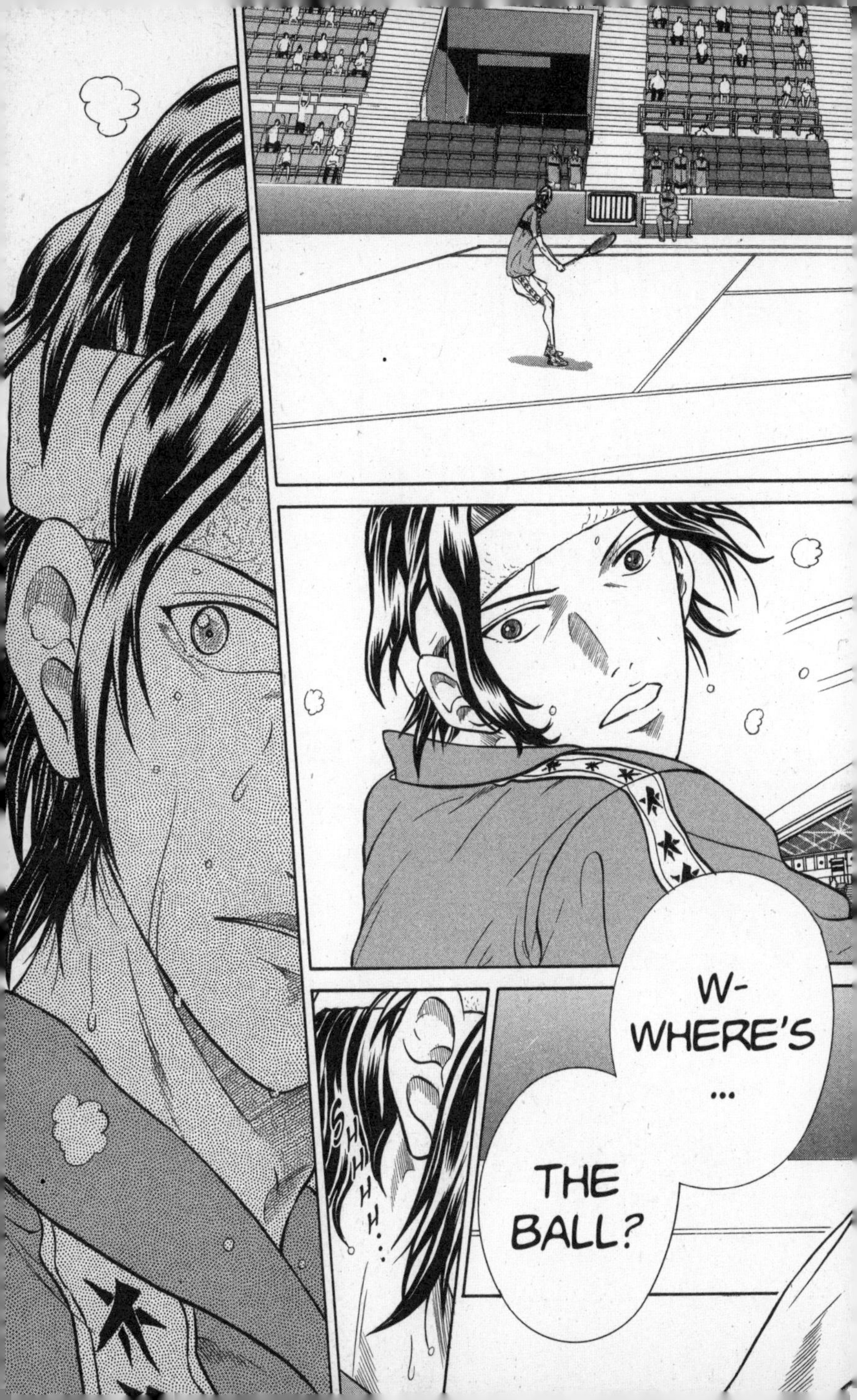
W- WHERE'S ... THE BALL?
SHHHH...

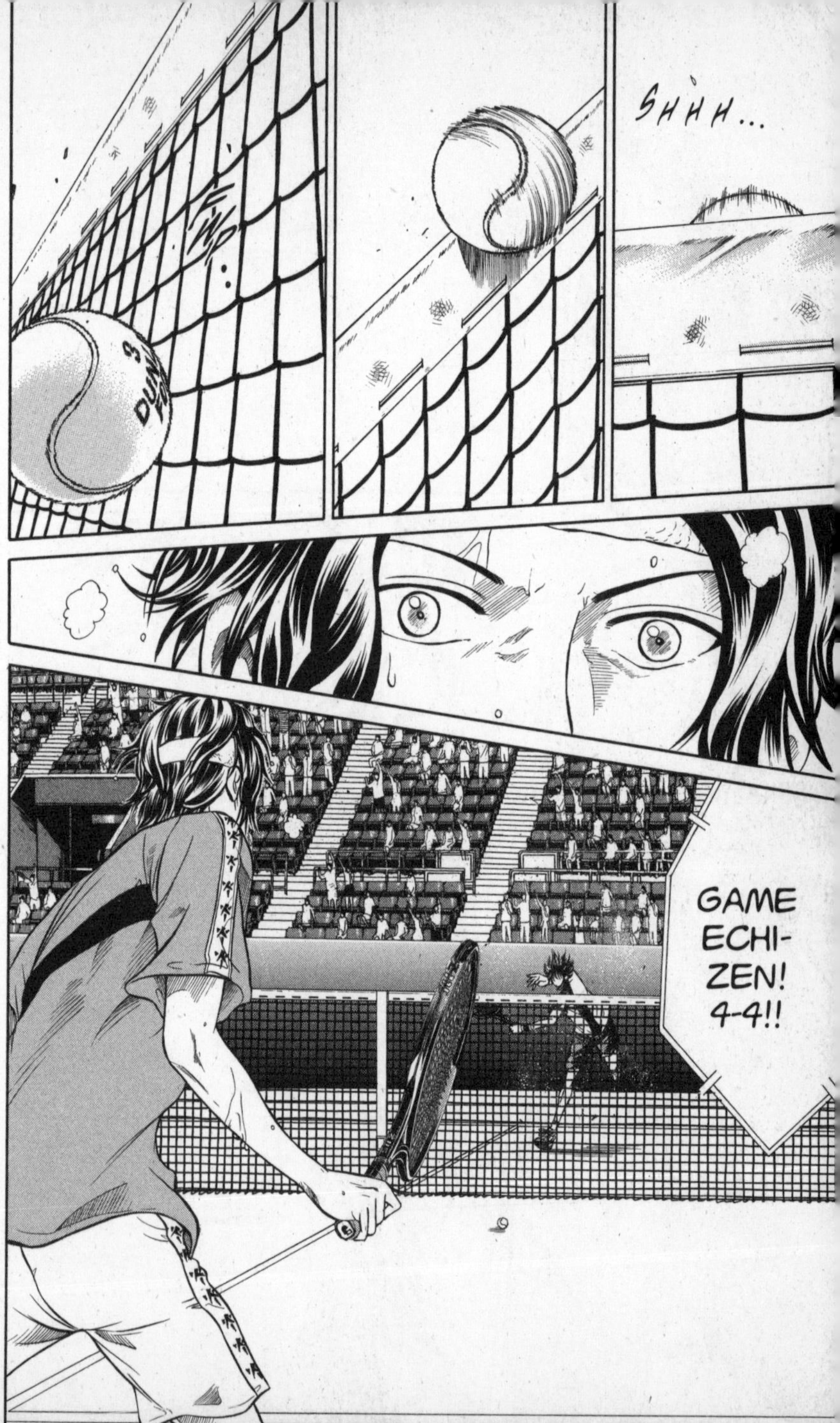
SHHH...
GAME ECHIZEN! 4-4!!

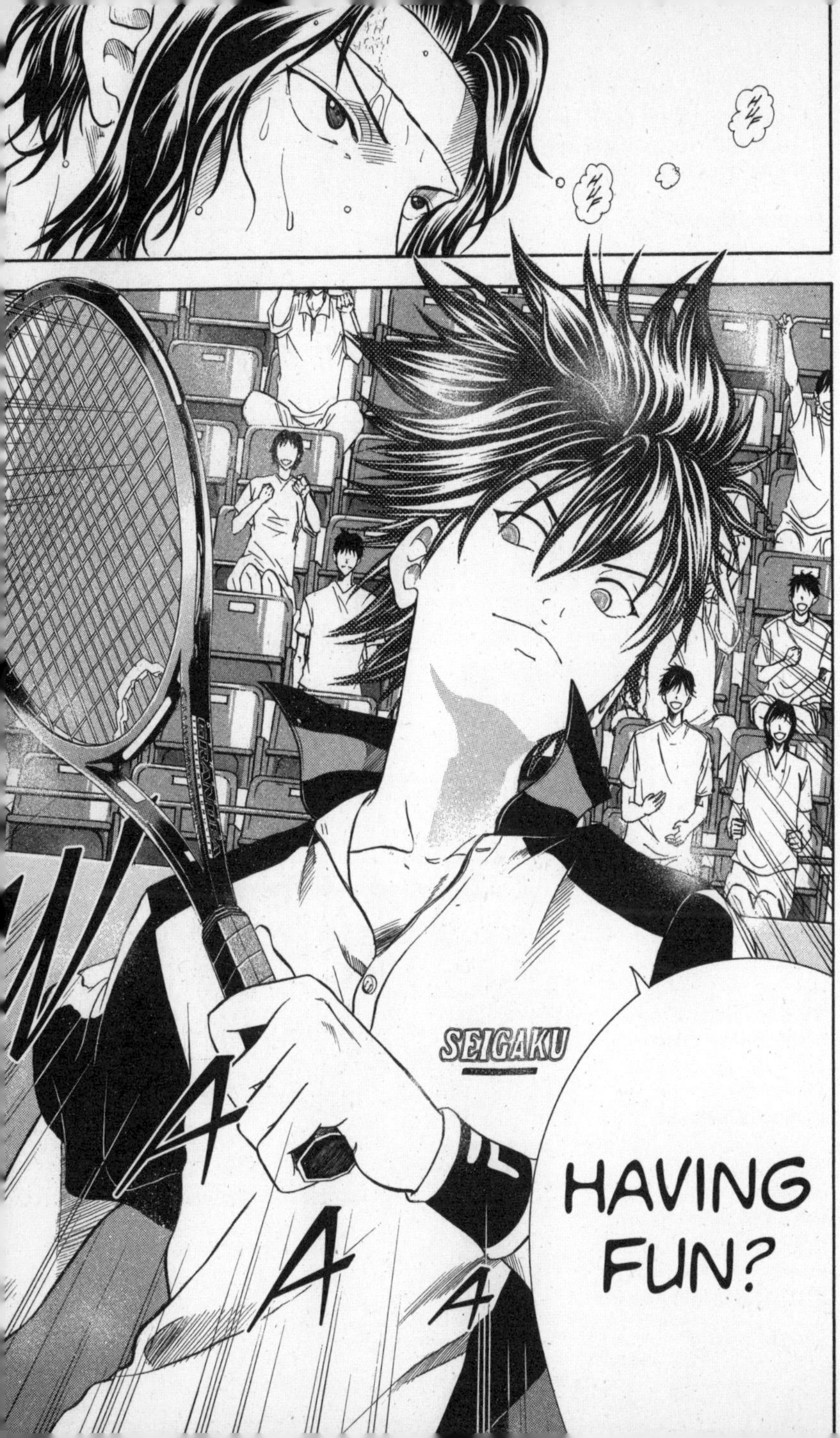
HUF
HUF
HAVING FUN?
SEIGAKU
WAAA

The can hitting game continued. Prizes included a Playstation 3, Nintendo DS, iPod Touch, tickets to an amusement park, and other things.

The cast of the musical begins to hit the cans.

The crowd erupts as punishment cards like "A lap around the court" and "Ten pushups" are drawn.

Unfortunately, the main cast did not win any prizes, but it was decided that the unclaimed prizes would be used for "The Prince of Tennis Cup Doubles Tournament" and the game was concluded.

Toshiyuki Toyonaga, who plays Kentaro Aoi in the anime, drawing the card saying "Touch an iPod Touch"! The voice actor for Aoi, Toyomizu (☹) →

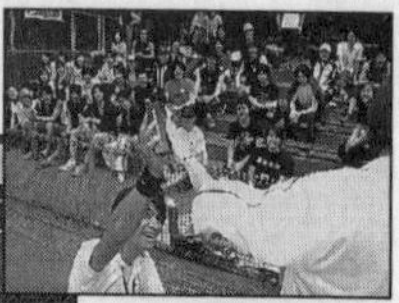

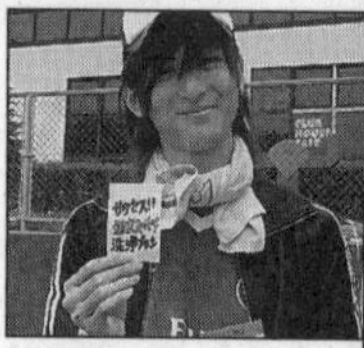

↑ Fukukawa, who played the fourth-generation Fuji, has won a Success brand brush.

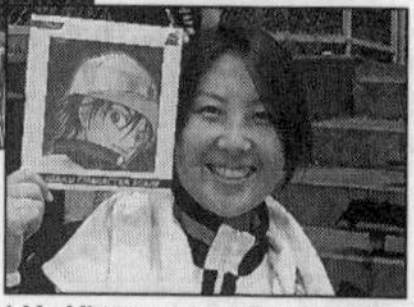

↑ Ms. Minagawa won a Ryoma scarf.

→ Unnecessarily cool? Kanata Irei (Kojiro Saeki)

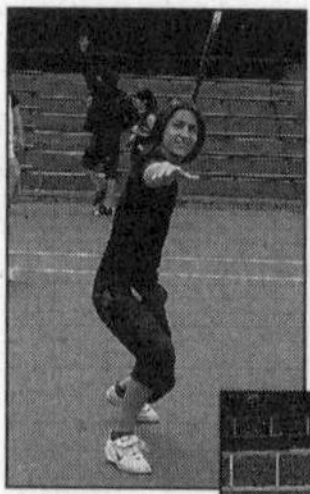

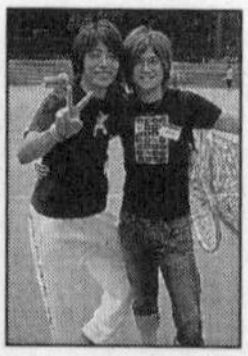

← Hiro Ogasawara, who plays fourth-generation Karamura, and Daisuke Watanabe (Kunimitsu Tezuka).

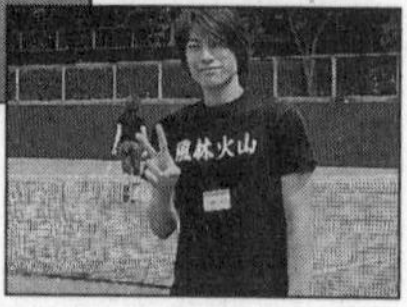
風林火山

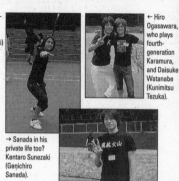

→ Sanada in his private life too? Kentaro Sunezaki (Genichiro Sanada).

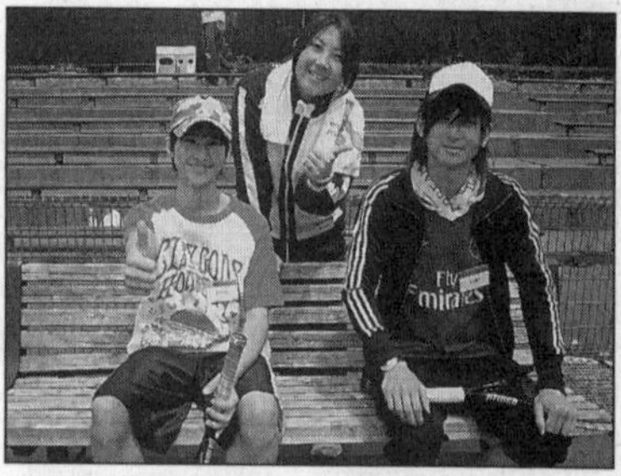

↑ Shogo Sakamoto, who played the fourth generation of Ryoma, commented, "It was really exciting today! I was happy to win some Prince of Tennis merchandise in the can hitting game. I had fun playing in the tournament as well. I lost, but it was fun seeing Masaaki Hara, who plays Horio, playing in the semifinals dressed like Ryoma. Thank you, Mr. Konomi."

Prince of Tennis Cup

Up next was the Prince of Tennis Cup.

It was a tournament where everybody drew straws and paired up to decide the No. 1 Golden Pair, but something unexpected happened.

Yasuka Saito, who played Rin Hirakoba, Noriko Namiki, who played Saori Shiba, and even creator Konomi, all experienced tennis players, lost in the first round.

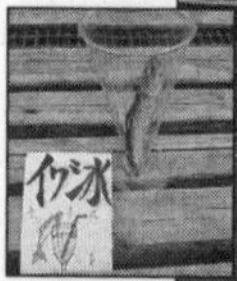
イワシ水

Sign: sardine water

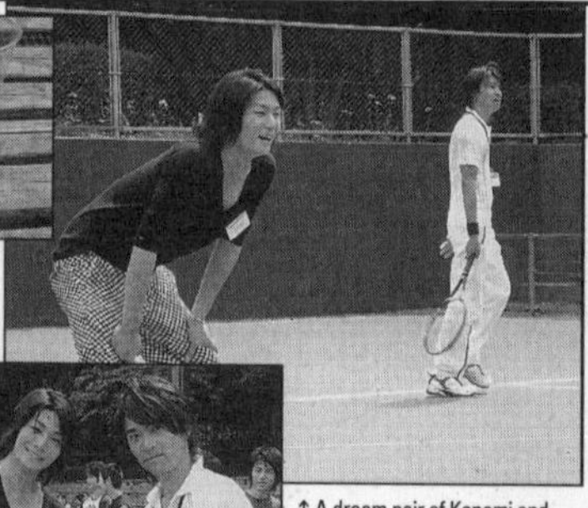

↑ A dream pair of Konomi and Ren Yagami (Seiichi Yukimura).

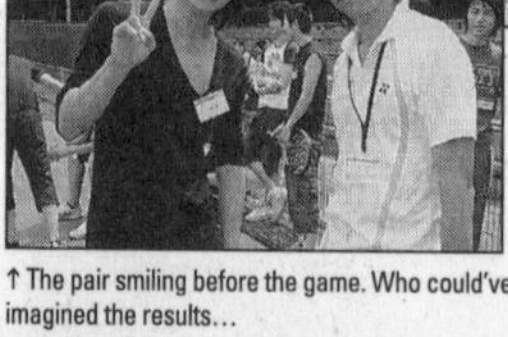

↑ The pair smiling before the game. Who could've imagined the results…

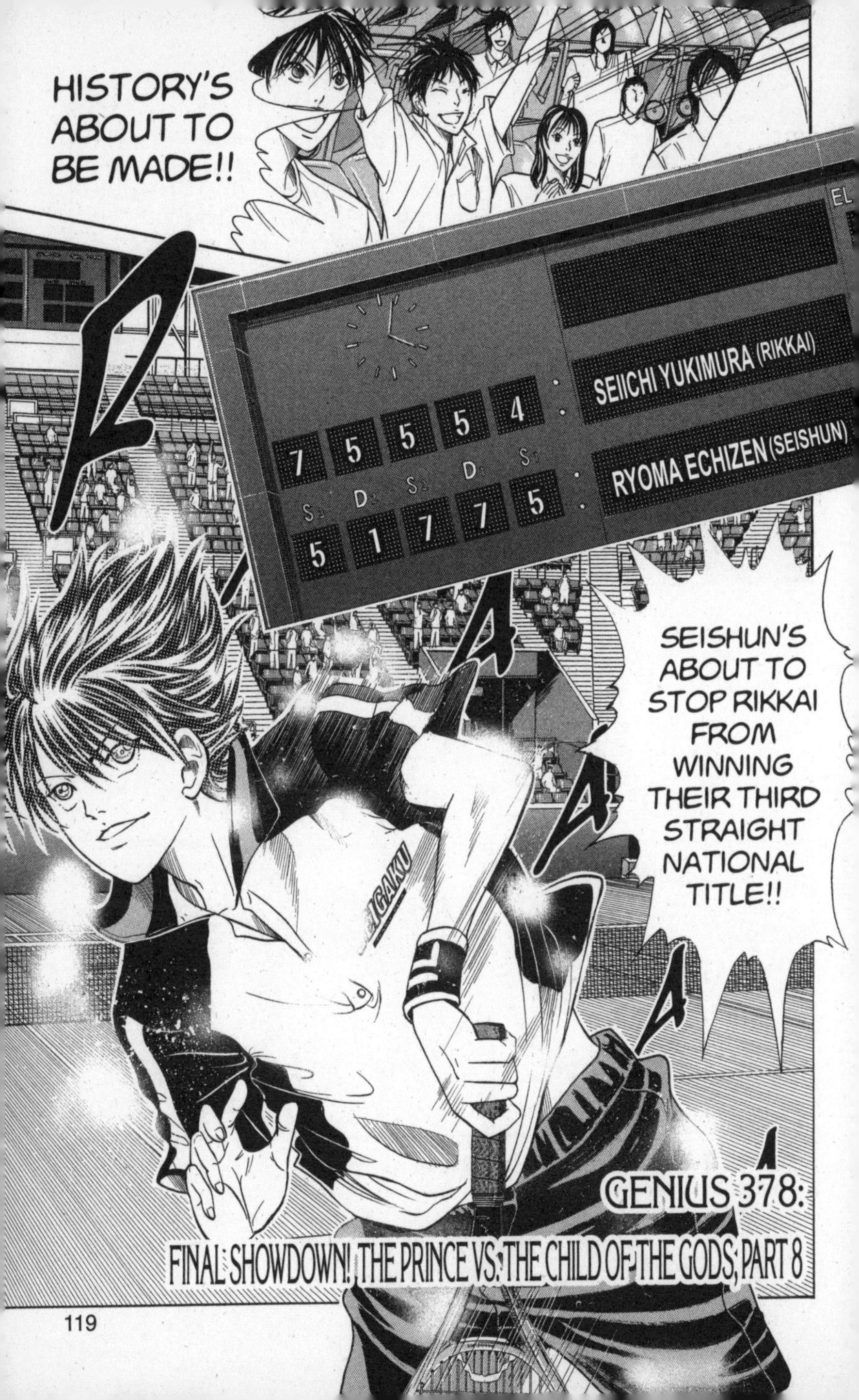
HISTORY'S ABOUT TO BE MADE!!
SEIICHI YUKIMURA (RIKKAI)
RYOMA ECHIZEN (SEISHUN)
7 5 5 5 4
S3 D2 S2 D1 S1
5 1 7 7 5
SEISHUN'S ABOUT TO STOP RIKKAI FROM WINNING THEIR THIRD STRAIGHT NATIONAL TITLE!!
GENIUS 378:
FINAL SHOWDOWN! THE PRINCE VS. THE CHILD OF THE GODS, PART 8

1st Match No. 3 Singles	2nd Match No. 2 Doubles		3rd Match No. 2 Singles	4th Match No. 1 Doubles		5th Match No. 1 Singles
Genichiro Sanada (9th Grade) Blood Type: A	Renji Yanagi (9th Grade) Blood Type: A	Akaya Kirihara (8th Grade) Blood Type: O	Masaharu Nio (9th Grade) Blood Type: AB	Jackal Kuwahara (9th Grade) Blood Type: O	Bunta Marui (9th Grade) Blood Type: B	Seiichi Yukimura (9th Grade) Blood Type: A

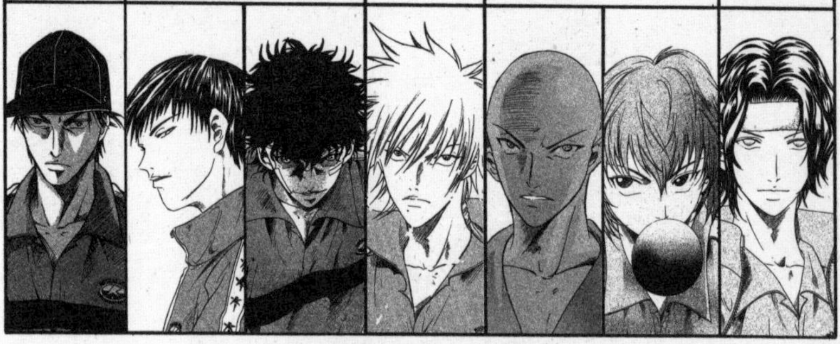

GENIUS 378: FINAL SHOWDOWN! THE PRINCE VS. THE CHILD OF THE GODS, PART 8

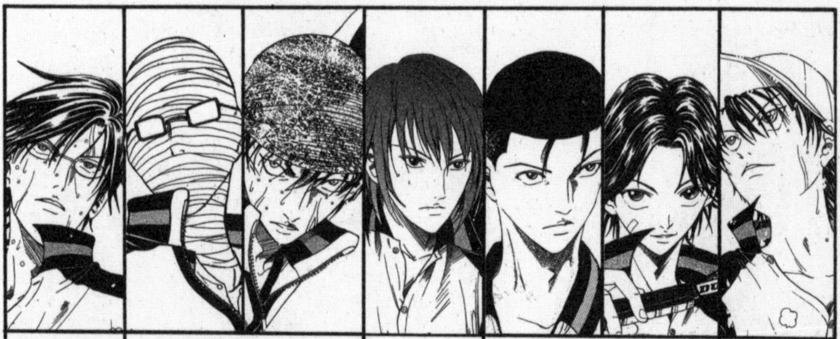

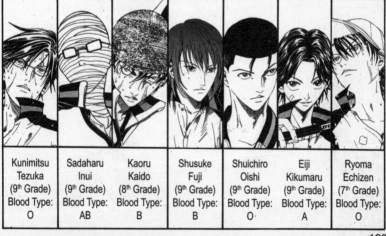

Kunimitsu Tezuka (9th Grade) Blood Type: O	Sadaharu Inui (9th Grade) Blood Type: AB	Kaoru Kaido (8th Grade) Blood Type: B	Shusuke Fuji (9th Grade) Blood Type: B	Shuichiro Oishi (9th Grade) Blood Type: O	Eiji Kikumaru (9th Grade) Blood Type: A	Ryoma Echizen (7th Grade) Blood Type: O

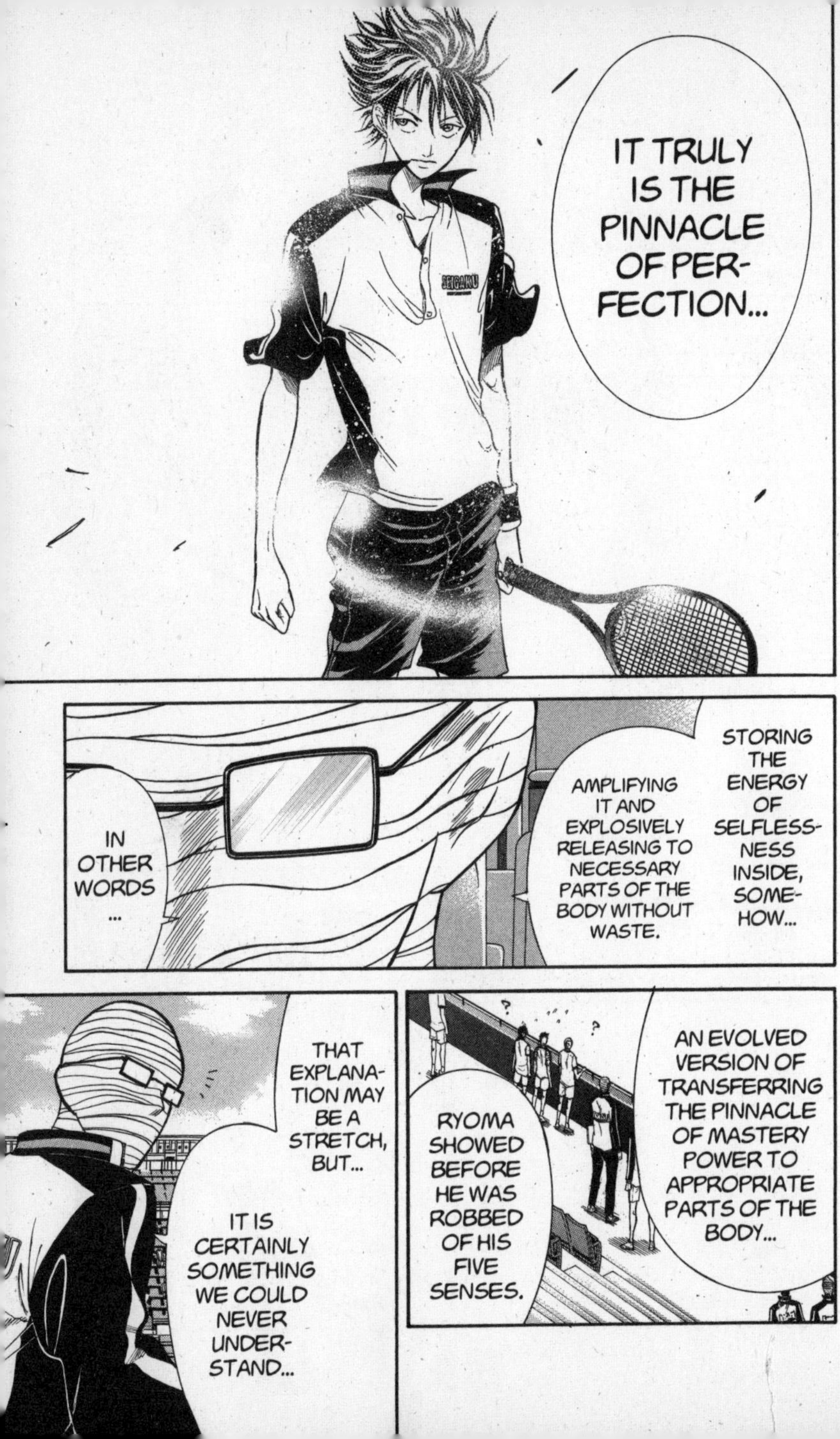
IT TRULY IS THE PINNACLE OF PER-FECTION...
STORING THE ENERGY OF SELFLESS-NESS INSIDE, SOME-HOW...
AMPLIFYING IT AND EXPLOSIVELY RELEASING TO NECESSARY PARTS OF THE BODY WITHOUT WASTE.
IN OTHER WORDS ...
AN EVOLVED VERSION OF TRANSFERRING THE PINNACLE OF MASTERY POWER TO APPROPRIATE PARTS OF THE BODY...
RYOMA SHOWED BEFORE HE WAS ROBBED OF HIS FIVE SENSES.
THAT EXPLANA-TION MAY BE A STRETCH, BUT...
IT IS CERTAINLY SOMETHING WE COULD NEVER UNDER-STAND...

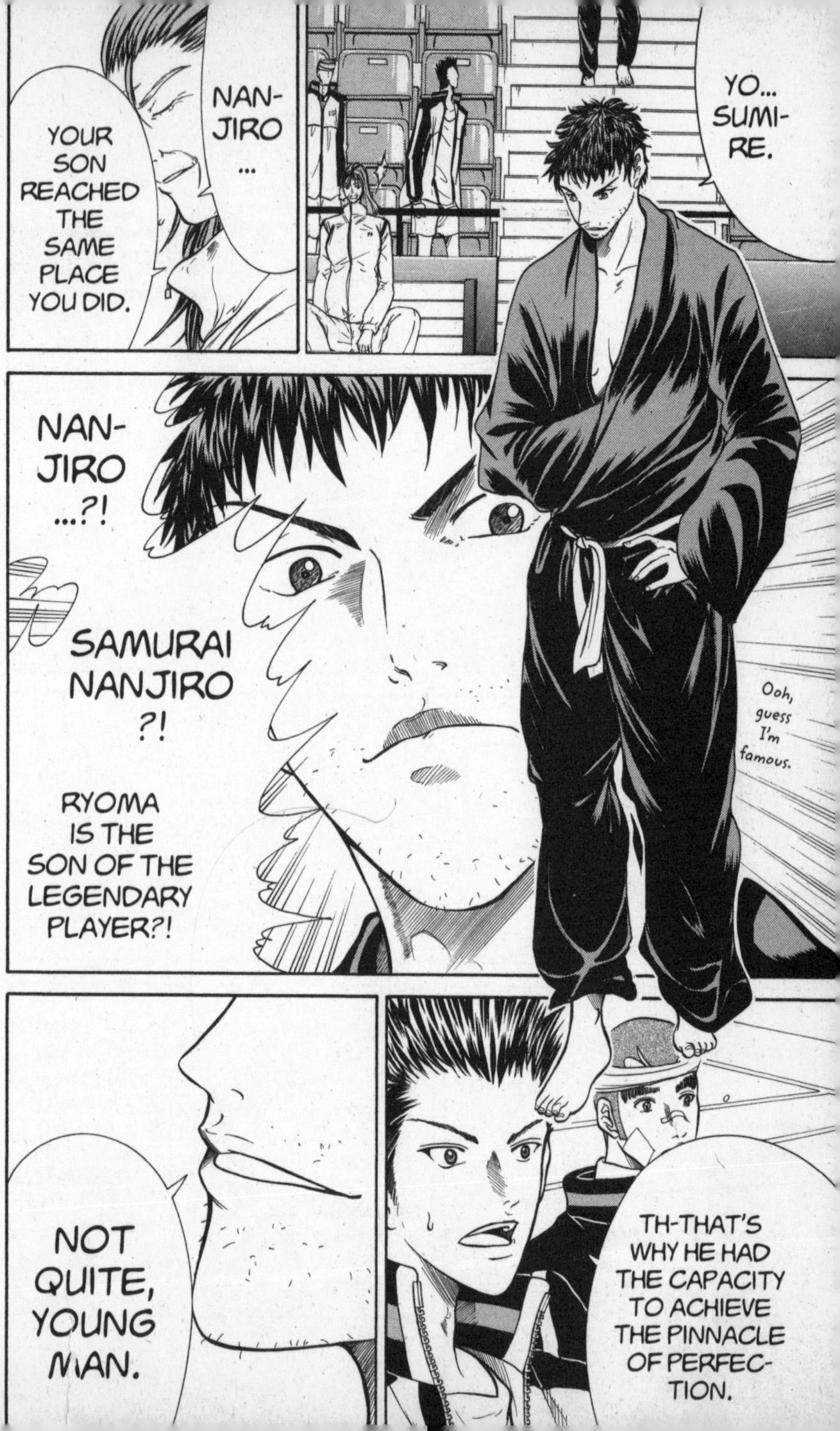
YO... SUMIRE.
NANJIRO...
YOUR SON REACHED THE SAME PLACE YOU DID.
NANJIRO...?!
SAMURAI NANJIRO?!
Ooh, guess I'm famous.
RYOMA IS THE SON OF THE LEGENDARY PLAYER?!
TH-THAT'S WHY HE HAD THE CAPACITY TO ACHIEVE THE PINNACLE OF PERFECTION.
NOT QUITE, YOUNG MAN.

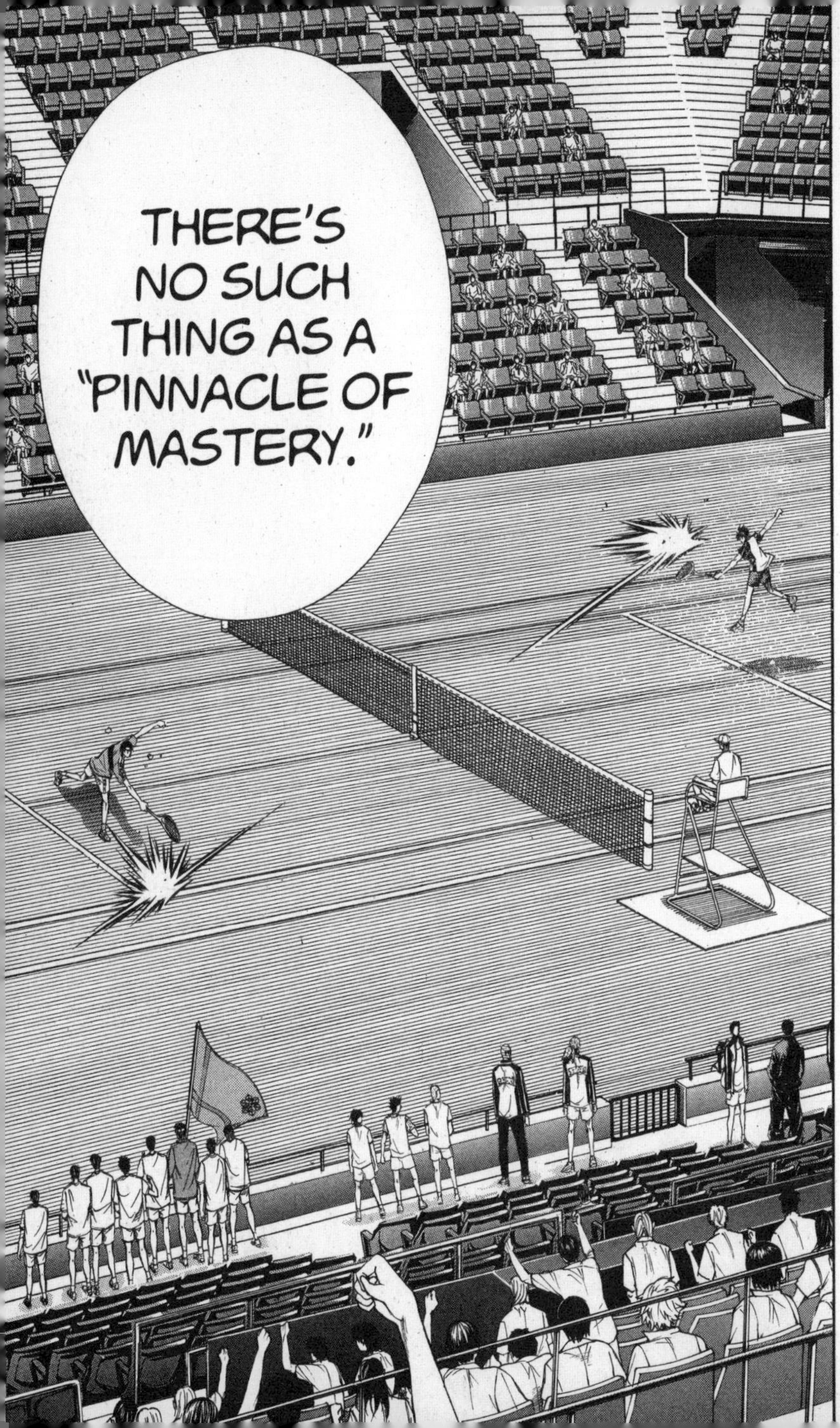
THERE'S NO SUCH THING AS A "PINNACLE OF MASTERY."

BUT...

WHAT?!

HOW SHOULD I PUT IT...

RYOMA'S HAVING FUN.

LOOKS LIKE...

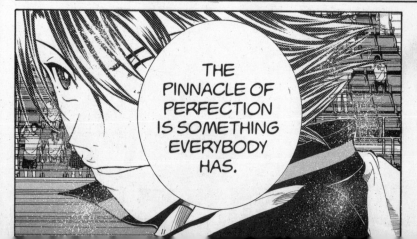

THE PINNACLE OF PERFECTION IS SOMETHING EVERYBODY HAS.

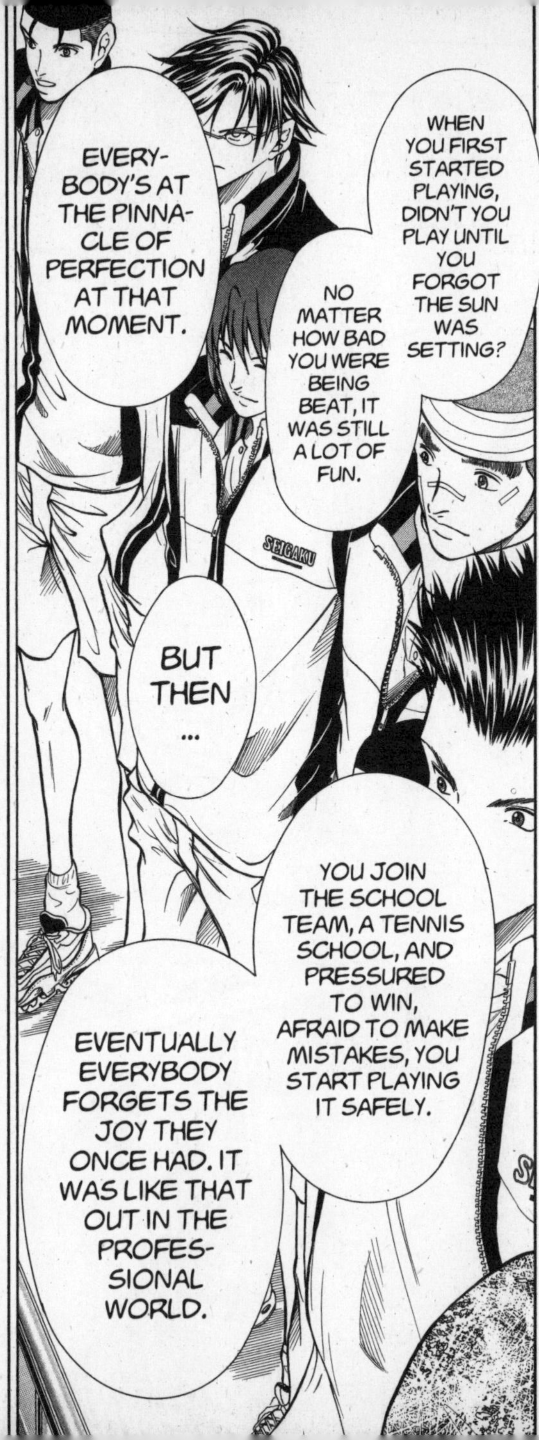
WHEN YOU FIRST STARTED PLAYING, DIDN'T YOU PLAY UNTIL YOU FORGOT THE SUN WAS SETTING?
NO MATTER HOW BAD YOU WERE BEING BEAT, IT WAS STILL A LOT OF FUN.
EVERY-BODY'S AT THE PINNA-CLE OF PERFECTION AT THAT MOMENT.
SEIGAKU
BUT THEN ...
YOU JOIN THE SCHOOL TEAM, A TENNIS SCHOOL, AND PRESSURED TO WIN, AFRAID TO MAKE MISTAKES, YOU START PLAYING IT SAFELY.
EVENTUALLY EVERYBODY FORGETS THE JOY THEY ONCE HAD. IT WAS LIKE THAT OUT IN THE PROFES-SIONAL WORLD.

THE FEELING EVERY-BODY HAS WHEN THEY FIRST DISCOVER THE GAME...

PLAYING FOR THE JOY OF THE GAME...

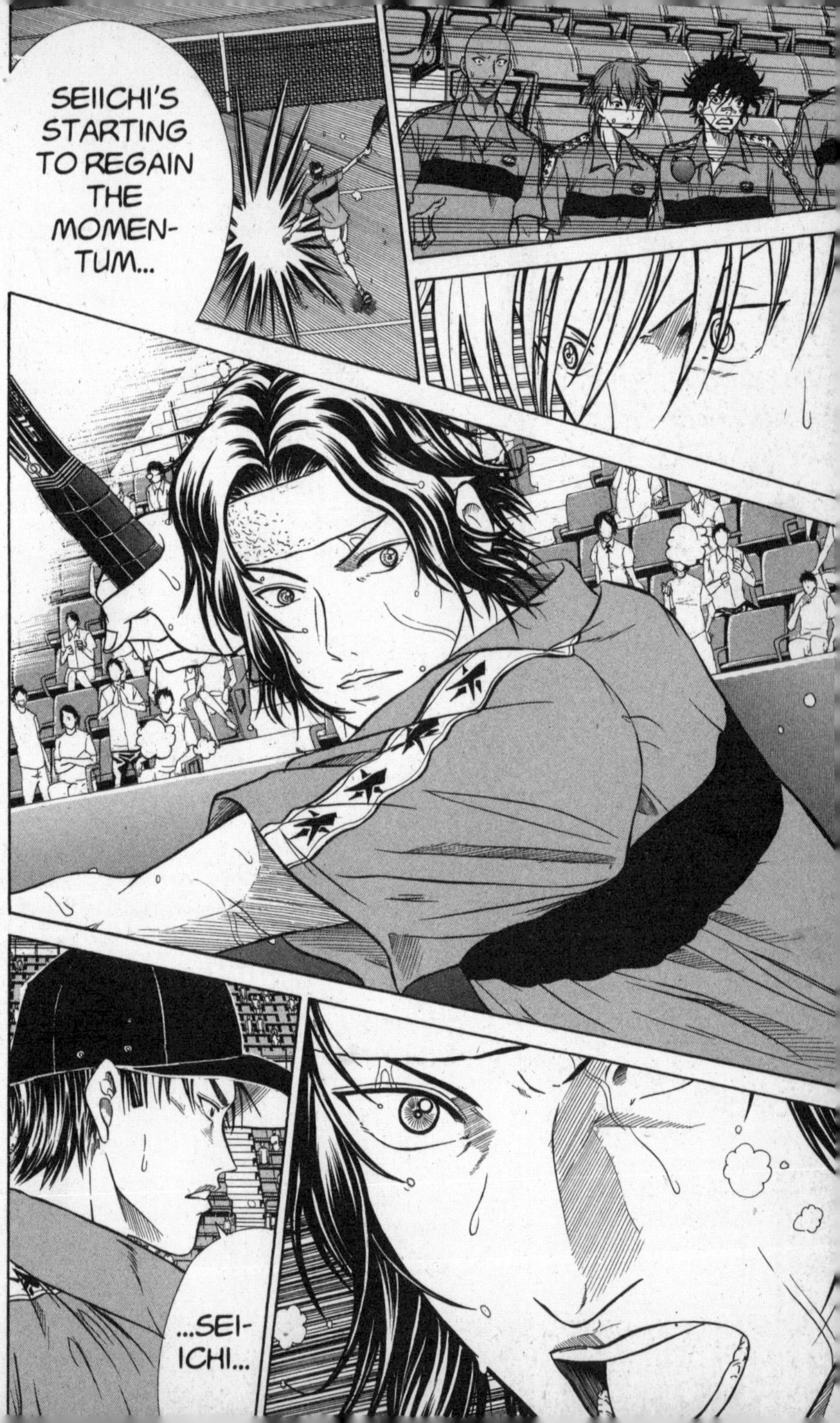
SEIICHI'S STARTING TO REGAIN THE MOMEN-TUM...
...SEI-ICHI...

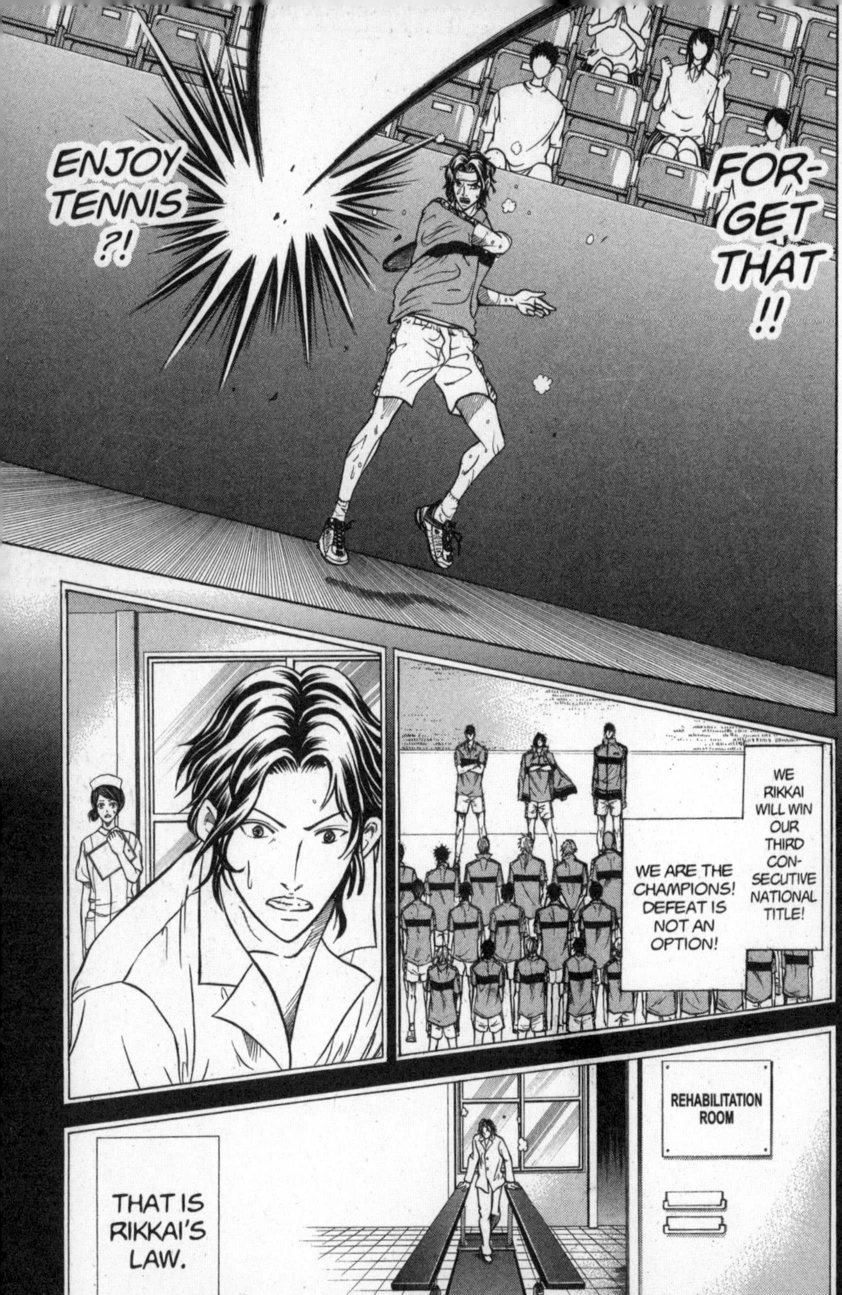
ENJOY TENNIS ?!
FOR-GET THAT !!
WE ARE THE CHAMPIONS! DEFEAT IS NOT AN OPTION!
WE RIKKAI WILL WIN OUR THIRD CON-SECUTIVE NATIONAL TITLE!
REHABILITATION ROOM
THAT IS RIKKAI'S LAW.

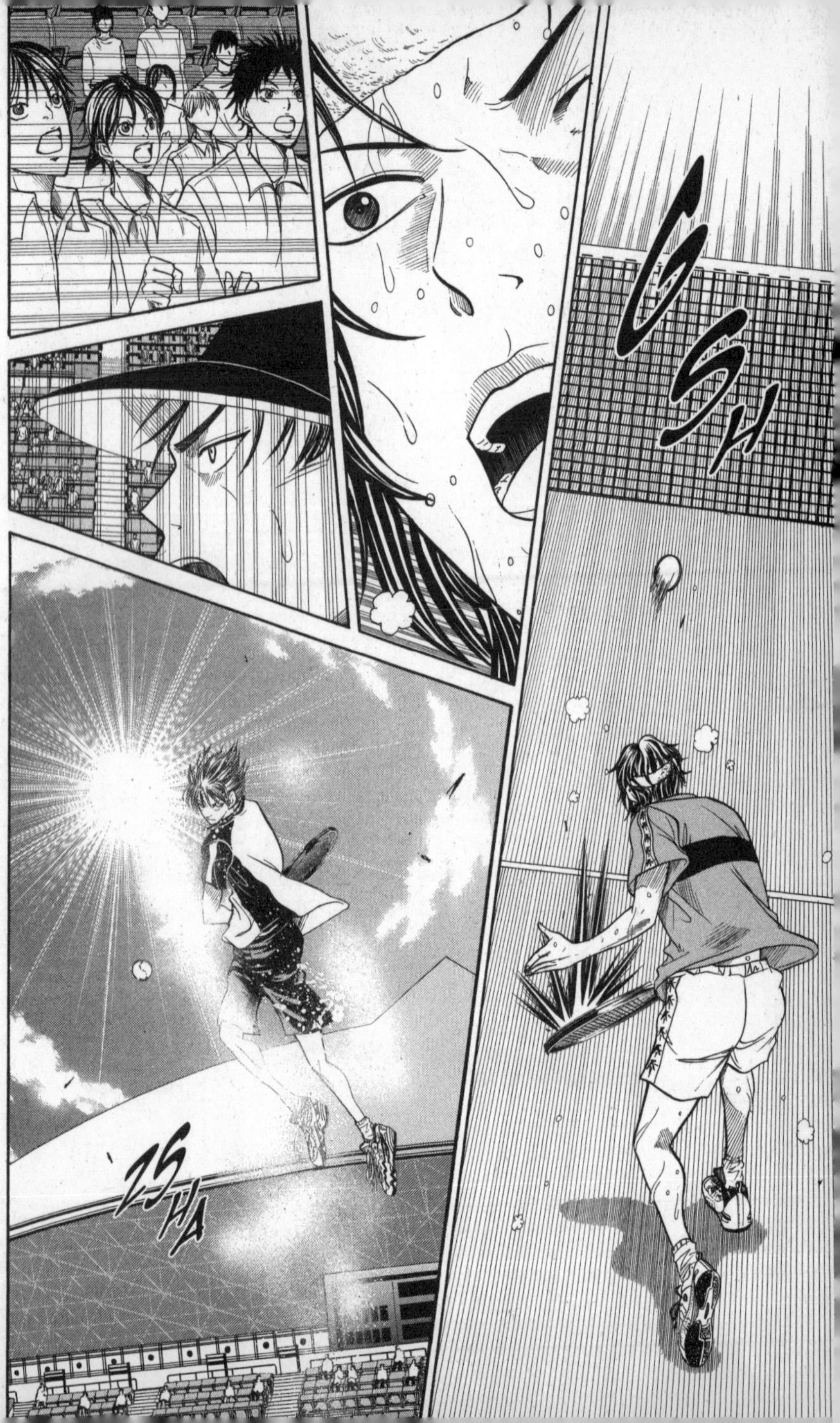
GISH
ZSHA

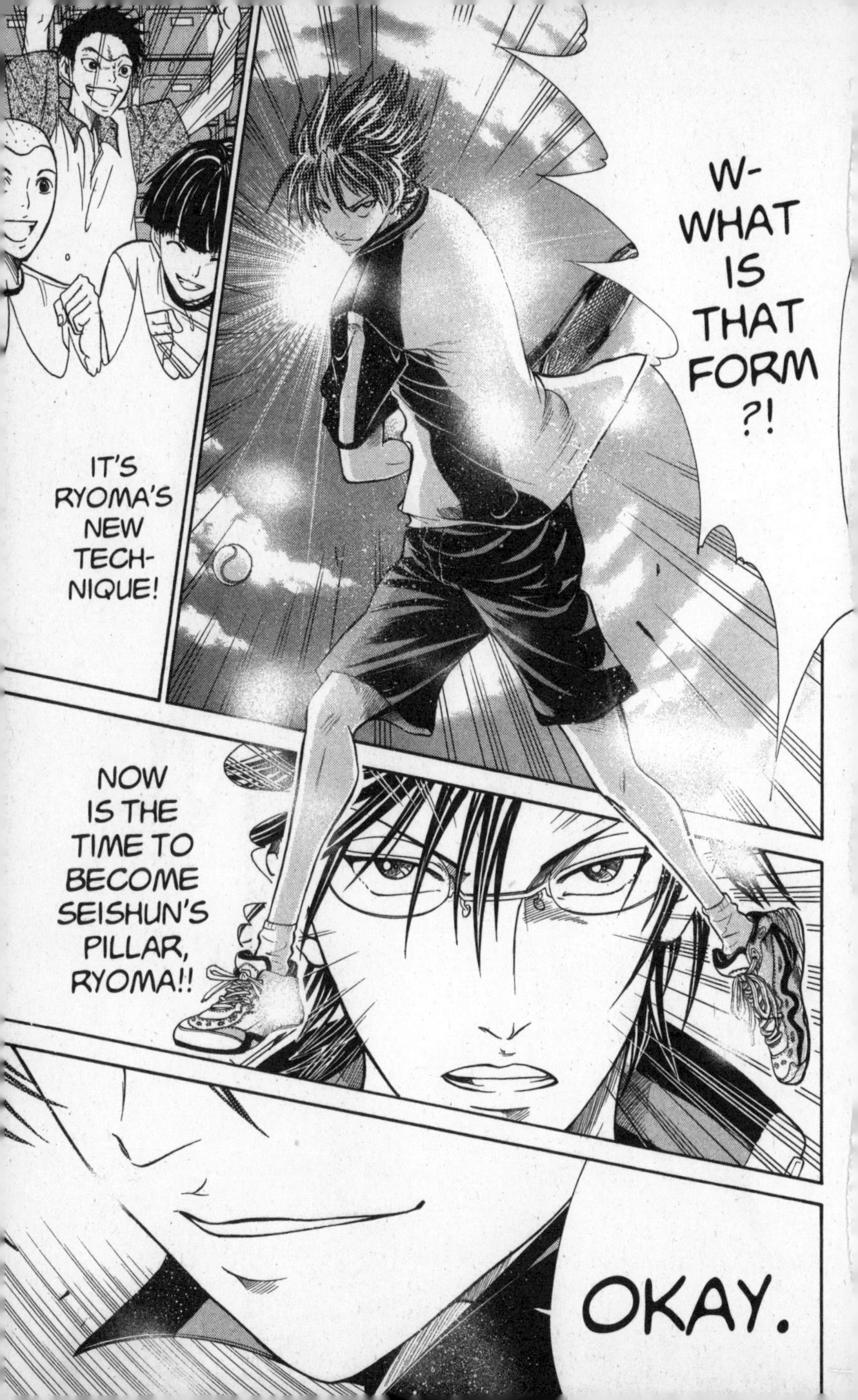
W-WHAT IS THAT FORM?!
IT'S RYOMA'S NEW TECH-NIQUE!
NOW IS THE TIME TO BECOME SEISHUN'S PILLAR, RYOMA!!
OKAY.

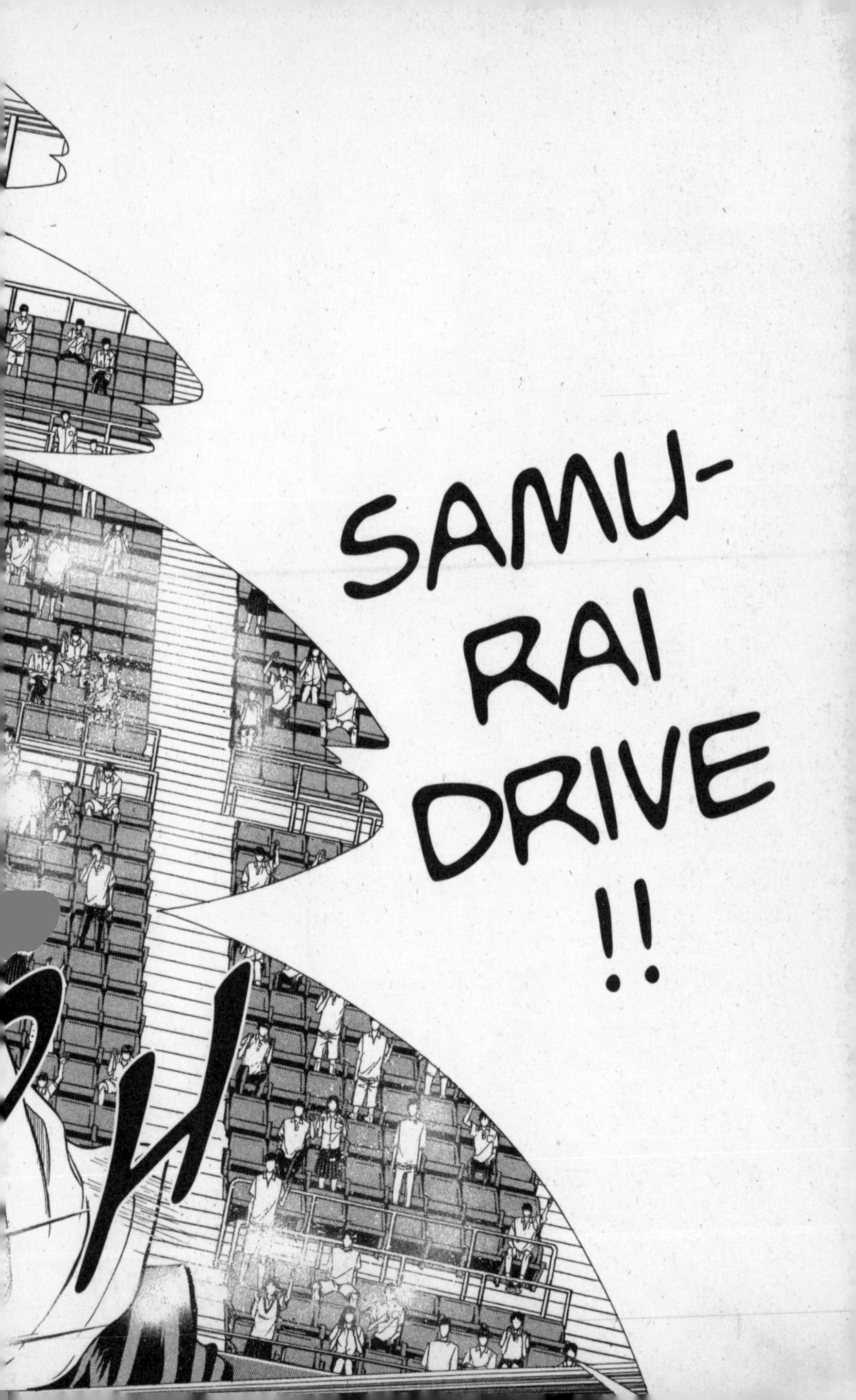
SAMU-
RAI
DRIVE
!!

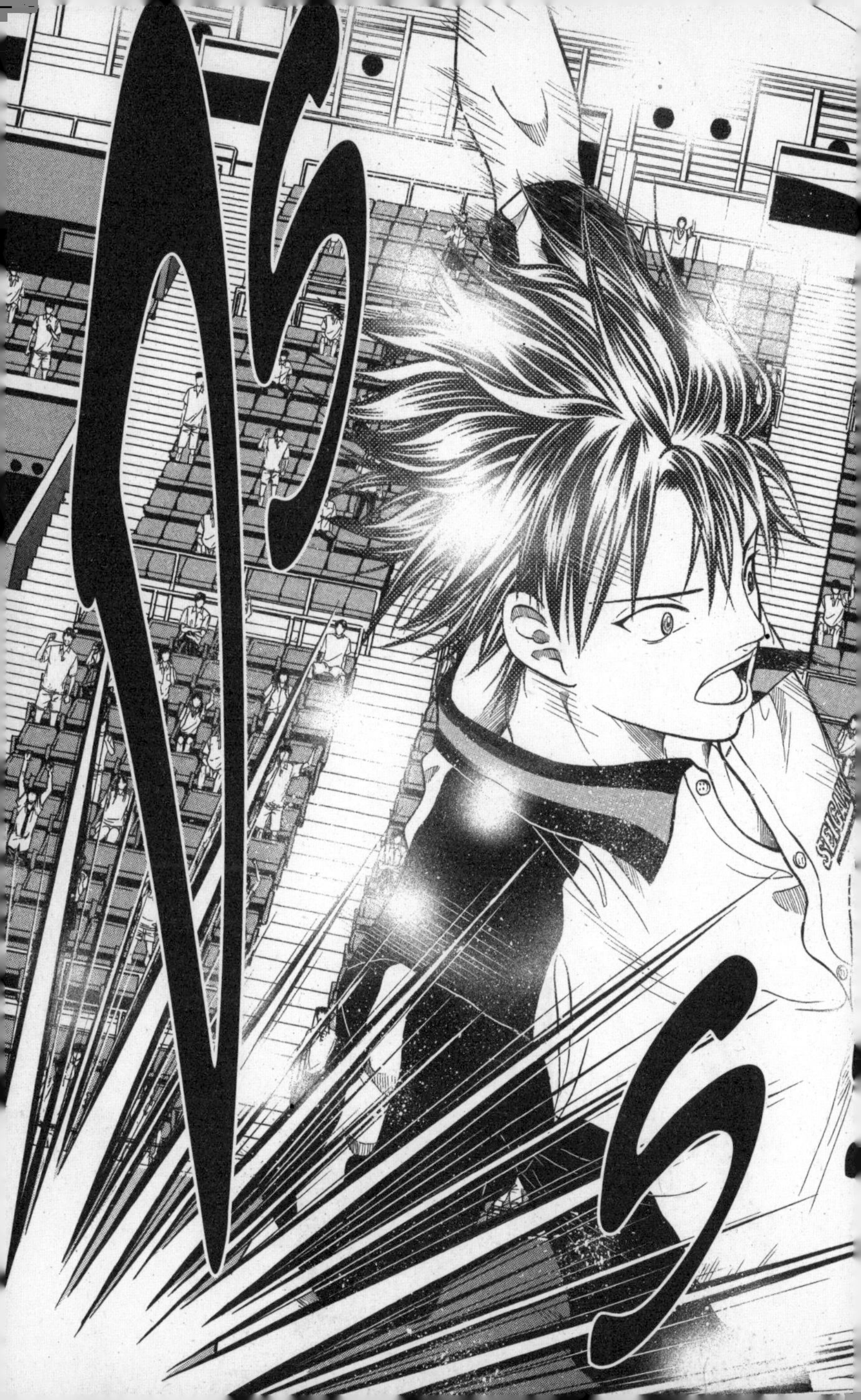

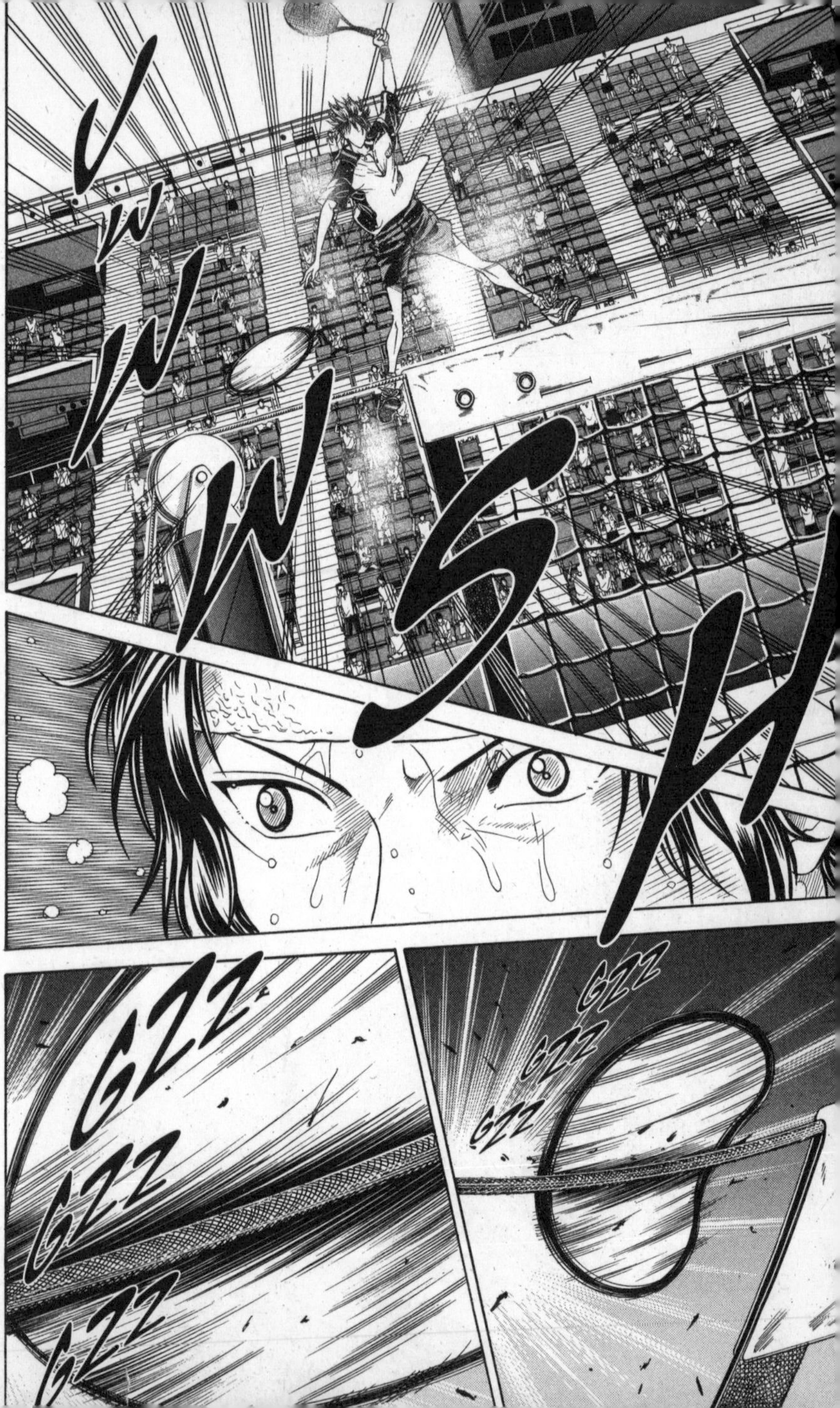
WWWSH
GZZ
GZZ
GZZ
GZZ
GZZ
GZZ

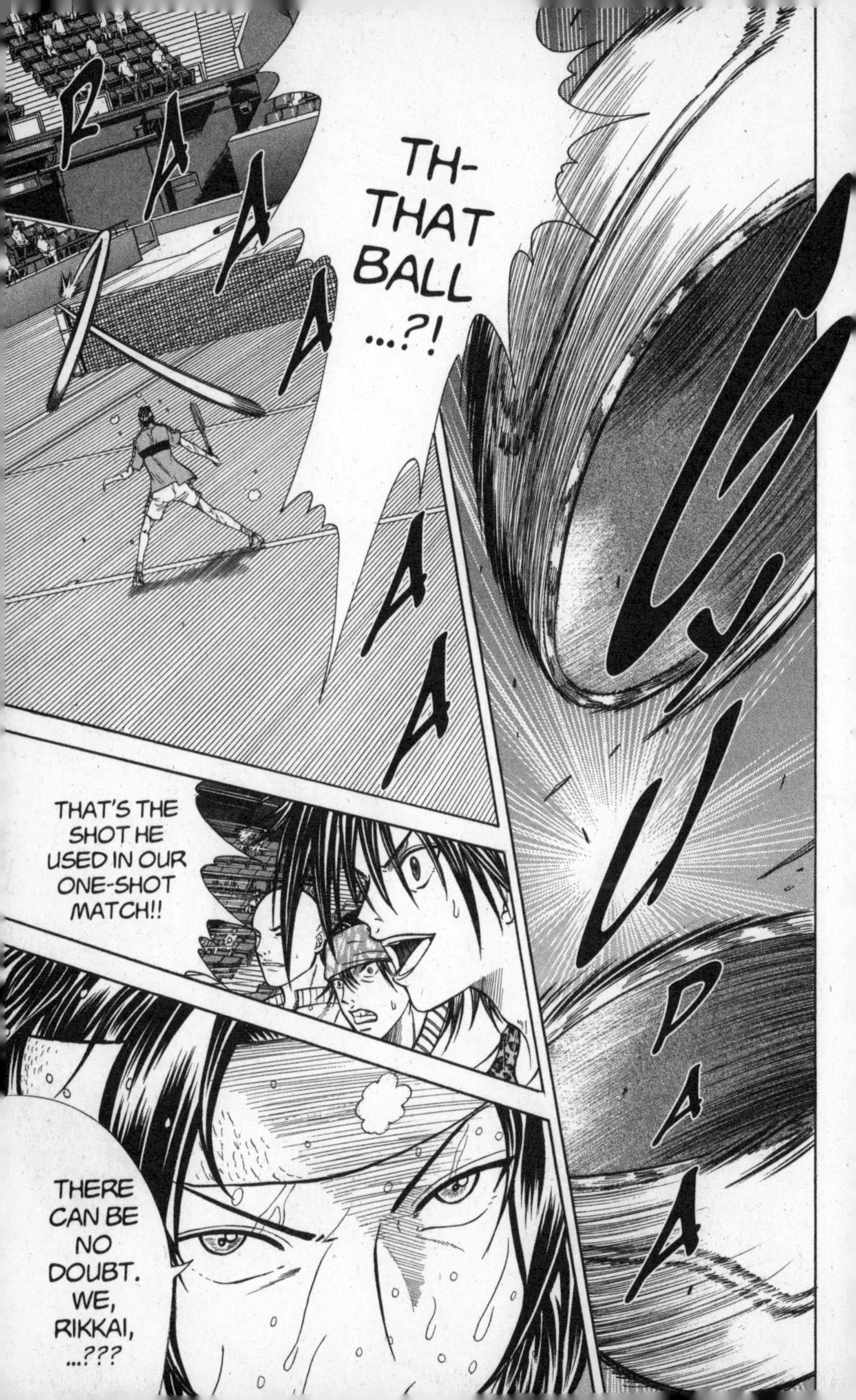
TH- THAT BALL ...?!
THAT'S THE SHOT HE USED IN OUR ONE-SHOT MATCH!!
THERE CAN BE NO DOUBT. WE, RIKKAI, ...???

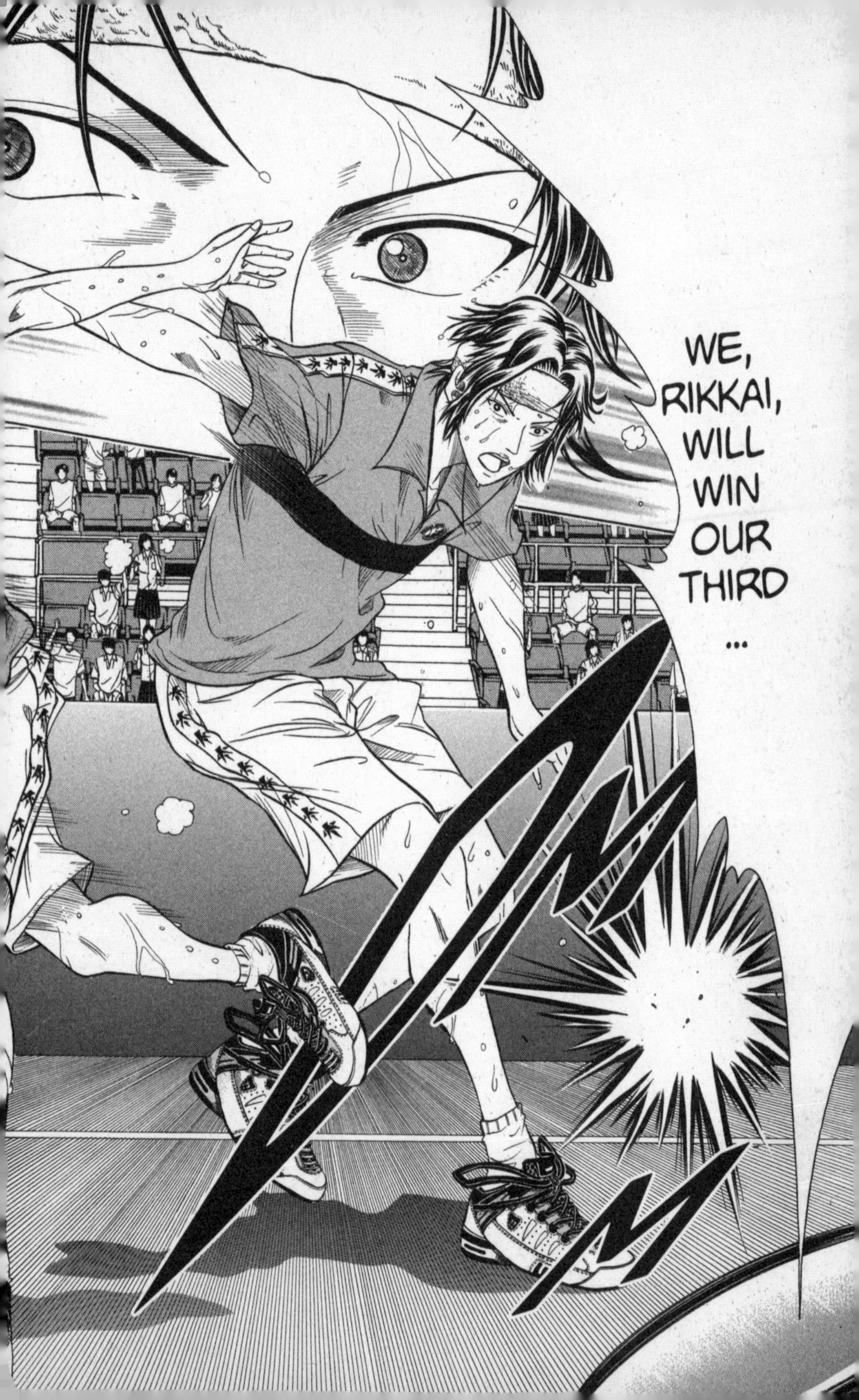
WE, RIKKAI, WILL WIN OUR THIRD ...

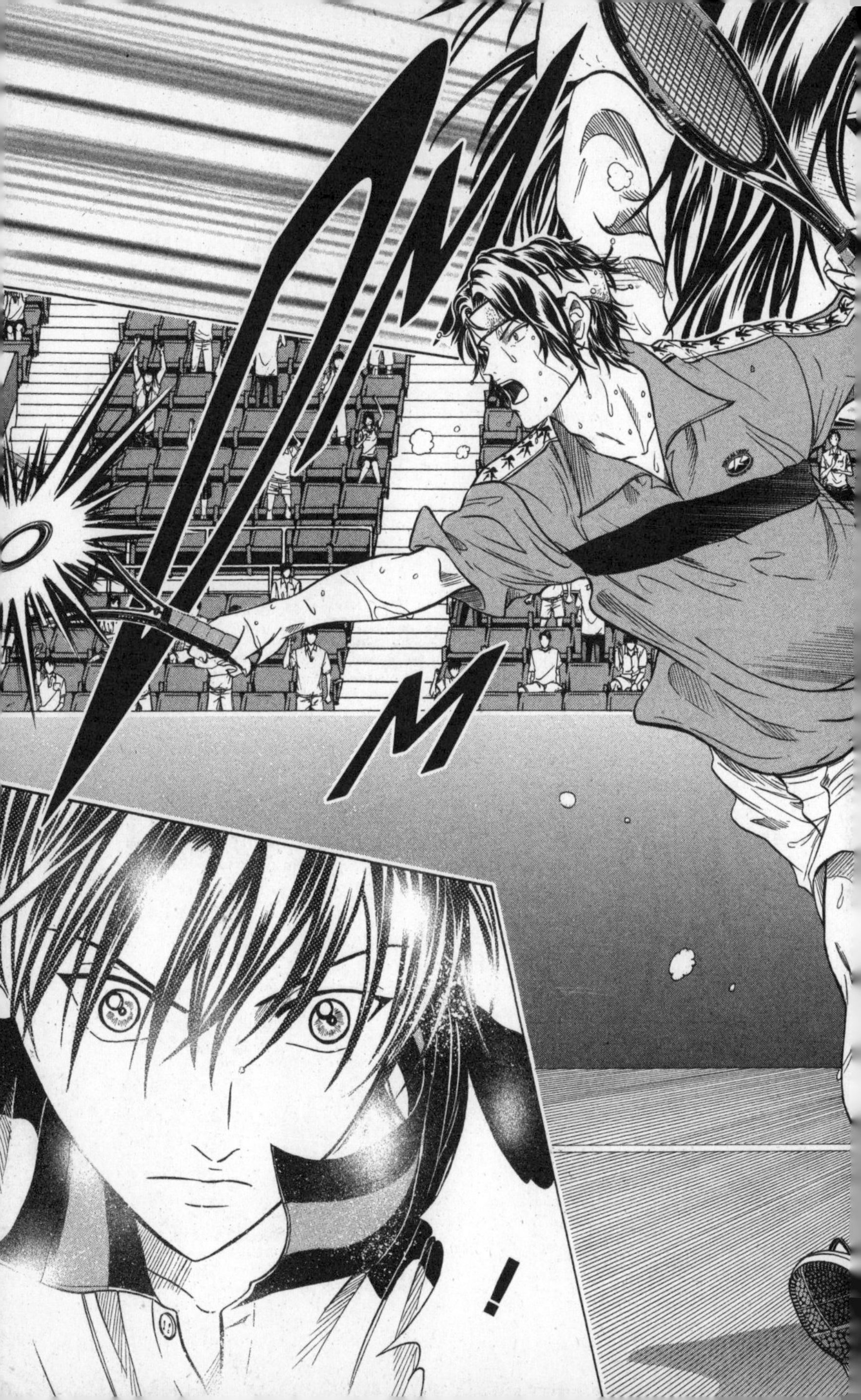
M
!

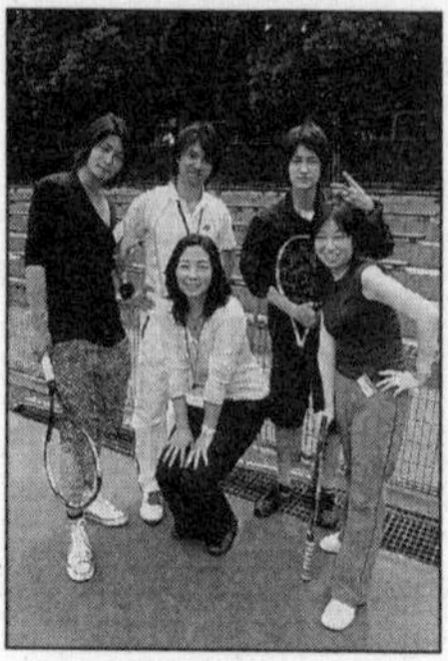

↑ From top left – Ren Yagami (Seiichi Yukimura), Konomi, Yuta Takahashi (fouth-generation Sadaharu Inui), Shusuke Fuij's voice Yuki Kaida. In the center is Prince of Tennis cheerleader Miho Nakai.

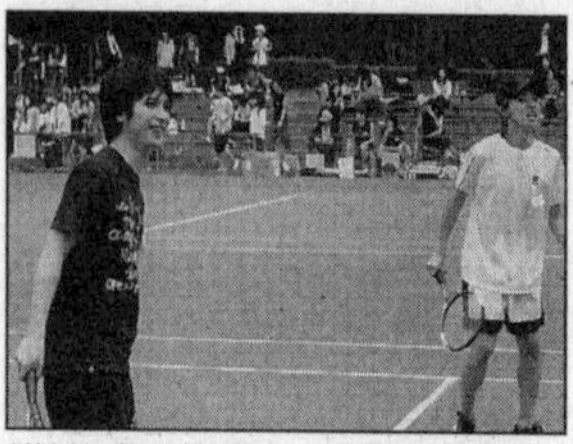

↑ Yuichiro Hirata (fourth-generation Kaoru Kaido) and Ren Kiriyama (Bunta Marui).

The players who advanced to the finals were on this court where the devil nests were Masaaki Hara (Horio) and MMV's (Marvelous Entertainment) Mamoru Ohi pair vs. Koji Watanabe (Takashi Kawamura) and fan representative Ms. Ohura.

Ms. Ohura was the only player who had any experience playing tennis. But the game was heated and filled with highlight reel moments.

The Masaaki Hara–Mamoru Ohi pair took control of the game. When it came to a critical moment, Masaaki took off his Seishun jersey.

But the Koji Watanabe–Ms. Ohura pair came back to bring the game to match-point. A tense moment. Somebody from the crowd yelled, "Maybe you should've kept your Seishun jersey on?" Despite being in the middle of the game, Masaaki ran off the court to put his jersey back on, and that is where the ball landed and the game was decided. Masaaki was left speechless and the crowd erupted in laughter. The Prince of Tennis Cup ended in laughter.

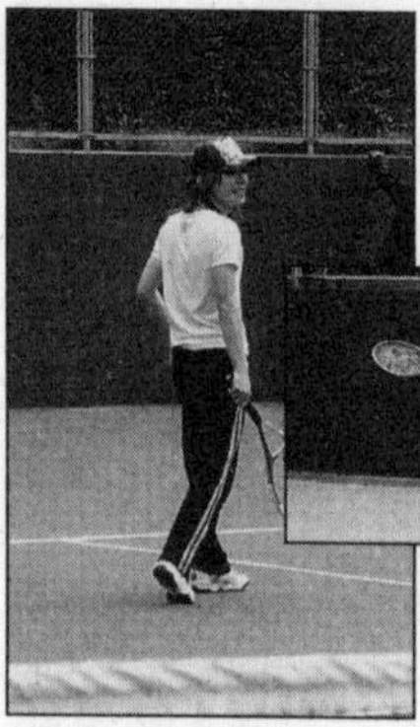

↑ Kimeru who sang the opening and ending song for the anime, the original Shusuke Fuji in the musical, temporarily playing as Ryoma. Sadly, he lost in the third round.

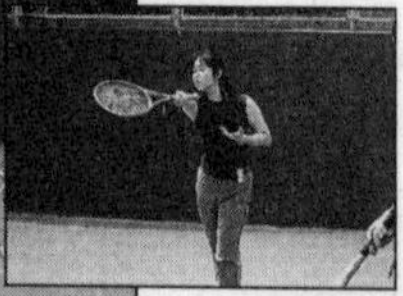

↑ This ball disappears.

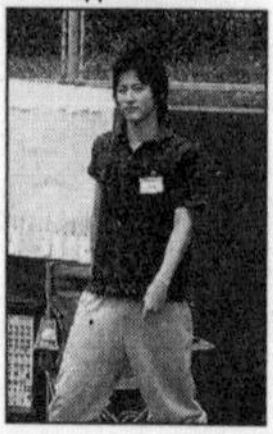

→ Baba, who plays Yagyu.

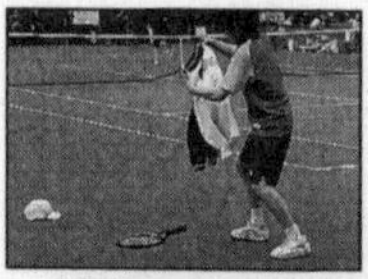

↑ Rushing to wear the jersey!!

Koji Watanabe–Ms. Ohura pair won an annual passport to TDL (Tokyo Disneyland), and Masaaki Hara, who lost, was awarded a Playstation 3 from the author for being the most memorable player.

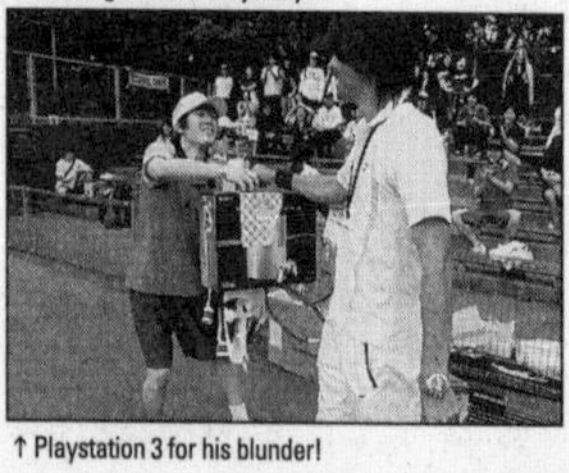

↑ Playstation 3 for his blunder!

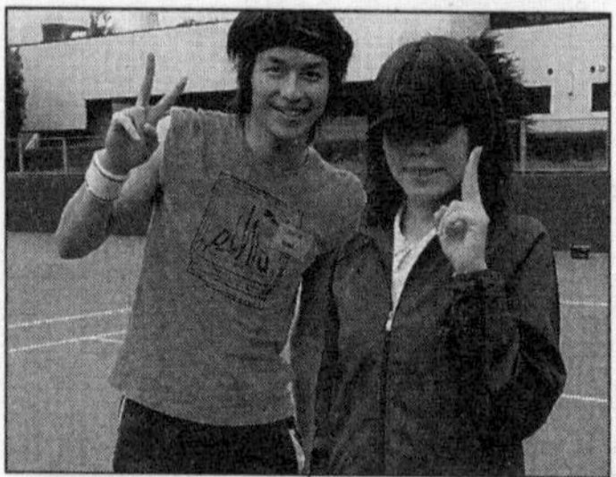

↑ Koji Watanabe commented:
I was nervous, but I had a lot of fun. I'm exhausted. I'll sleep well tonight.

↑ Ms. Ohura commented:
I was very excited to be able to participate in such a wonderful event. Thank you very much. I didn't think we would win, so I'm very happy. I'm glad I attended tennis school.

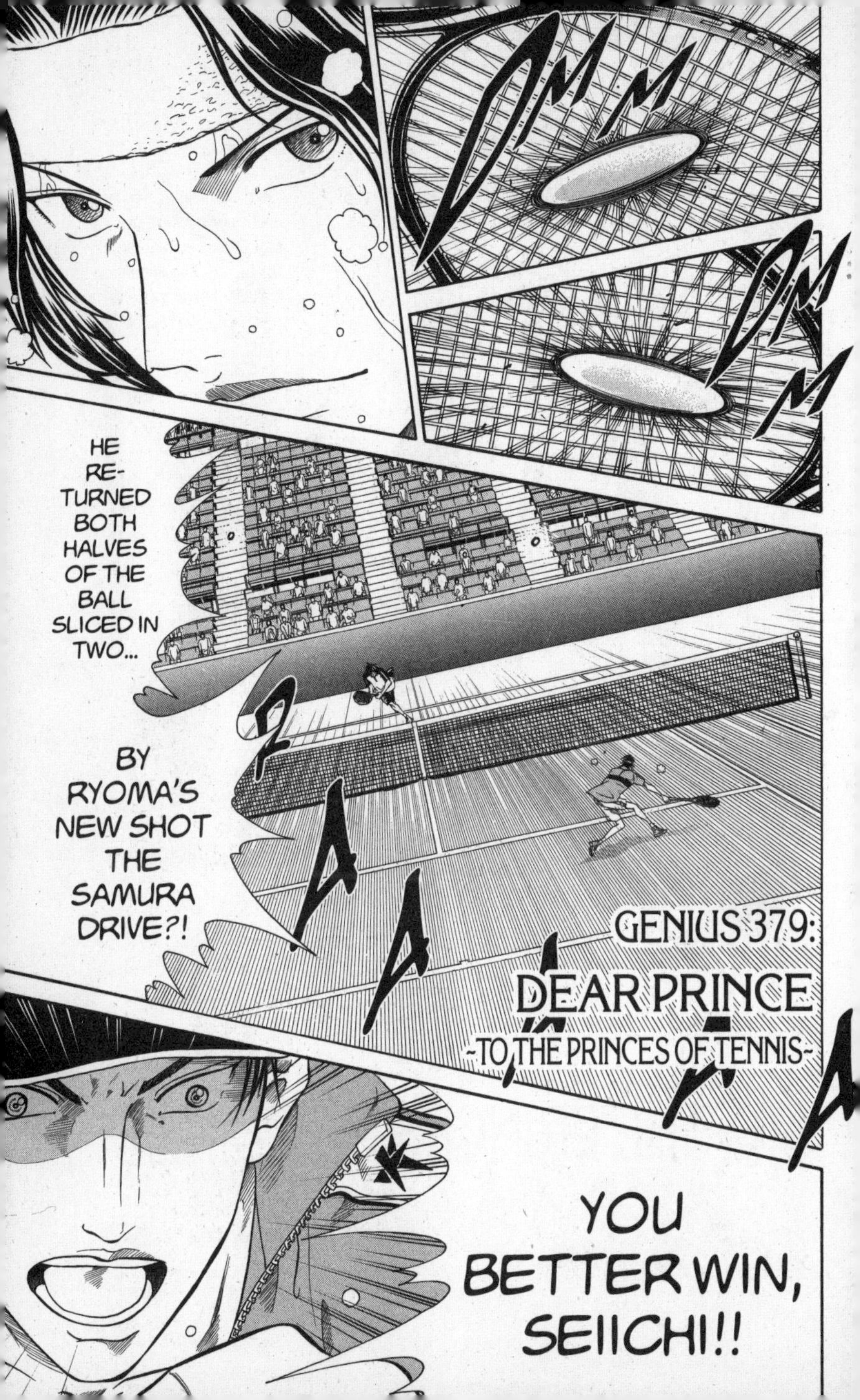

DOMM
DOMM
HE RE-TURNED BOTH HALVES OF THE BALL SLICED IN TWO...
BY RYOMA'S NEW SHOT THE SAMURA DRIVE?!
GENIUS 379:
DEAR PRINCE
~TO THE PRINCES OF TENNIS~
YOU BETTER WIN, SEIICHI!!

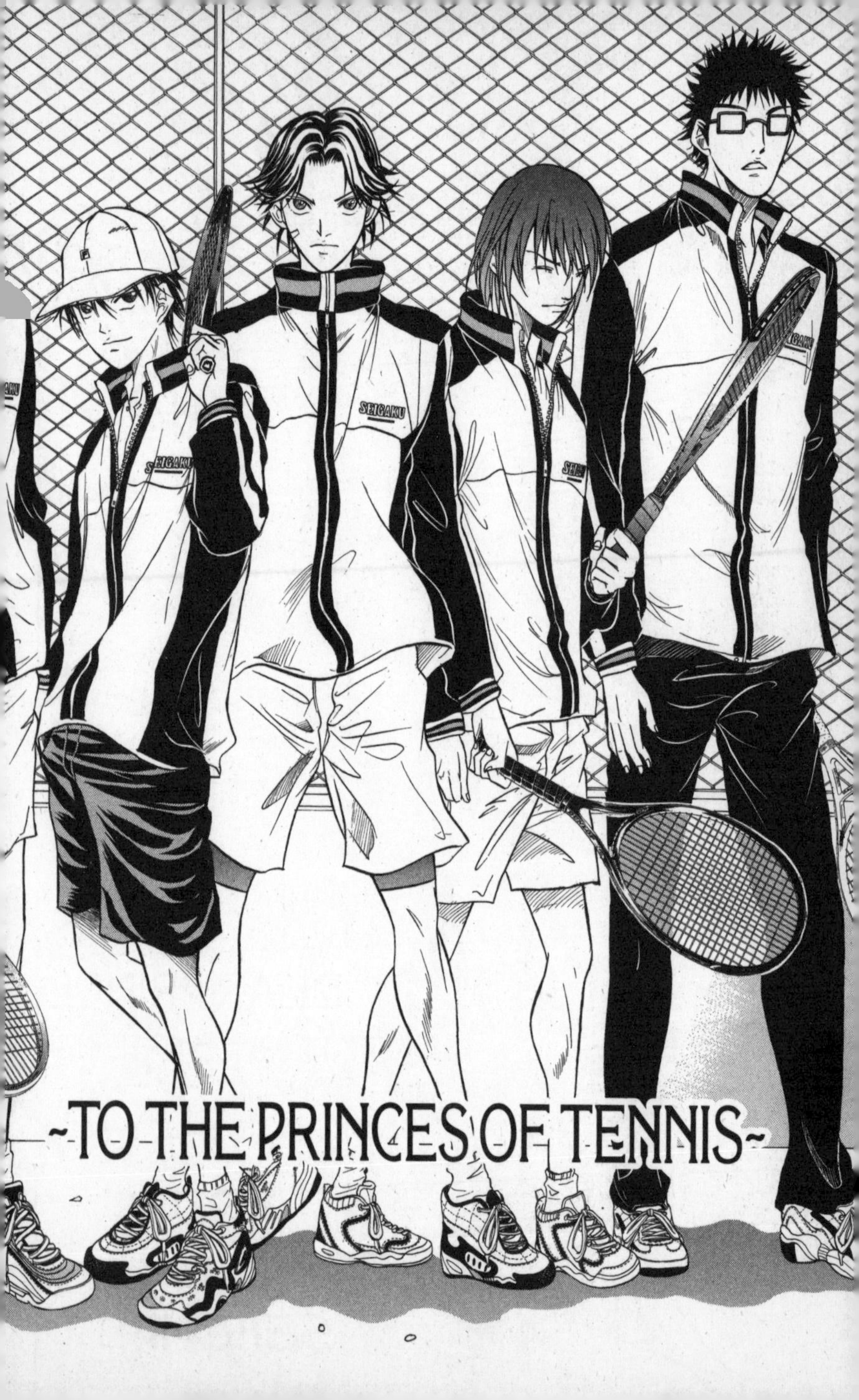
~TO THE PRINCES OF TENNIS~
SEIGAKU

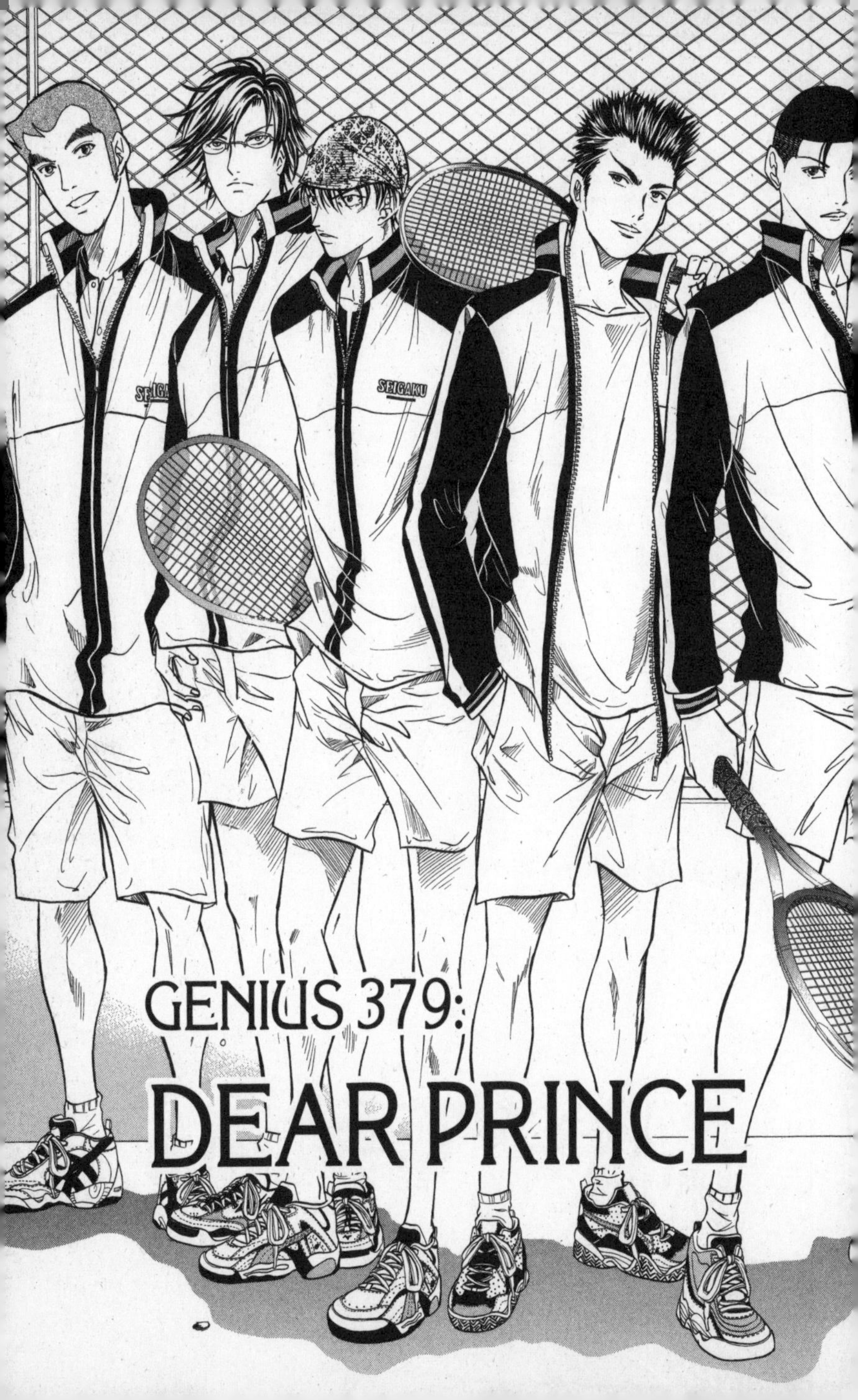
SEIGAKU
GENIUS 379:
DEAR PRINCE

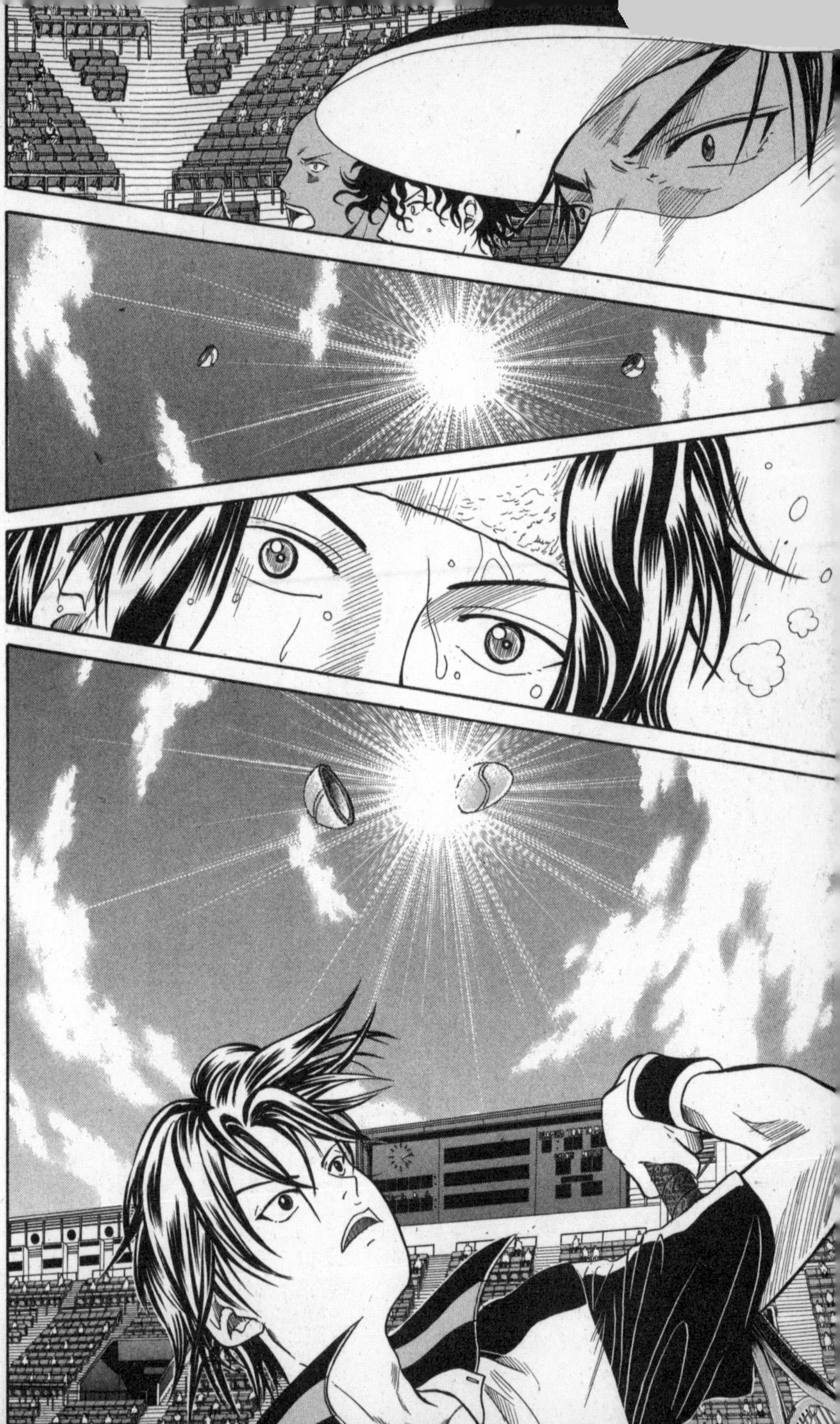

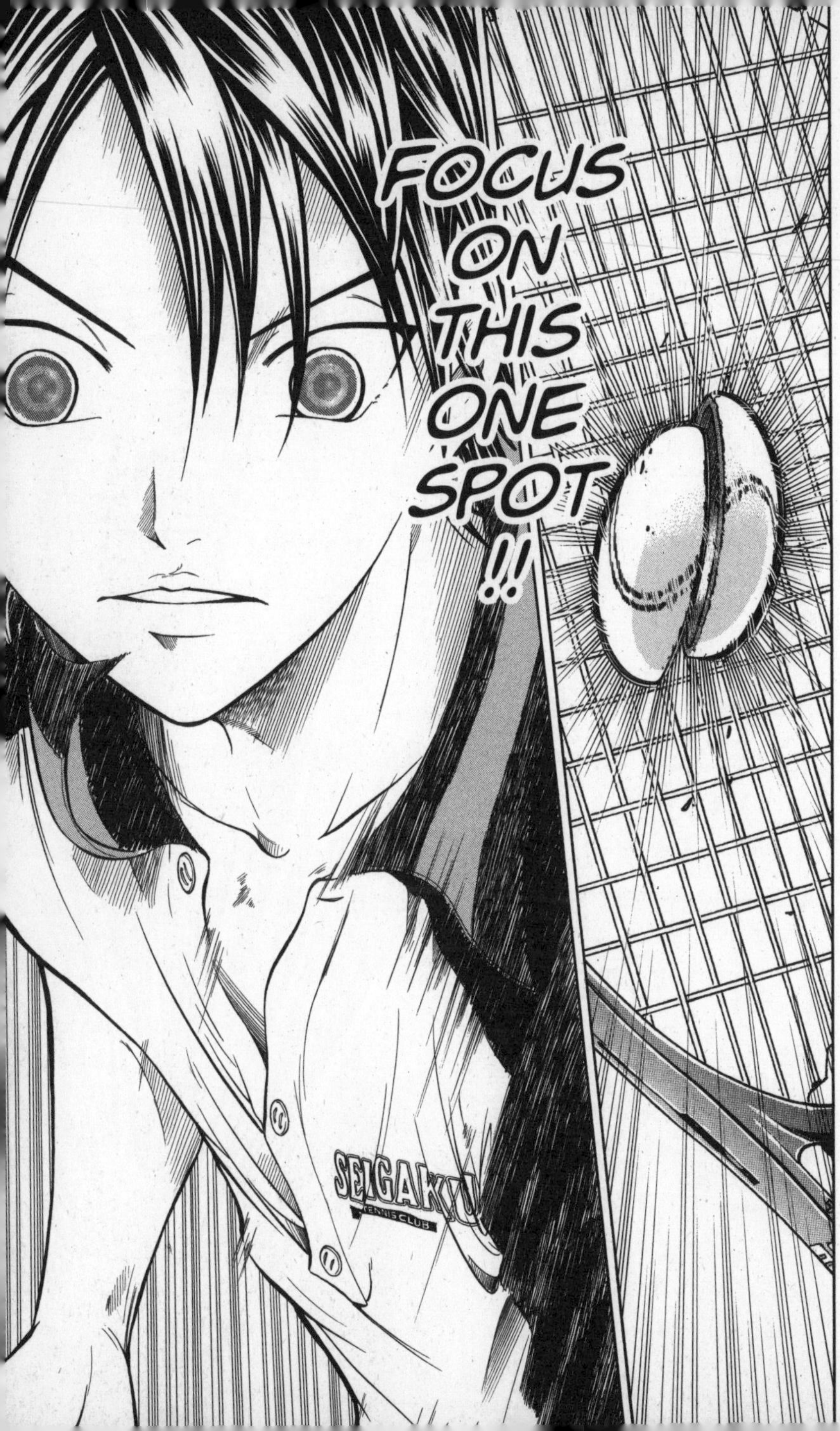
FOCUS ON THIS ONE SPOT!!
SEIGAKU TENNIS CLUB

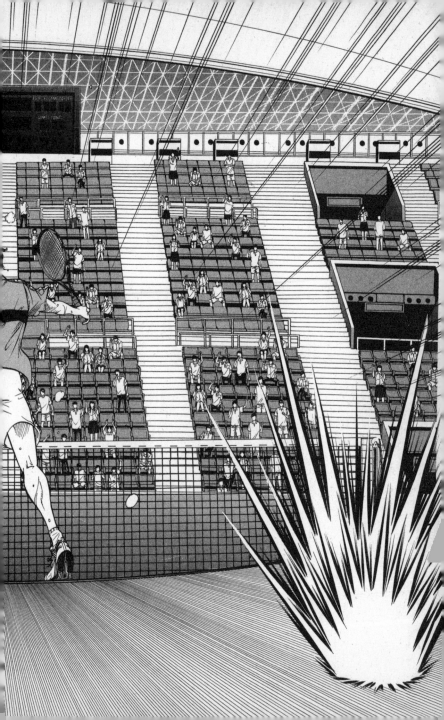

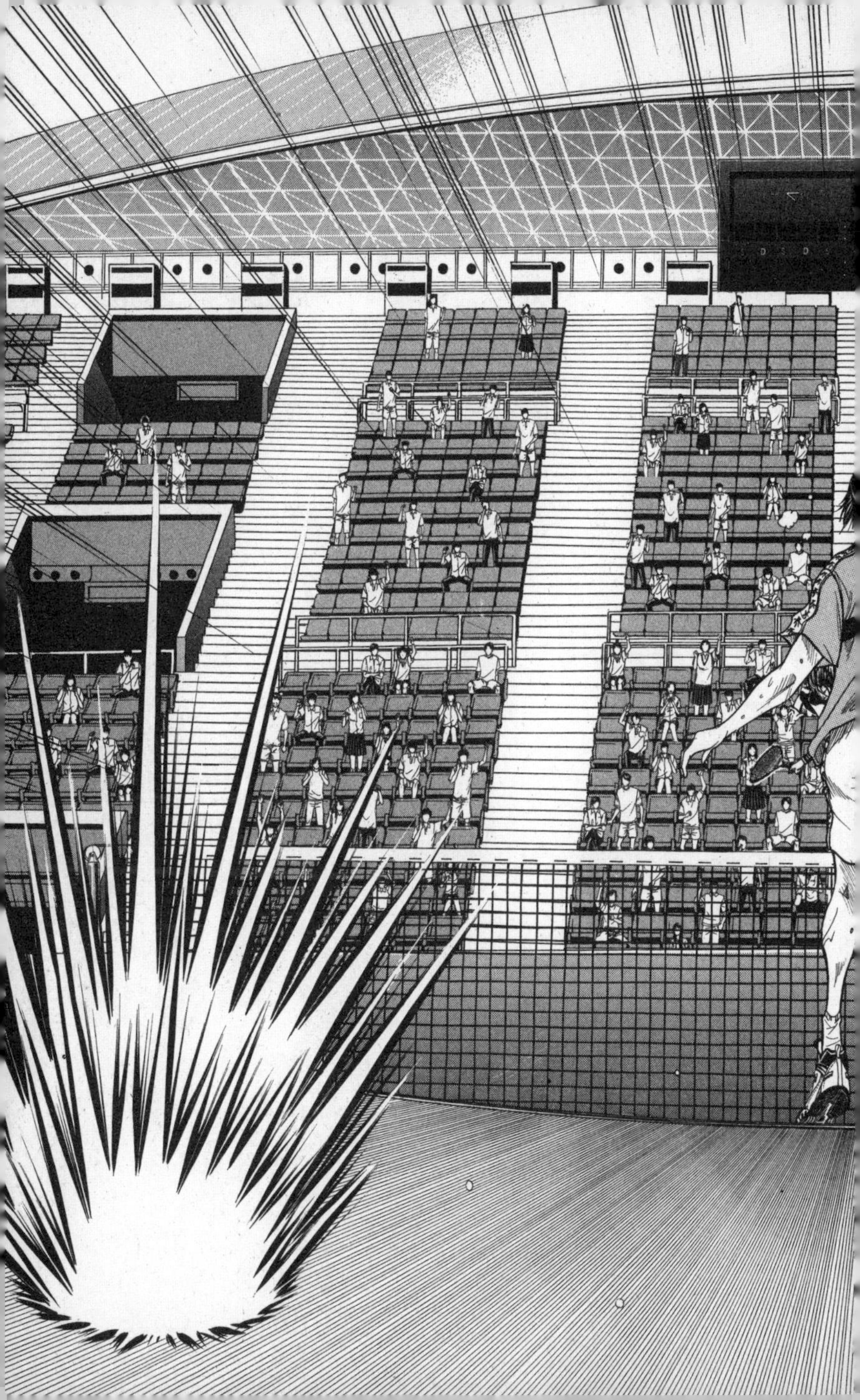

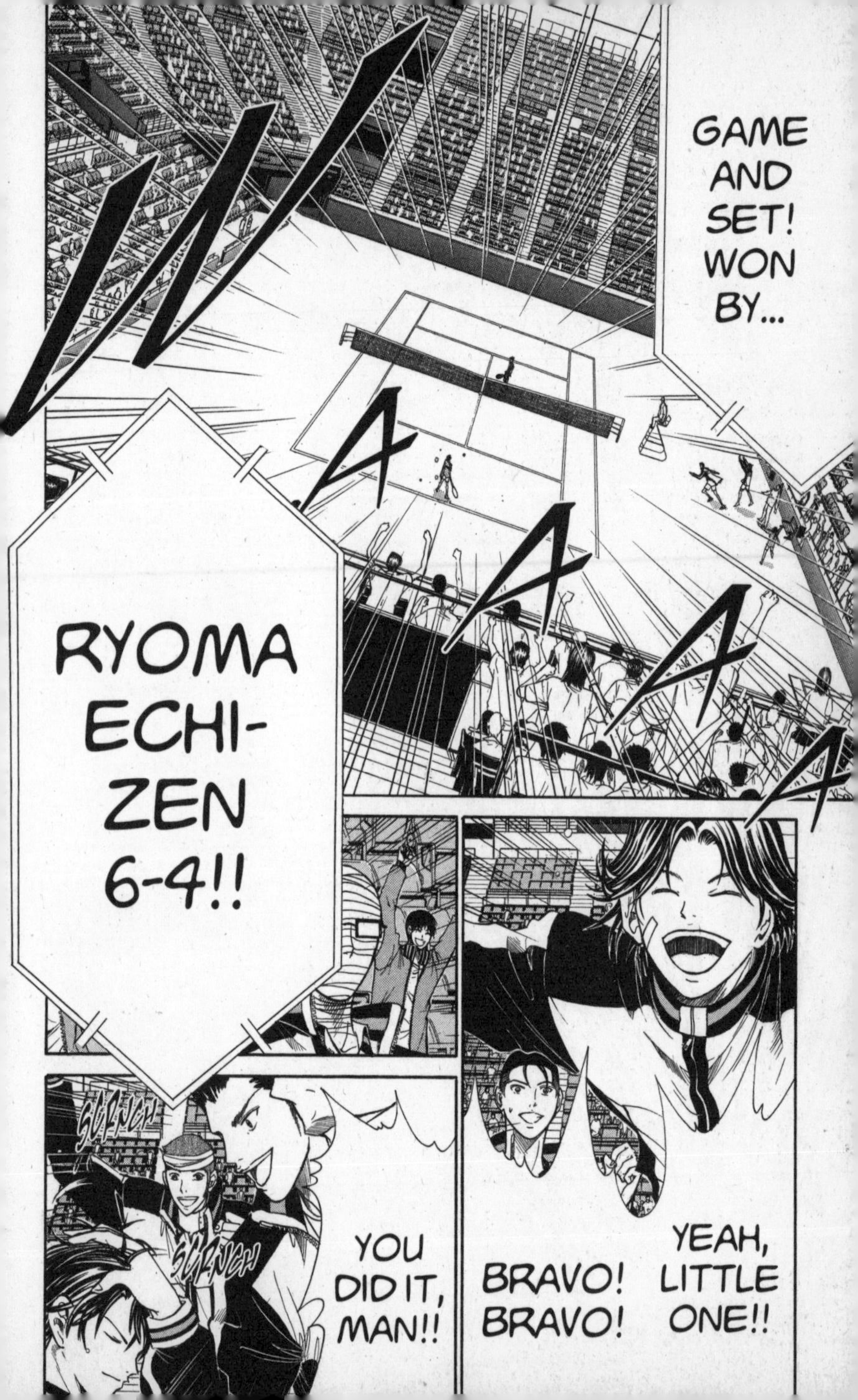
GAME AND SET! WON BY...
WAAAA
RYOMA ECHIZEN 6-4!!
YEAH, LITTLE ONE!!
BRAVO! BRAVO!
YOU DID IT, MAN!!

LET'S GO, KUNI-MITSU...

WE'RE THE BEST IN THE COUNTRY.

... YEAH.

EVEN YOU CAN LAUGH LIKE THAT HUH?

Hehe

Ahem

....! PRETEND YOU NEVER SAW THAT.

NOT SO FAST, KUNI-MITSU.

WAAAAA

SEIGAKU

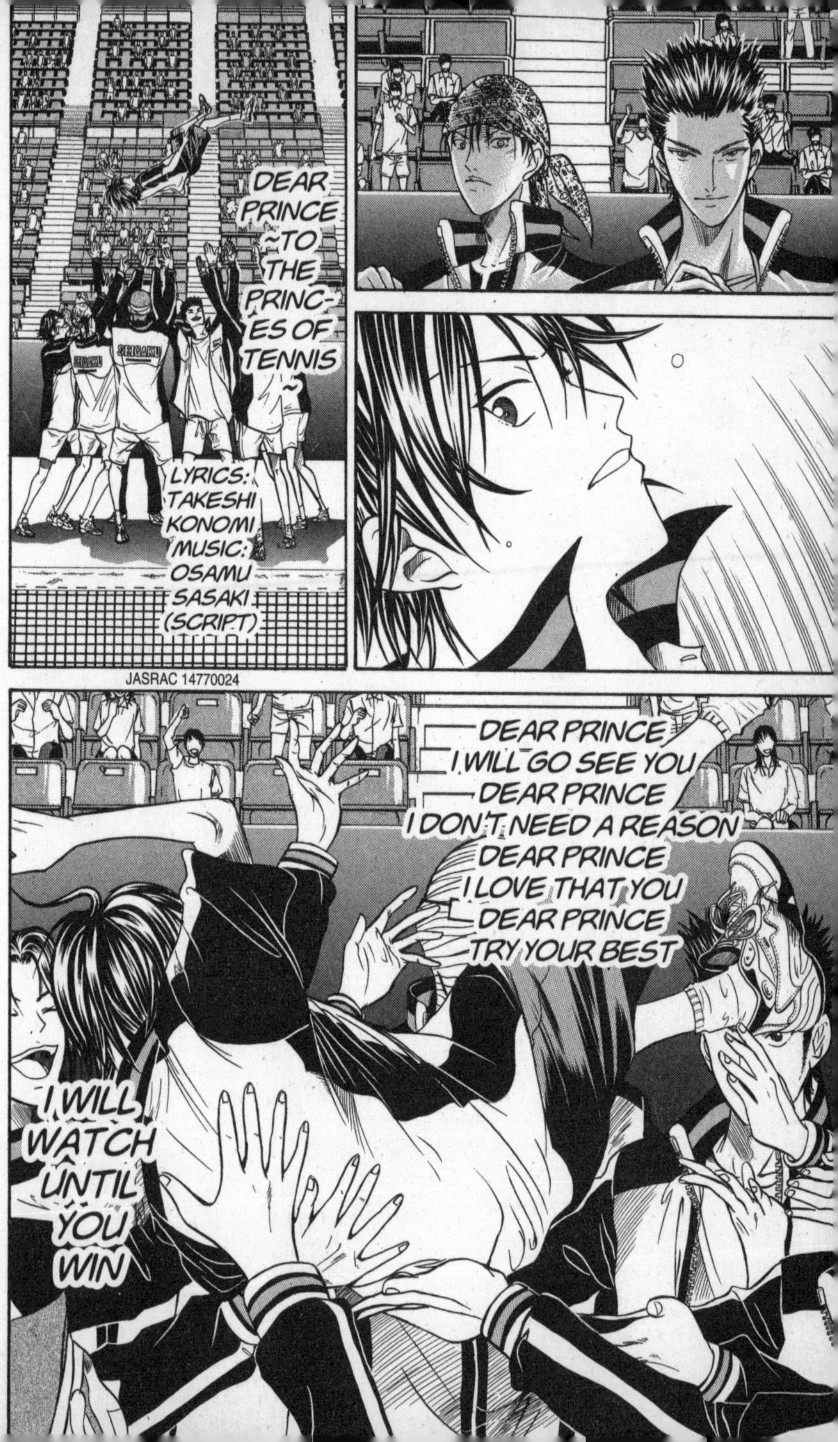
DEAR PRINCE ~TO THE PRINC-ES OF TENNIS~
LYRICS: TAKESHI KONOMI MUSIC: OSAMU SASAKI (SCRIPT)
JASRAC 14770024
DEAR PRINCE I WILL GO SEE YOU DEAR PRINCE I DON'T NEED A REASON DEAR PRINCE I LOVE THAT YOU DEAR PRINCE TRY YOUR BEST
I WILL WATCH UNTIL YOU WIN

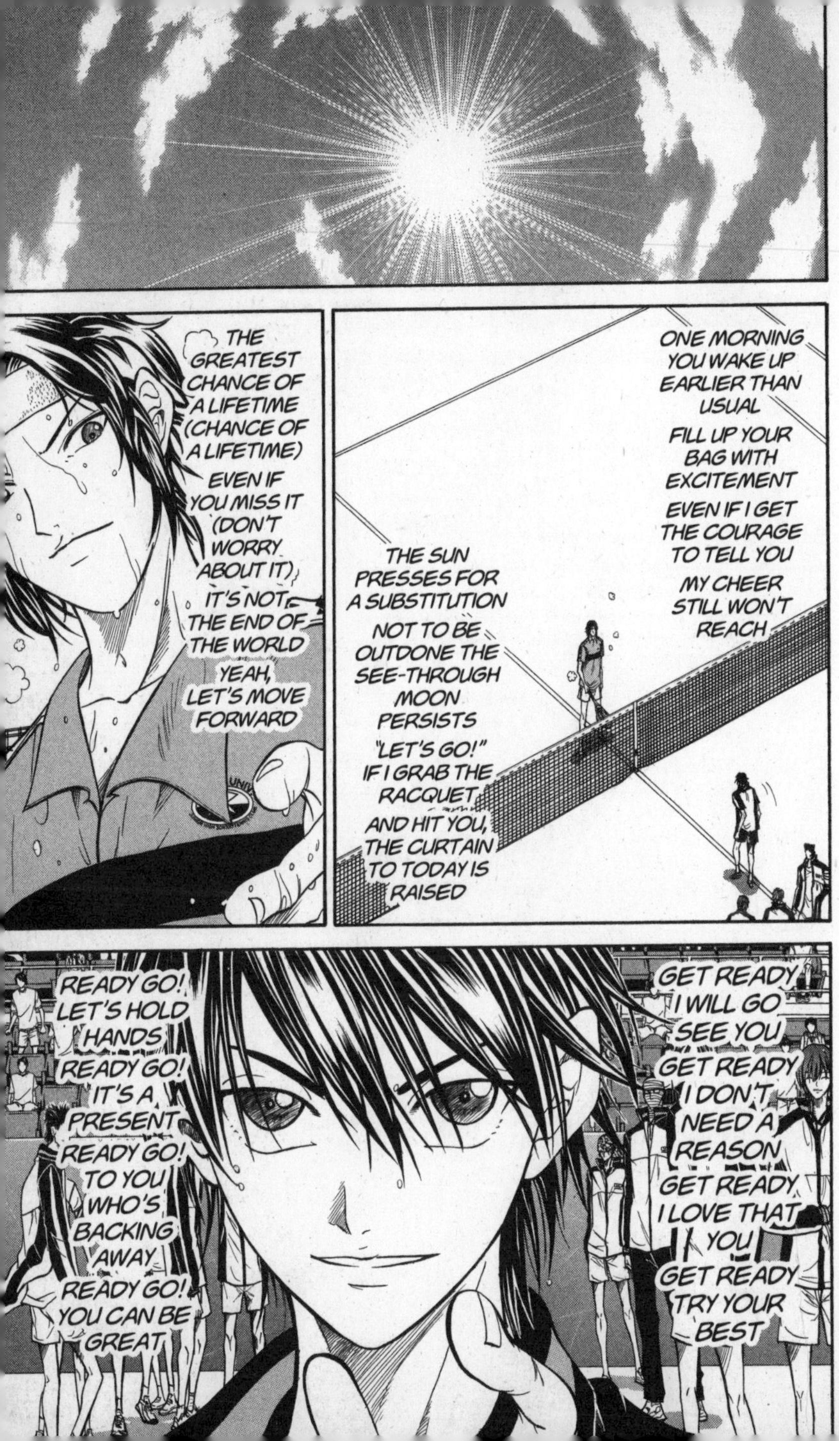
ONE MORNING YOU WAKE UP EARLIER THAN USUAL
FILL UP YOUR BAG WITH EXCITEMENT
EVEN IF I GET THE COURAGE TO TELL YOU
MY CHEER STILL WON'T REACH
THE SUN PRESSES FOR A SUBSTITUTION
NOT TO BE OUTDONE THE SEE-THROUGH MOON PERSISTS
"LET'S GO!" IF I GRAB THE RACQUET
AND HIT YOU, THE CURTAIN TO TODAY IS RAISED
THE GREATEST CHANCE OF A LIFETIME (CHANCE OF A LIFETIME)
EVEN IF YOU MISS IT (DON'T WORRY ABOUT IT)
IT'S NOT THE END OF THE WORLD
YEAH, LET'S MOVE FORWARD
GET READY I WILL GO SEE YOU
GET READY I DON'T NEED A REASON
GET READY I LOVE THAT YOU
GET READY TRY YOUR BEST
READY GO! LET'S HOLD HANDS
READY GO! IT'S A PRESENT
READY GO! TO YOU WHO'S BACKING AWAY
READY GO! YOU CAN BE GREAT

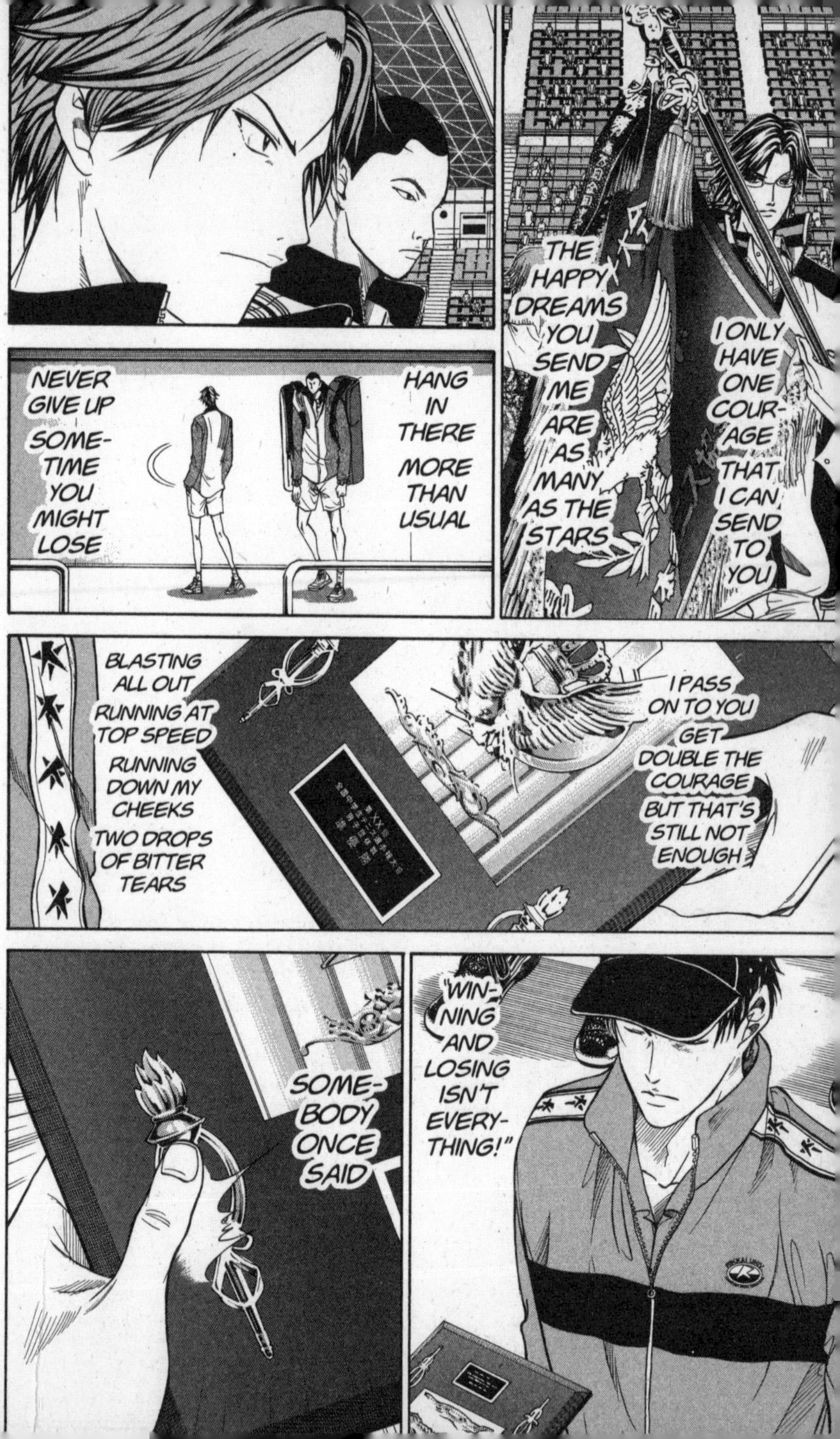
I ONLY HAVE ONE COURAGE THAT I CAN SEND TO YOU
THE HAPPY DREAMS YOU SEND ME ARE AS MANY AS THE STARS
HANG IN THERE
MORE THAN USUAL
NEVER GIVE UP
SOMETIME YOU MIGHT LOSE
I PASS ON TO YOU
GET DOUBLE THE COURAGE
BUT THAT'S STILL NOT ENOUGH
BLASTING ALL OUT
RUNNING AT TOP SPEED
RUNNING DOWN MY CHEEKS
TWO DROPS OF BITTER TEARS
"WINNING AND LOSING ISN'T EVERYTHING!"
SOMEBODY ONCE SAID

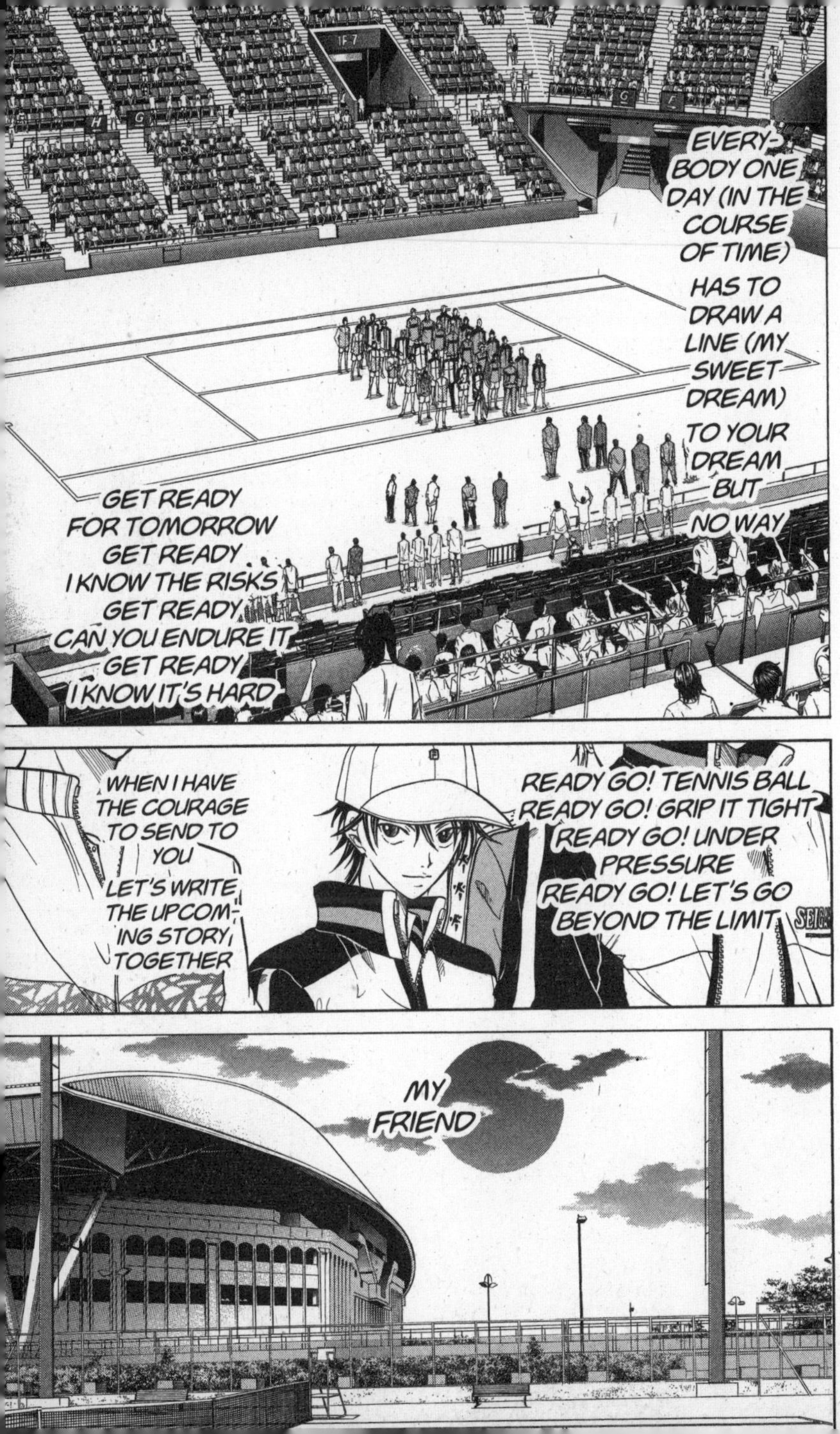
EVERYBODY ONE DAY (IN THE COURSE OF TIME) HAS TO DRAW A LINE (MY SWEET DREAM) TO YOUR DREAM BUT NO WAY
GET READY FOR TOMORROW GET READY I KNOW THE RISKS GET READY CAN YOU ENDURE IT GET READY I KNOW IT'S HARD
READY GO! TENNIS BALL READY GO! GRIP IT TIGHT READY GO! UNDER PRESSURE READY GO! LET'S GO BEYOND THE LIMIT
WHEN I HAVE THE COURAGE TO SEND TO YOU LET'S WRITE THE UPCOMING STORY TOGETHER
MY FRIEND

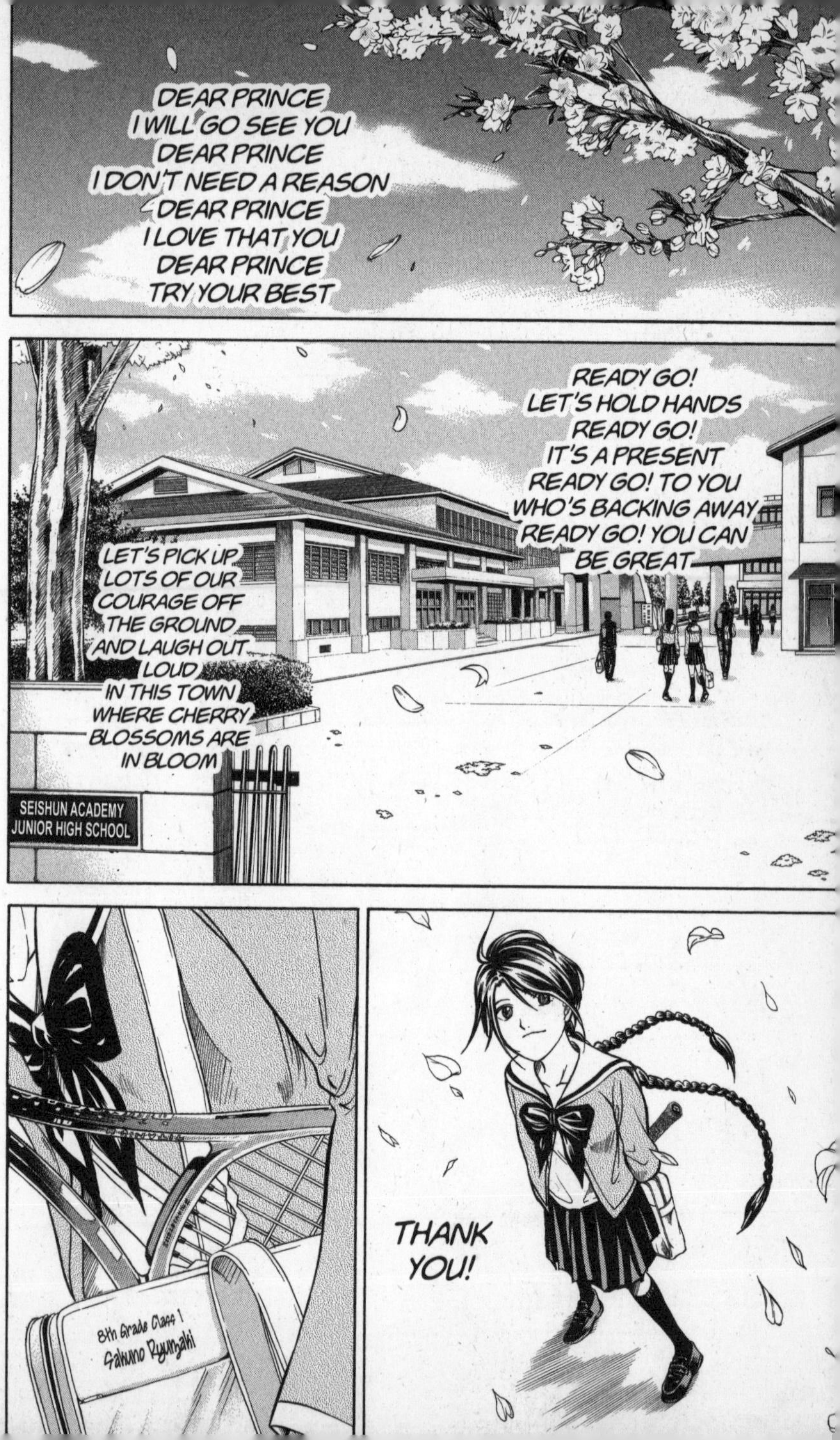
DEAR PRINCE
I WILL GO SEE YOU
DEAR PRINCE
I DON'T NEED A REASON
DEAR PRINCE
I LOVE THAT YOU
DEAR PRINCE
TRY YOUR BEST
READY GO! LET'S HOLD HANDS READY GO! IT'S A PRESENT READY GO! TO YOU WHO'S BACKING AWAY READY GO! YOU CAN BE GREAT
LET'S PICK UP LOTS OF OUR COURAGE OFF THE GROUND AND LAUGH OUT LOUD IN THIS TOWN WHERE CHERRY BLOSSOMS ARE IN BLOOM
SEISHUN ACADEMY JUNIOR HIGH SCHOOL
THANK YOU!
8th Grade Class 1
Sakuno Ryuzaki

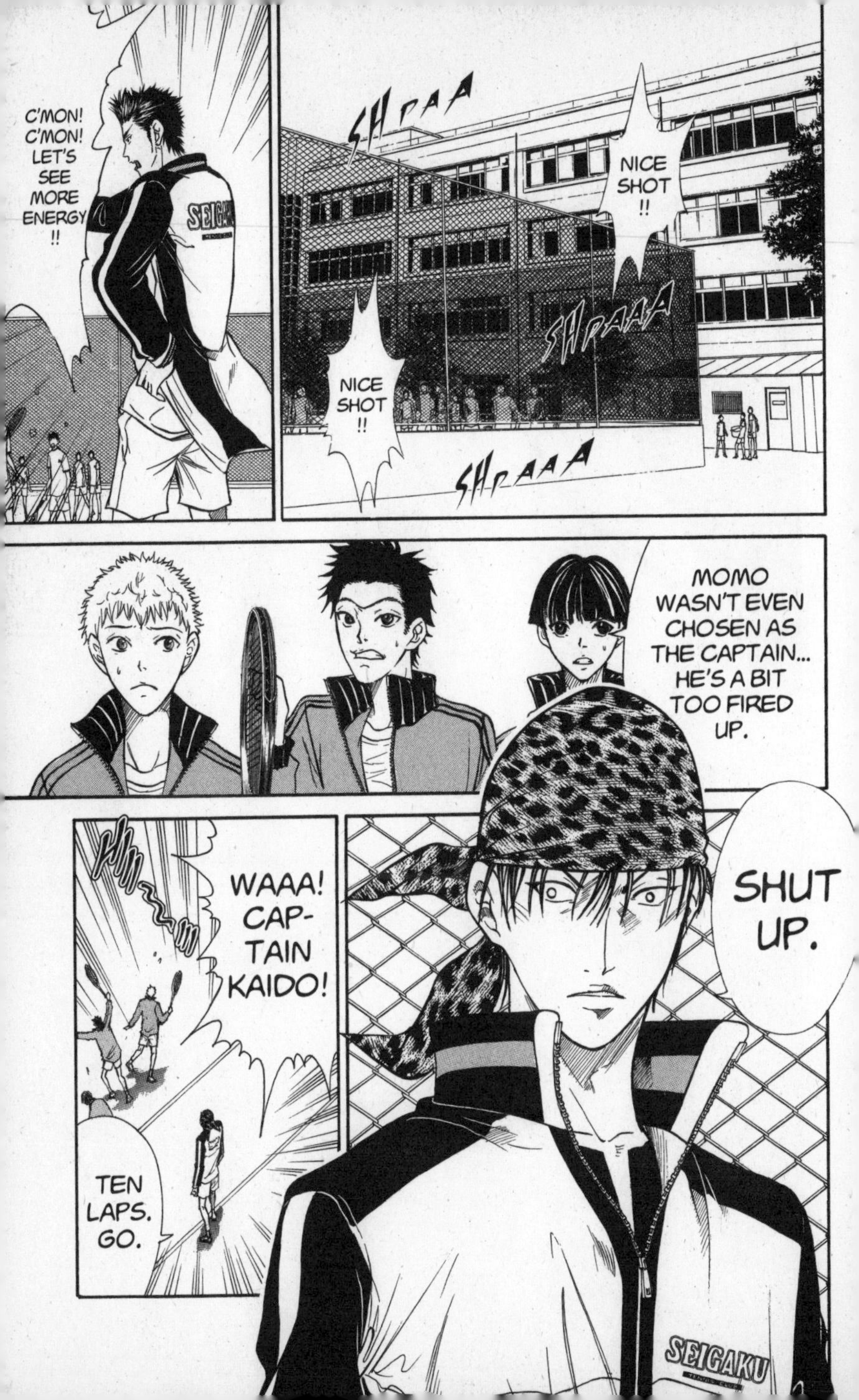
SHPAA
NICE SHOT !!
SHPAAA
NICE SHOT !!
SHPAAA
C'MON! C'MON! LET'S SEE MORE ENERGY !!
SEIGAKU
MOMO WASN'T EVEN CHOSEN AS THE CAPTAIN... HE'S A BIT TOO FIRED UP.
SHUT UP.
WAAA! CAP-TAIN KAIDO!
TEN LAPS. GO.
SEIGAKU

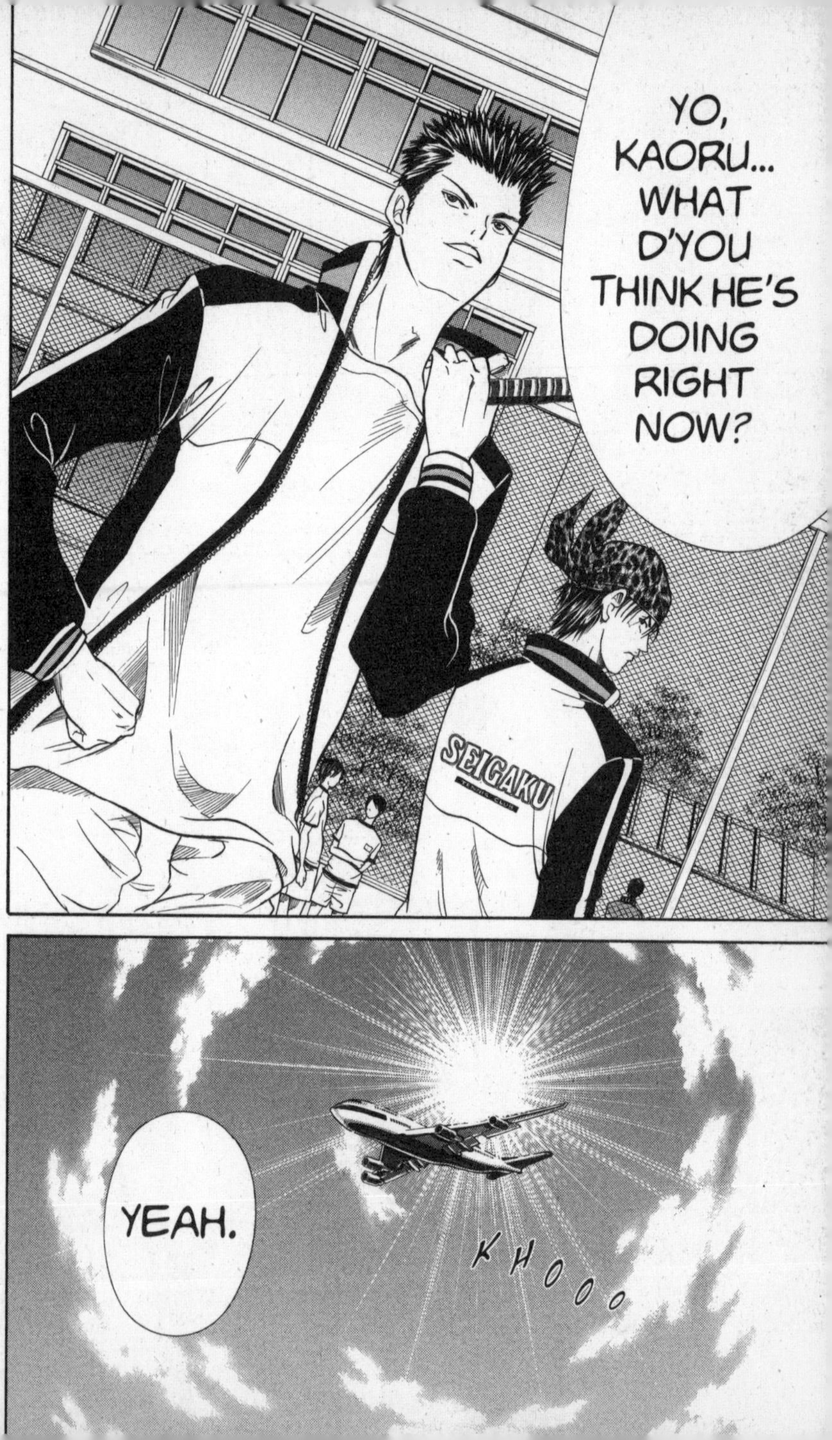
YO, KAORU... WHAT D'YOU THINK HE'S DOING RIGHT NOW?
SEIGAKU
YEAH.
KHOOO

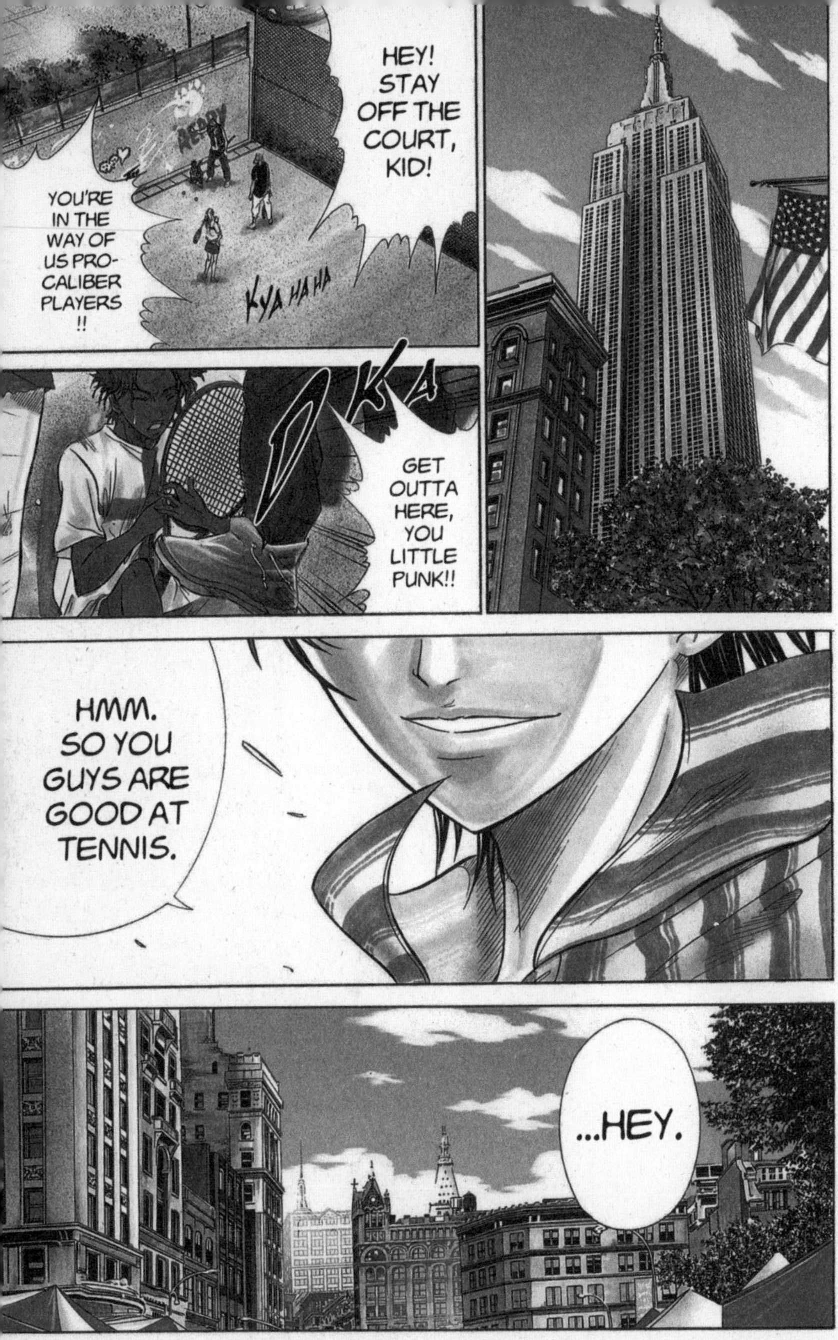

HEY! STAY OFF THE COURT, KID!
YOU'RE IN THE WAY OF US PRO-CALIBER PLAYERS!!
KYA HAHA
DOKA
GET OUTTA HERE, YOU LITTLE PUNK!!
HMM. SO YOU GUYS ARE GOOD AT TENNIS.
...HEY.

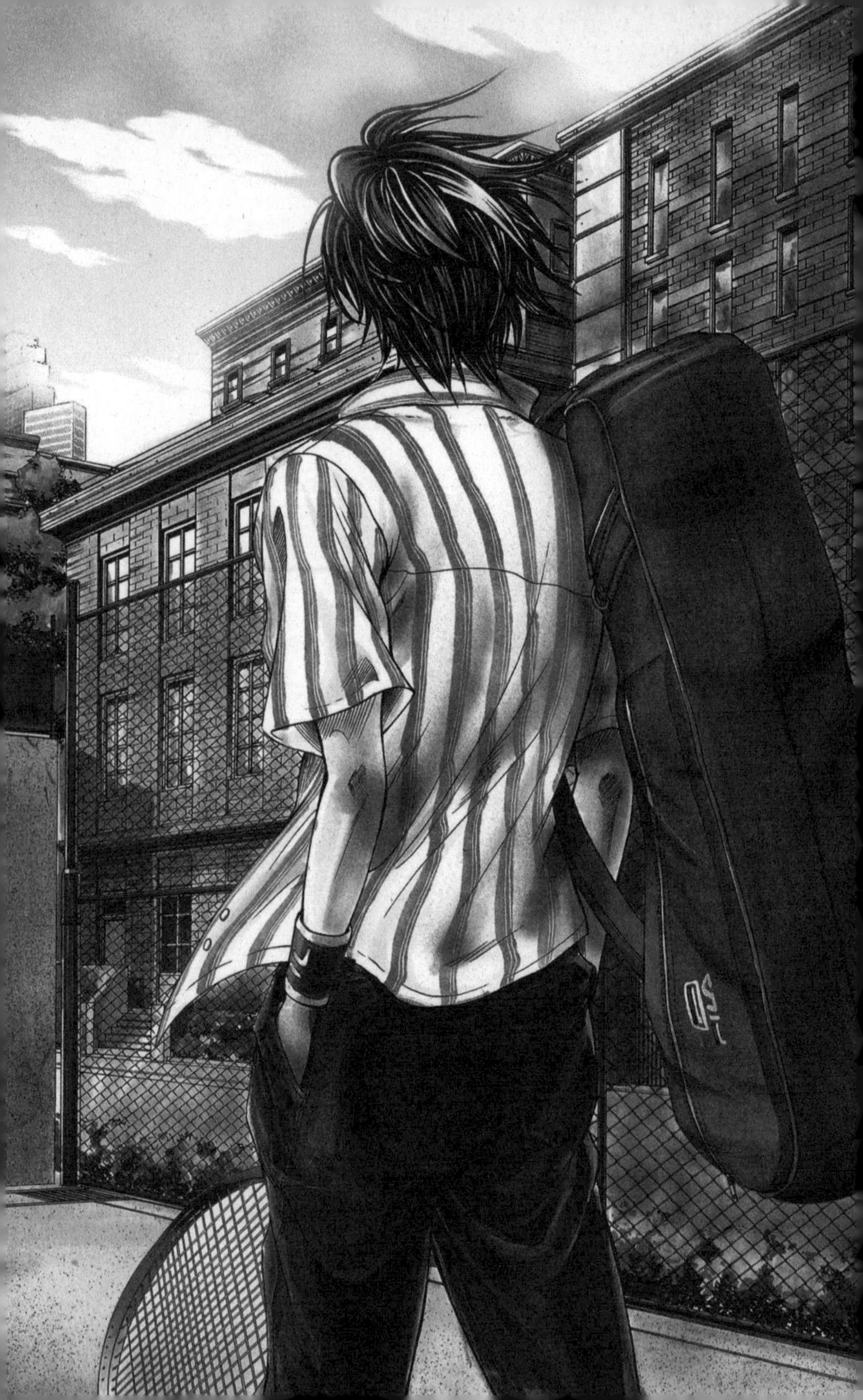

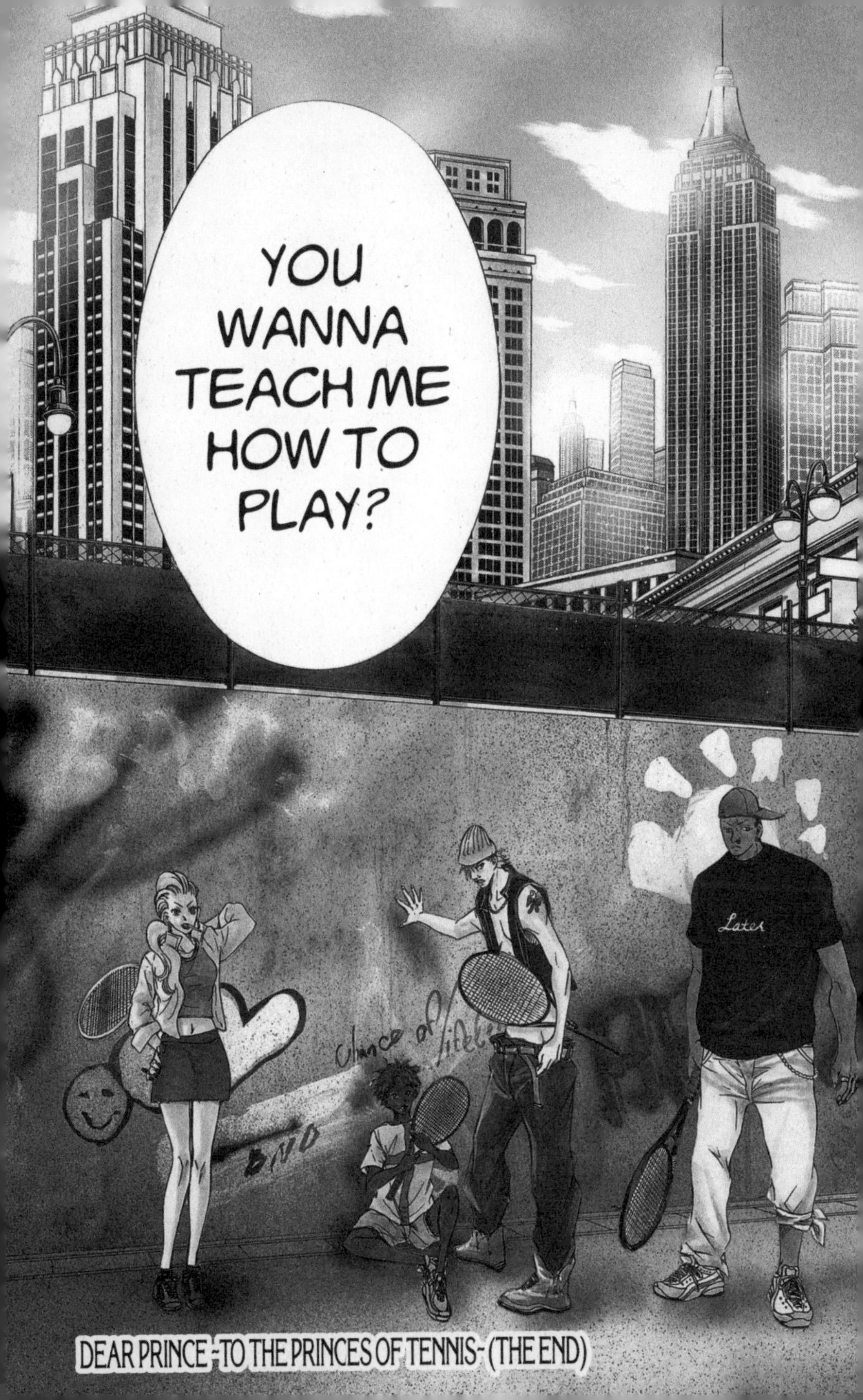
YOU WANNA TEACH ME HOW TO PLAY?
Later
DEAR PRINCE -TO THE PRINCES OF TENNIS- (THE END)

The top says: Mr. Takeshi Konomi
Great Work on Prince of Tennis!

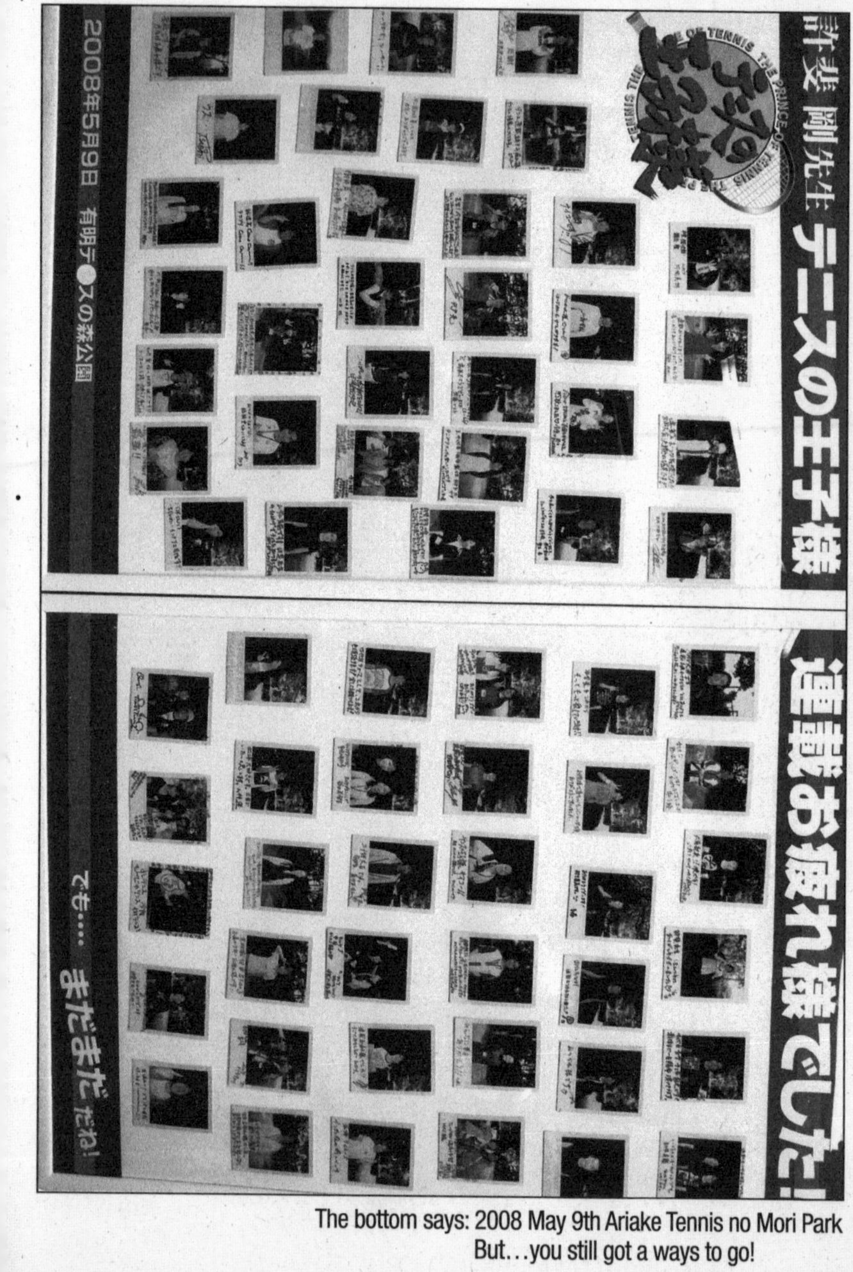
許斐 剛先生 テニスの王子様 連載お疲れ様でした!
THE PRINCE OF TENNIS
テニスの王子様
2008年5月9日 有明テ●スの森公園
でも…. まだまだだね!

The bottom says: 2008 May 9th Ariake Tennis no Mori Park
But…you still got a ways to go!

Battle of Ariakegahara

Two o'clock. The cast of the musical leaves the court to rehearse for *Dream Live*.

After the author bid farewell to them and sent them off, the "Mixed Doubles East–West Game, the Battle of Ariakegahara" was held.

The remaining members split into East and West to compete for the most wins. The losing team must drink Inui's Last Drink, the "Farewell Drink."

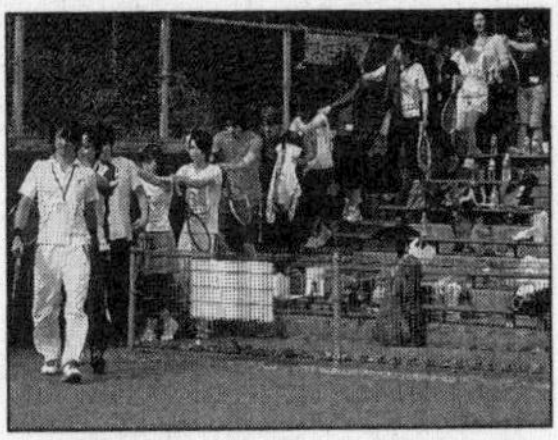

↑ West Squad Konomi Team turning into a battle group.

We all split into our teams to practice, but when the West–Konomi Team came back, they were truly an army.

↓ Announcers from Nelke Planning

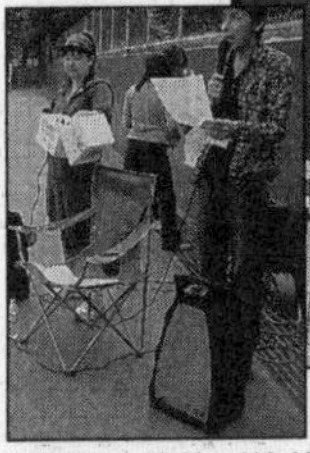

↑ Ms. Nogami (left) and Mr. Matsuda (right) got laughs as if they were a husband-wife comedy duo.

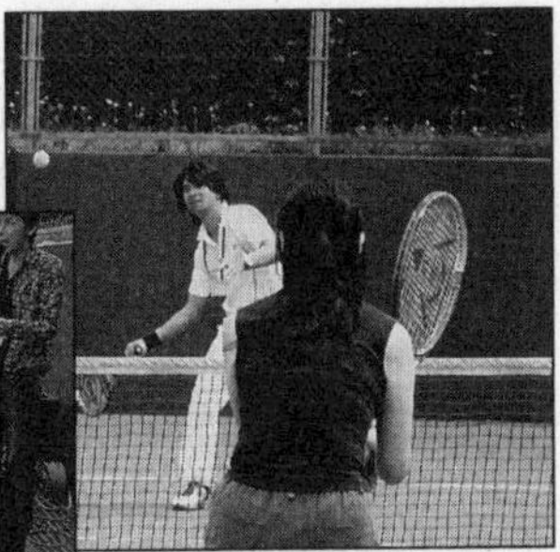

↑ Grudge match. Author Pair vs. Kaida Pair's tense moment! Where will this ball go?

When the East–Kataoka Producer Team huddled up, Ryutaro Okiayu (Kunimitsu Tezuka) brought his team together by saying "Let's stay focused."

It was nine pairs vs. nine pairs, so whoever won five games first would win. West–Konomi Team falls to three wins and four losses! They cannot afford to lose another game.

And that is when the long-awaited Konomi Pair steps in. Facing them is none other than Yuki Kaida, who beat the author in the first round of the Prince of Tennis Cup.

↓ East Squad . ↓ West Squad

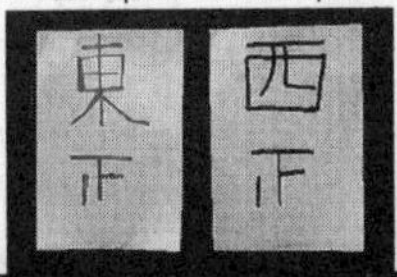
東
西

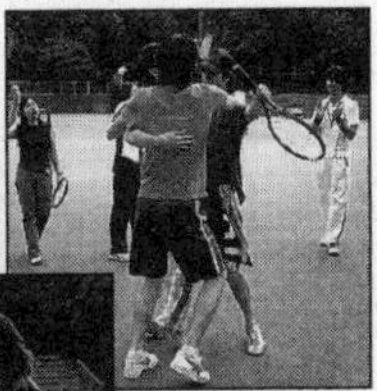

↑ West Squad rejoicing.

The author takes a drink of water and throws the bottle toward the bench. With the sound of that thump, the author's intensity is felt by the crowd.

Seeing that, Yuki Kaida also takes a drink of water and throws the bottle toward the bench. Sparks fly between them!

The Konomi Pair won. An overwhelming victory that made us question his first round loss! Yuki Kaida graciously accepts defeat.

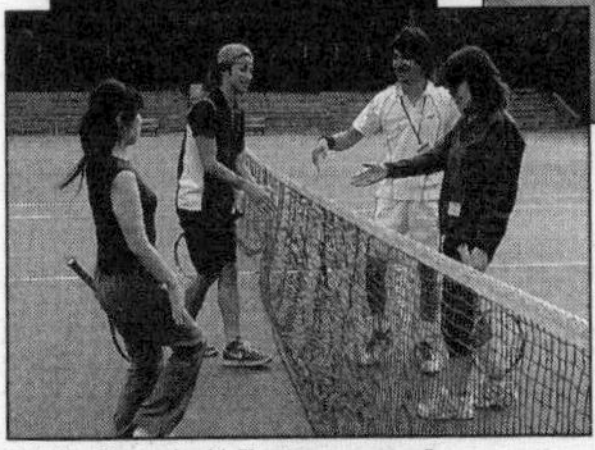

↑ Author Konami said, "I got my revenge."

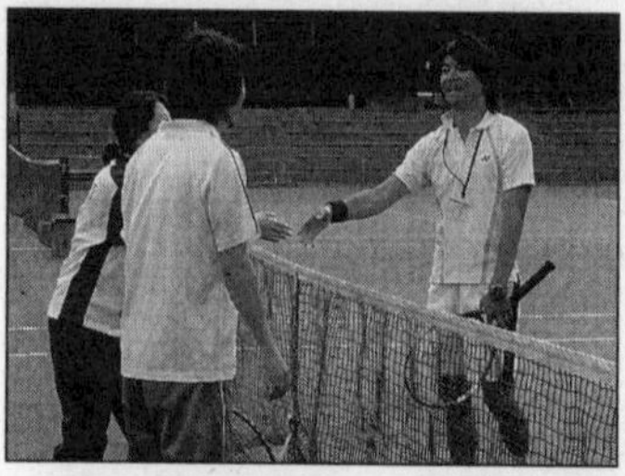

Up comes the last pair. But West–Konomi Team, due to the lack of players, could not put together the final pair.

The East Squad's final pair is Ms. Minagawa and the director of the live-action film, Mr. Abe.

The West Squad sends out Takeshi Konomi to face them by himself. A two-against-one battle.

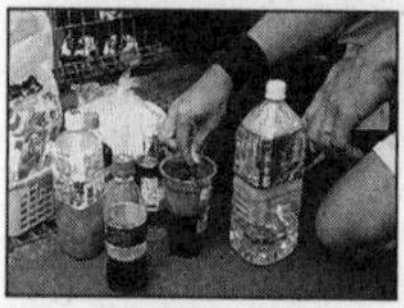

↑ Inui making his Farewell Drink

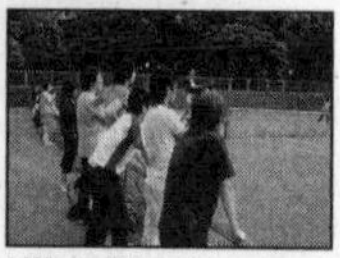

↑ What will the outcome be...

As expected, the crowd gets fired up and both sides loudly cheer for their teams. It was the moment when the excitement was at its highest throughout the whole event.

And...

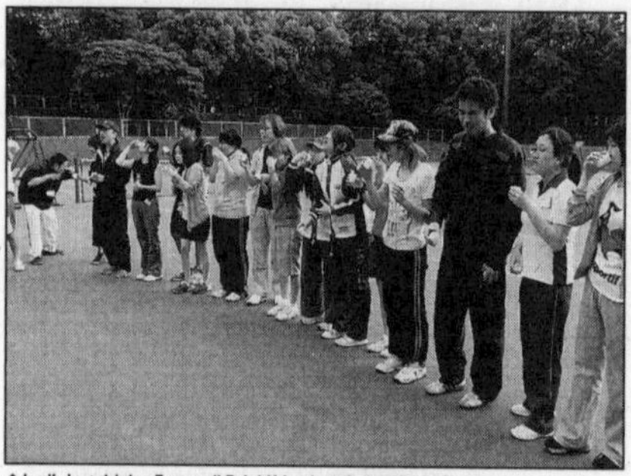

↑ Inui's last drink – Farewell Drink!! Look at their expressions!

The West–Kataoka Team holding the Farewell Drink.

Ms. Minagawa winces at the strange liquid that looks as if it was scooped out from the gutters of hell.

The entire East Squad reluctantly drinks it up! The winners, West–Konomi Team, watches them groan with beaming smiles on their faces.

That ended the Prince of Tennis Serialization Completion Memorial Party.

Although they had to drink the Farewell Drink, the East Squad looked fulfilled. The West Squad as well, of course.

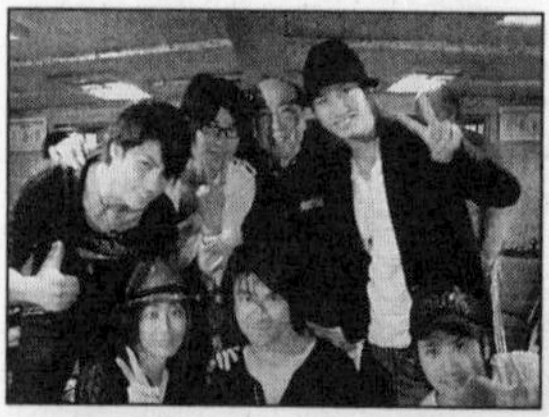

But that was not the end. It wasn't called the Daytime Portion for nothing–the evening portion was still left.

The evening portion included a monja *[a type of Japanese pan-fried batter with various ingredients – Ed.]* party on a houseboat. With members of SCRIPT that sang the theme song for *The Prince of Tennis* movie joining, over fifty of us boarded the houseboat.

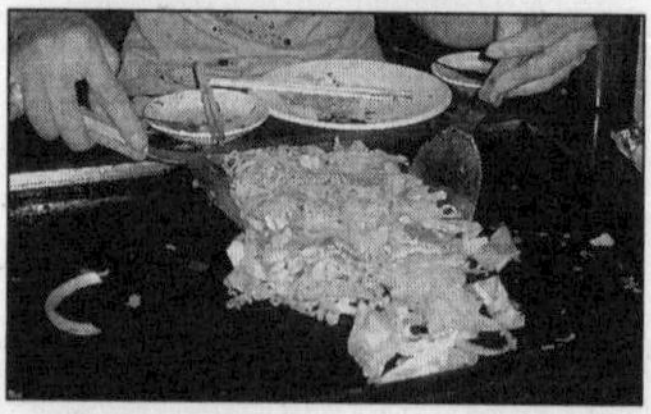

Character songs from the anime played inside the houseboat and everybody began to hum along.

The party continued on with everybody eating and drinking.

A rock-paper-scissors tournament was held for the prizes left over from the day portion.

↑ Monja party heating up. The view was great too!

The prizes left over were two DSs, an iPod Touch, and an autograph from the author (w/illustration of Shusuke).

Everybody prepares for the rock-paper-scissors tournament with serious expressions on their faces. Toshiyuki Toyonaga (Kentaro Aoi) who drew the 'touch an iPod Touch' card was eager for revenge.

And that is exactly what he got. He won the rock-paper-scissors game to win the iPod Touch. I guess these things do happen. It goes without saying that it was exciting.

With everything concluded and the boat on its way back to the pier, there was a surprise gift from everybody to the author.

↑ A surprise for the author! Author Konomi thanking everybody.

A beautiful bouquet of roses and two big panels with the words "Mr. Takeshi Konomi Great Work on *The Prince of Tennis*!" written on them.

The panel had pictures and comments from everybody that attended the event.

The author was filled with emotions. A word from the author, a round of applause, and the party ended.

It was a party fitting for the ending of a long nine-year serialization...

After the event

Ms. Minagawa's comment:
An unbelievable fourth place finish, paired up with Momo from the musical. I wish we could've won...tut. Thank you for a great event, Mr. Konomi!!

Comments from the six fan representatives

Aihara: I thought it was a joke when I received the invitation. I had a lot of fun and was sad to see it end. To Mr. Konomi for his planning and to the staff, thank you so much.

Shimizu: I am only twenty-two years old, but it is the greatest memory of my life. Thank you.

Iwamoto: It was a dreamlike day. Thank you very much. I will never forget it. Even in my next life!

Ohura: I always wanted to play tennis with Mr. Konomi, so I had a great time. I was really lucky to be paired up with Mr. Konomi for the doubles tournament. It will be a lifelong memory. Thank you.

Iwai: You're the best!! I love you♥.

Iwahara: Thank you so much for inviting me today. I love you.

-Special Novella-
Shoot Toward Graduation

Written by Takeshi Konomi

Three days after winning a tough battle against the champions Rikkai, after Seishun's tennis team led by Kunimitsu Tezuka won their national title, Ryoma Echizen left for America...

Months go by as a matter of fact, like turning pages of a Weekly Shonen Jump. Just as the cherry blossoms are about to bloom, the 26th graduation for Seishun Academy is about to take place.

Two girls walk briskly across campus carrying what looks to be colorful handmade paper flowers decorating a large sign with the word "Graduation" written on it.

"Be careful not to trip, Sakuno! Watch where you're..." Tomoka falls.

Tomoka Osakada—yes, that girl in Ryoma's cheering group.

"Are you okay, Tomoka...?"

Sakuno worriedly peeks from behind the sign. They see that five or six of the flowers have fallen off the sign. They look at each other.

"Oops... It fell off, but oh well!"

"No, Tomo."

"I guess not, huh?"

Tomoka laughs innocently as she sticks her tongue out.

"Then I'll go get some tape, so wait here!" Tomoka says and quickly turns the corner of the campus and disappears.

"..."

The warm spring sun wraps Sakuno, who stands there stunned. But the situation drastically changes in an instant.

A galumphing clothed gorilla appears and roars.

It was Mr. Saitoda the P.E. teacher.

"Hey! Hurry up and take that sign to the front gate!"
The gori...Saitoda fiercely pounds his chest.

Sakuno struggles to run carrying the sign that is almost as big as her. She runs frantically.

The roaring from behind grows quieter.

Sakuno, who successfully escaped, arrives near the gate. Her heart is still pounding. Then she hears a voice from the front.

"Hey, where's the graduation ceremony taking place?"

The sign is too big for Sakuno to see who is in front of her. She can only manage to see the person's feet.

"Uh, um...in the gymnasium...it's...it's to the right."

The owner of the voice begins to move his feet to the right. But it quickly stops, spins around and heads to the left.

"Hmm. As usual."

Recognizing the voice, she hurriedly lowers the sign and stares in the direction of the voice.

The wind wildly flutters Sakuno's French braid along with the cherry blossom petals.

The graduation ceremony progresses and Principal Ishikawa's speech is long and painful.

"He talks forever as usual. He begins everything with 'Uh...' too much. It's the 75th time already," utters Momoshiro, attending the ceremony as a student representative.

"Just be quiet! Can't you at least be quiet during graduation! You dope!"

Kaido, another student representative sitting behind him, glares. They both stand up and get in each other's faces.

"You want some of this, you snake?!"

"Fine. Let's step outside!!"

They both realize something.

Everybody is staring at them.

They both sit in embarrassment.

"Those two..."

Oishi feels his stomach in pain to the very end.

"Diploma presentation!"

The graduates receive their diplomas from Principal Ishikawa, whose motto is "Mind and Body."

"Ninth Grade Class 1 Number 12, Kunimitsu Tezuka."

"Yes!"

Everybody holds their breath watching his dignified walk up to the stage.

He is highly trusted not only by his classmates, but by the teachers for leading the tennis team to a national title as the captain while serving as Student Council president.

He firmly grasps his diploma with both hands and bows deeply.

"Ninth Grade Class 2 Number 3, Shuichiro Oishi."

"Yes!"

Tears overflow in his eyes as he stares directly in front of him.

"Ninth Grade Class 4 Number 5, Takashi Kawamura."

"Y-yes..."

Taka, looking nervous, steps up onto the stage. Of course his right arm and right leg move together. His movement stops as he receives his diploma.

"Raaaaa! Great Graduation!!"

Principal Ishikawa adjusts his glasses. "Uh...okay. Next student."

The crowd erupts in laughter.

"Ninth Grade Class 6 Number 7, Eiji Kikumaru."

"Yo!"

He softly accepts his diploma, then backflips off the stage. The crowd applauds his beautiful acrobatics.

On Kikumaru's face, who responds to the crowd by waving his hand, is a big smile.

"Ninth Grade Class 6 Number 14, Shusuke Fuji."

"Yes."

Fuji steps onto the stage with a gentle expression.

The female students' sights are glued to his supple and beautiful posture.

"Ninth Grade Class 11 Number 2, Sadaharu Inui."

"...Yes."

"I am the 8,364th graduate. At this pace, this school will..."

"Uh... be quiet."

Principal Ishikawa mercilessly cuts him off. The graduation is drawing to a close.

"Graduate Representative's statement — Kunimitsu Tezuka."

"Yes!"

A dignified voice echoes in the gymnasium. As Tezuka steps onto the stage, everybody's eyes are on him.

"We were able to spend a fulfilling time at this school. There will be many obstacles in our lives. But with the things we learned here over the last three years, the time we spent with friends, everything we were able to gain by being in school clubs, we will be able to overcome them!"

"That's our Captain..."

Kaido happily nods to Momoshiro's words.

Kunimitsu's speech continues.

It is rare to hear Kunimitsu, usually a man of few words, talk this much.

"When this graduation ceremony ends, I will leave for Germany. It was my experience at this school that helped me make my decision to become a professional tennis player. I will work hard not to embarrass myself. And..."

The tennis team regulars Oishi, Fuji, Kikumaru, Kawamura, and Inui listen closely.

"...Everybody..."

Coach Ryuzaki, looking intently at them, also closes her eyes.

"Oishi, Fuji, Inui, Kikumaru, Kawamura... Thank you so much. I am grateful."

The ex-tennis team, graduating regulars, though a little confused, appear happy at Tezuka's unexpected remark.

The gymnasium is wrapped in a warm air, and one by one the attendants begin applauding.

The graduation ceremony reaches its end with a big round of applause.

"Captain...there's something I've been regretting."

The crowd buzzes.

A tennis ball comes roaring toward the stage from the very back row. Tezuka firmly catches the ball with his left hand. Without batting an eye, of course.

At the entrance of the gymnasium where the ball was shot from, there's a boy in shorts wearing a cap and gripping a racquet tightly in his left hand.

"Ryoma!!" Momo yells out.

Echizen lifts the bill of his cap. His usual confident eyes are visible.

"Will you play me one more time?"

Ignoring Oishi's unease, Tezuka firmly responds.

"Sure."

Two men separated by a net stand face to face on the Seishun Tennis Team's court.
Everybody knows how fierce the game that is about to take place will be.
But the crowd that gathers around appear strangely happy, as if they were waiting for this face-off.
And the cherry blossom petals flutter in the big blue sky.

The End

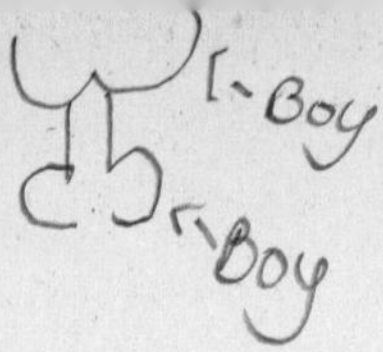
Boy
Boy

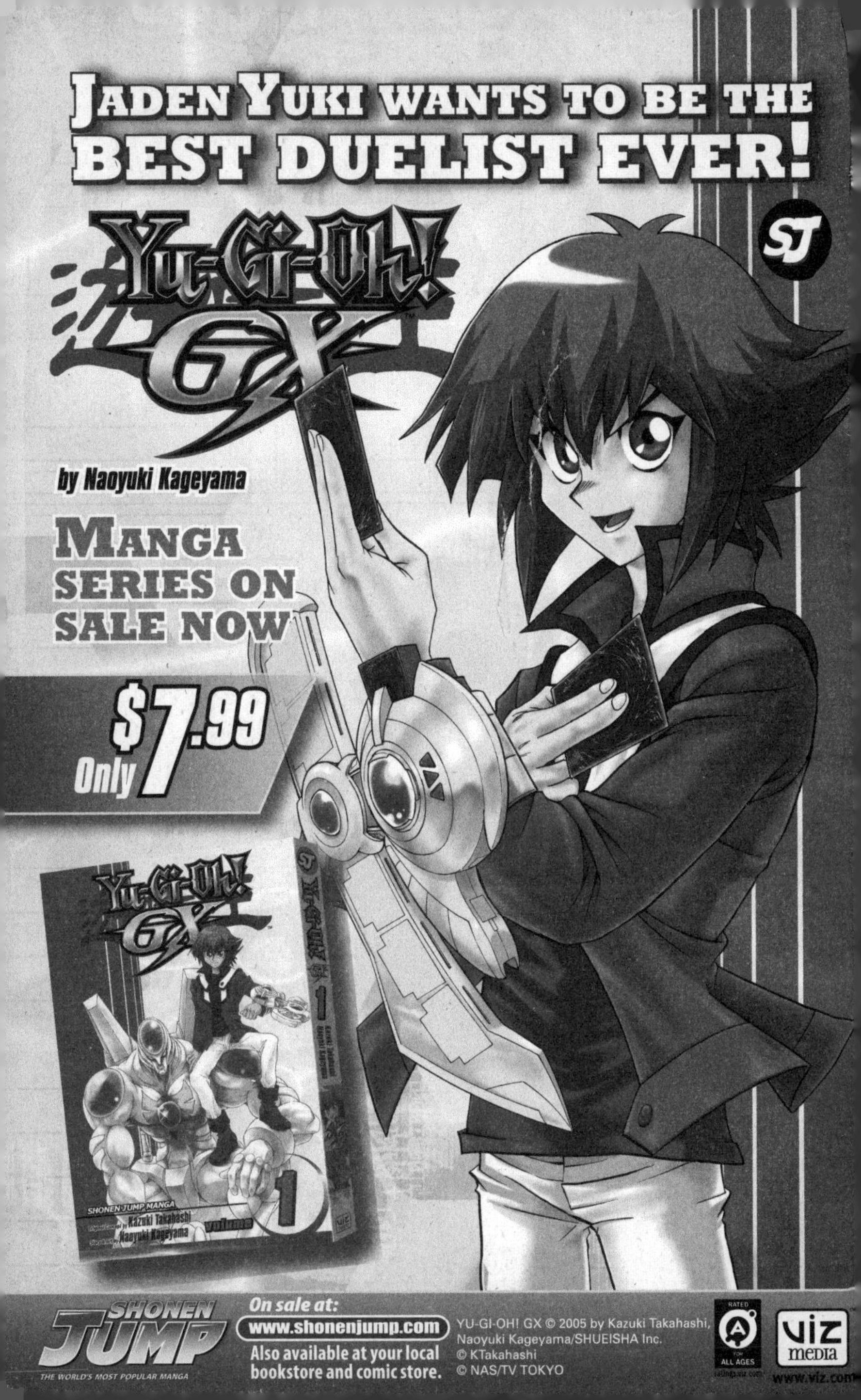
JADEN YUKI WANTS TO BE THE
BEST DUELIST EVER!
SJ
YU-GI-OH! GX
by Naoyuki Kageyama
MANGA
SERIES ON
SALE NOW
Only $7.99
YU-GI-OH! GX
SHONEN JUMP MANGA
Kazuki Takahashi
Naoyuki Kageyama
1
SHONEN JUMP
THE WORLD'S MOST POPULAR MANGA
On sale at:
www.shonenjump.com
Also available at your local
bookstore and comic store.
YU-GI-OH! GX © 2005 by Kazuki Takahashi,
Naoyuki Kageyama/SHUEISHA Inc.
© KTakahashi
© NAS/TV TOKYO
RATED
A
FOR
ALL AGES
viz media
www.viz.com

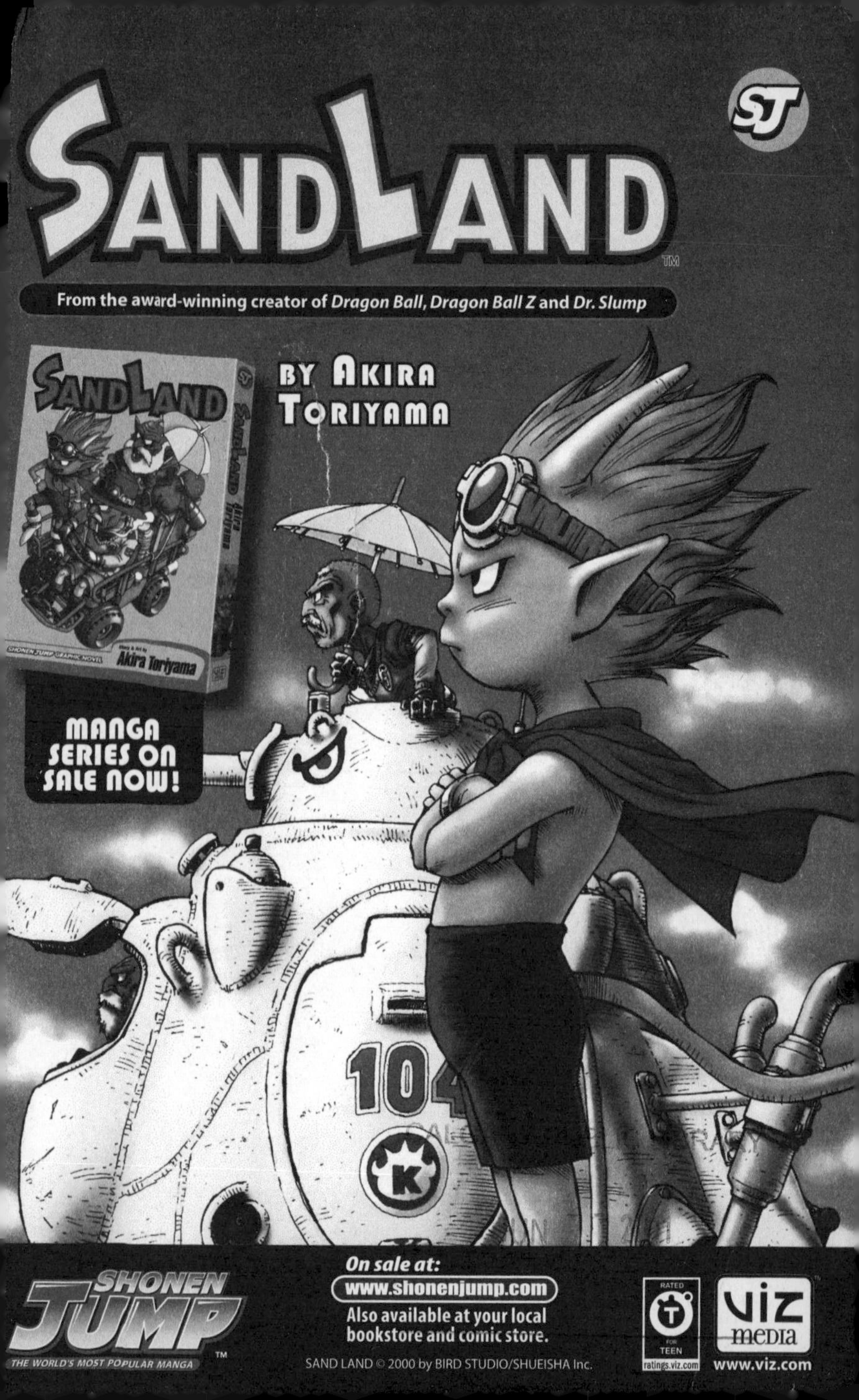
SANDLAND™
From the award-winning creator of Dragon Ball, Dragon Ball Z and Dr. Slump
BY AKIRA TORIYAMA
SANDLAND
SHONEN JUMP GRAPHIC NOVEL
Akira Toriyama
MANGA SERIES ON SALE NOW!
104
SHONEN JUMP™
THE WORLD'S MOST POPULAR MANGA
On sale at:
www.shonenjump.com
Also available at your local bookstore and comic store.
SAND LAND © 2000 by BIRD STUDIO/SHUEISHA Inc.
RATED T FOR TEEN
ratings.viz.com
viz media
www.viz.com